Department
for Transport

New Roads and Street Works Act 1991 Specification for the Reinstatement of Openings in Highways

Third Edition

Code of Practice for England

Approved by the Secretary of State under Section 71
of the New Roads and Street Works Act 1991

April 2010

Published by TSO (The Stationery Office) and available from:

Online
www.tsoshop.co.uk

Mail, Telephone, Fax & E-mail
TSO
PO Box 29, Norwich, NR3 1GN
Telephone orders/General enquiries:
0870 600 5522
Fax orders: 0870 600 5533
E-mail: customer.services@tso.co.uk
Textphone 0870 240 3701

TSO@Blackwell and other Accredited Agents

Department for Transport
Great Minster House
33 Horseferry Road
London SW1P 4DR
Telephone 0300 330 3000
Web site www.gov.uk/dft

ISBN 978 0 11 553141 5

Ninth impression 2015

Printed in Great Britain on material containing 75% post-consumer waste and 25% ECF pulp.

J003022883 C3 04/15

Contents

Foreword

Under section 71 of the New Roads and Street Works Act 1991 (NRSWA) an Undertaker executing street works must when reinstating the street comply with whatever specification may be prescribed for materials to be used and standards of workmanship to be observed. The Undertaker must also ensure that the reinstatement conforms to prescribed performance standards – in the case of an interim reinstatement, until a permanent reinstatement is effected, and, in the case of a permanent reinstatement, for the prescribed period after completion of the reinstatement.

The Secretary of State for Transport has approved this Code under powers to issue codes of practice under section 71 of the NRSWA.

The Code incorporates the requirements set out in the following regulations:

- The Street Works (Reinstatement) Regulations 1992, SI 1992 No.1689;
- The Street Works (Reinstatement) (Amendment) Regulations 1992, SI 1992 No. 3110; and
- The Street Works (Reinstatement) (Amendment) (England) Regulations 2002, SI 2002 No. 1487.

Street works have been a devolved matter in Scotland and Wales since the promulgation of constitutional changes with effect from 1999.

This edition of the Code of Practice was prepared by a working party of the Highway Authorities and Utilities Committee (HAUC), and was the subject of extensive consultation with interested organisations. On the working party were representatives of the National Joint Utilities Group (NJUG) (of which the majority of utilities are members), Joint Authorities Group (JAG) (representing local authorities in their capacity as highway authorities) and the Department for Transport. Sections which have changed in this version of the code include:

- Materials to comply with new EN standards
- Reinstatement Edge Preparation
- Cut Back
- Proximity of Reinstatements to Iron Work and other fixed features
- Edge Regularity
- Match of surface in high amenity areas

- Compaction
- Edge treatment at verges
- Manhole covers and frames
- Water presence
- Binder penetration and equivalence
- Alternative reinstatement materials Appendix A9 of the Code
- Modular Paving and use of Natural Materials
- Reinstatement construction thickness; and
- Correcting ambiguities, clarifying and simplifying the text.

This third edition of the Specification for the Reinstatement of Openings in Highways has been approved by The Secretary of State for Transport for use in England only. The 'Notes for Guidance' section does not form part of the statutory code. This version of the Code of Practice will come into operation on 1 October 2010 and replaces the second edition in England.

Definitions

Aggregate Abrasion Value (AAV)	the standard measure of an aggregate's resistance to abrasion.
Authority	unless otherwise stated, in this Specification and Definitions, 'the Authority' refers to the Authority as defined in the Act.
BBA/HAPAS	British Board of Agrément/Highway Authorities Product Approval Scheme – a recognised body giving approval for products and processes.
Bond Coat	Bond coats are proprietary materials certified by HAPAS, generally formulated to enable heavier application rates than are possible with tack coats and to provide greater cohesion between bituminous layers.
CBGM	Cement Bound Granular Material.
CBR	Californian Bearing Ratio: a measure of the load bearing strength of a granular or unbound material.
Composite construction	a structure where the road is composed of lean mix concrete or other cement bound granular material, normally with bituminous surfacing layers.
Cut-back	see 'stepped joint'.
Cycle track	a way constituting or comprised in a highway, being a way over which the public have a right of way on pedal cycles only, with or without a right of way on foot.
Deep openings	all excavations and trenches in which the depth of cover over the buried apparatus is greater than 1.5 metres. Trenches with a depth of cover that is intermittently more than 1.5 metres for lengths of less than 5 metres are not deemed to be deep openings.

Emergency works works whose execution at the time when they are executed is required in order to put an end to, or to prevent the occurrence of, circumstances then existing or imminent for which the person responsible for the works believes on reasonable grounds to be existing or imminent which are likely to cause danger to persons or property.

Flexible construction a structure where the Base is composed of either bituminous material or granular material, or a combination thereof.

Footpath a way over which the public have a right of way on foot only, not being a footway.

Footway a way comprised in a highway, which also comprises a carriageway, being a way over which the public have a right of way on foot only.

Geosynthetic materials a generic term describing a product at least one of whose components is made from a synthetic or natural polymer, in the form of a sheet or a 3D structure, used in contact with soil and/or other materials in geotechnical and civil engineering applications.

HBM Hydraulically Bound Materials.

HD Highway Design Standard- A section of the Design Manual for Roads and Bridges (DMRB) issued by the Stationery Office – Standards for Highways.

Immediate Reinstatement works comprising the orderly replacement of excavated material, reasonably compacted to finished surface level, usually with a cold-lay surfacing.

Interim reinstatement the orderly placement and proper compaction of reinstatement layers to finished surface level, including any temporary materials.

Intervention restoration of a reinstatement which does not comply with the performance standards, to a condition complying with those standards.

LA Los Angeles Abrasion Value – measure of the resistance to abrasion of an aggregate.

Major projects standard works which have been identified specifically in the Undertaker's annual operating programme or which, if not specifically identified in that programme, are normally planned at least 6 months in advance of works commencing.

Modular construction a structure where the surface is composed of setts, concrete blocks, brick pavers or paving slabs etc. laid on appropriate sub-construction.

msa	million standard axles.
Narrow trenches	all trenches of 300 mm surface width or less, with a surface area greater than 2 square metres.
Pen	the penetration grade of a bituminous binder.
Permanent reinstatement	the orderly placement and proper compaction of reinstatement layers up to and including the finished surface level.
Permitted	An allowable alternative to the preferred material – see also 'Preferred'.
Preferred	The favoured choice between a number of options – see also 'Permitted'.
PSV	Polished Stone Value.
PTV	Pendulum Test Value – a measure of the frictional properties of a surface using a Pendulum test device.
Rigid construction	a structure where the surface slab also performs the function of the Base; is of pavement quality concrete and may be reinforced. Under certain circumstances, as defined in Section S7, a rigid road that has been overlaid may be deemed to be a composite construction for the purpose of this Specification.
Road & footway structure	includes the surface course, binder course, base and sub-base.
SHW	Specification for Highway Works, published as Volume 1 of the Manual of Contract Documents for Highway Works (MCHW1) Standards for Highways.
Small excavations	all openings with a surface area of 2 square metres or less. For the purposes of this Specification, test holes up to 150 mm diameter are not excavations and shall be reinstated in accordance with the requirements of Section S11.
SRV	Skid Resistance Value – a measure of the frictional properties of a surface using a Pendulum test device.
Stepped joint	the practice whereby the width of the reinstatement of the binder course and/or surface course is made wider than the reinstatement below it to provide higher resistance to water ingress.

Street the whole or any part of any of the following, irrespective of whether it is a thoroughfare:

a) any highway, road, lane, footway, alley or passage,

b) any square or court, and

c) any land laid out as a way whether it is for the time being formed as a way or not; and for the avoidance of doubt includes land on the verge of a street or between two carriageways. Where a street passes over a bridge or through a tunnel, references to the street include that bridge or tunnel. (NRSWA section 48 etc.).

Street Manager Ref. New Roads and Street Works Act Section 49 (4).

Tack Coat Conventional bitumen emulsions conforming to BS EN 13108 classes C40B4 or C60B3 used to enhance the adhesion of the overlying bituminous layer which might be impaired due to minor dust problems or insufficient free bitumen on the surface of the layer to be overlaid.

The Act unless otherwise stated in this Specification and Definitions, 'the Act' refers to the New Roads and Street Works Act 1991.

Traffic sign has the same meaning as in the Road Traffic Regulation Act 1984.

Trim-line The cut face that defines the outer edge of an excavation.

Trimback The area between trim-lines excavated around a fixed feature to permit adequate reinstatement.

TRL Transport Research Laboratory.

UKAS the organisation that has introduced a national scheme for the accreditation of Laboratories used for the testing of materials.

Undertaker unless otherwise stated in this Specification and Definitions, 'the Undertaker' refers to the Undertaker as defined in the Act and is the person in whom a statutory right to execute works is vested or the holder of a street works licence.

Urgent works works which fall short of emergency works but are of sufficient urgency to warrant immediate action either to prevent further deterioration of an existing situation or to avoid an Undertaker becoming in breach of a statutory obligation.

Verge that part of the highway outside of the carriageway, which may be slightly raised but is exclusive of embankment or cutting slopes, and generally grassed.

Wheel Tracking A test to determine the resistance to deformation (rutting), primarily of surface courses.

S0 Preamble to the Specification

S0.1 General

This Specification is a Code of Practice outlining a national standard applicable to all Undertakers when carrying out reinstatement as a part of executing street works. Broadly, the Specification and its appendices prescribe materials that may be used, the expected standards of workmanship and performance standards to be complied with at both interim and permanent reinstatement stages for the duration of the Guarantee Period (defined in Section S1.2).

There is a strong focus in this Specification on sustainability by encouraging the first time completion of permanent reinstatements, material recycling and the reuse of materials to minimise the carbon footprint of the reinstatement operation.

S0.2 Outline of the specification

The Specification 'S' Sections are logically ordered, reflecting what practitioners need to know before commencing works, what will be required in order to complete the works and the obligations upon Undertakers once the works are completed.

Sections S1 and S2 respectively set out in advance of any reinstatements, the general parameters associated with reinstatements and the expected performance requirements.

Sections S3, S4 and S5 follow the normal sequence of operations carried out by Undertakers when breaking up or opening up the street and laying new or maintaining apparatus, namely, excavation, placing surround material to apparatus and the backfilling of the openings above the surround to apparatus to the underside of the specified unbound and bound material layers, which comprise the designed structure of the reinstatement.

Sections S6 and S7 set out the detailed requirements and permissible reinstatement methods for the bound materials in carriageways. Limitations on the use of preferred and permissible materials (more fully detailed in Appendices A1 and A2) are described. Sections S8 and S9 similarly set out the requirements for reinstatements in footways and verges.

Section S10 sets out the fundamental requirements for compaction of all permissible reinstatement materials, including guidance as to the degree of compaction necessary to comply with the Code of Practice, thereby supporting the required end performance of the whole reinstatement.

Sections S11 and S12 respectively cover ancillary activities which might be encountered during street works and the prescribed remedial measures in the event that the reinstatement is defective and/or causes settlement beyond the limits of the reinstatement.

S0.3 Outline of the Appendices

The Appendices are an integral part of this Code of Practice, setting out significant amounts of technical detail, including the design of different reinstatements using materials and thickness specified in the Appendices. This reflects the various categories of surfaces normally encountered in reinstatements, which includes carriageways, footways and verges.

Incorporation of this type of detail into the Specification 'S' Sections was considered likely to impede the general flow of those clauses. Whilst the Appendices stand alone as sections of the Code of Practice, they in essence complement the Specification 'S' Sections.

S0.4 Outline of the Notes for Guidance

Where considered beneficial, Notes for Guidance sections complementary to the Specification 'S' Sections and some of the Appendices have been included in the Code of Practice. However, Notes for Guidance are by definition notes or details which are thought to be useful to support practitioners to both understand and use the Specification and Appendices. They sit outside the Code of Practice and are not enforceable under law.

S0.5 Using the Specification and Appendices to undertake the correct reinstatement

Specific to the reinstatement-related aspects within the Code of Practice, readers and practitioners will find reference to reinstatement materials in numerous parts of the Specification 'S' Sections and Appendices. These include:

- the overall class of materials, such as Hot Rolled Asphalts, Stone Mastic Asphalts, Asphalt Concretes and traditional Concretes used in some roads;
- different types of mixture within each class of material, such as Hot Rolled Surface Course and Hot Rolled Binder Course – *these tend to relate to the relative position of the mixture within the overall reinstatement (generally the layer) and reflect the design function of the layer*;
- different preferred (and permissible) mixtures for different layers;
- different thicknesses of mixture layers;
- specific requirements and limitations for surface courses.

Each of the above references has been intentionally assigned to different parts of the Code of Practice and it is essential that these are all taken into account when selecting the correct reinstatement design in a specific category of surface.

The reinstatement of flexible roads (and footways) is particularly more complex at the reinstatement design selection stage. To assist practitioners, Figure S0.1 sets out the intended materials selection process for flexible (and composite) carriageways.

Figure S0.1 Flexible Reinstatement Material Selection Process

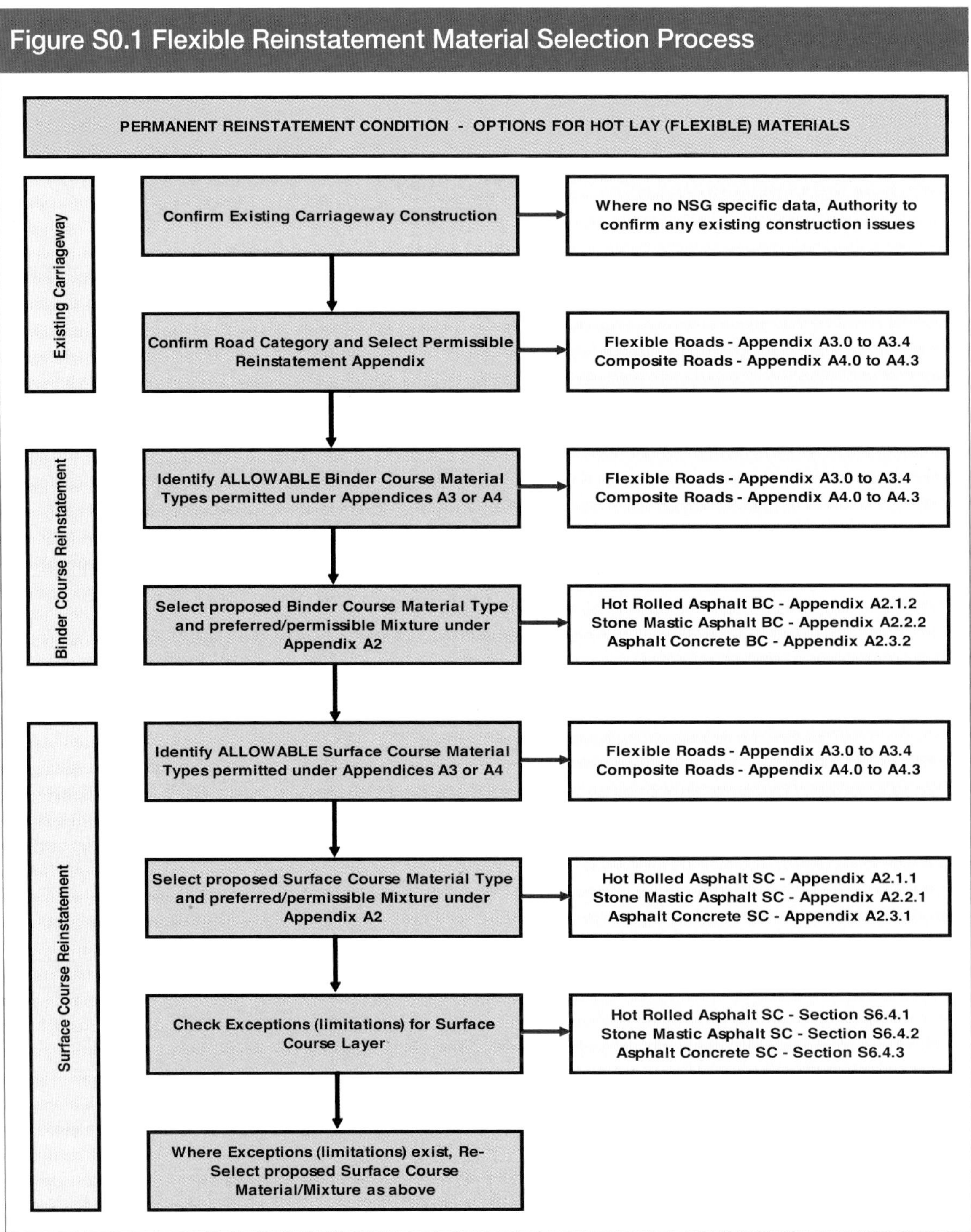

S1 Operational Principles

S1.1 General

This Specification incorporates new terminology introduced under the European EN 13108 series of standards for asphalt, the term asphalt in this case referring to mixtures of bituminous binder and aggregate. These became effective in January 2008. Readers and practitioners should therefore be familiar with the new terms used in this Specification, as follows:

"asphalt concrete"	replaces the previous	"coated materials (bituminous mixtures) to BS4987"
"base"	replaces the previous	"base (roadbase)"

Readers and practitioners should note that reference to "asphalt" is NOT limited to "hot rolled asphalt".

S1.1.1 An Undertaker executing street works shall carry out the excavation and reinstatement in accordance with this Specification. Where this Specification allows alternatives, the Undertaker shall select one of the permitted options. Regardless of which alternative is selected, the Undertaker shall guarantee the performance of the reinstatement to the relevant standards, for the relevant guarantee period.

S1.1.2 The reinstatement shall be carried out using a permitted method incorporating the highest degree of immediate permanent reinstatement appropriate, in the opinion of the Undertaker, to the prevailing circumstances.

S1.1.3 If, at any time during a guarantee period, the reinstatement fails the relevant performance requirements of this Specification, the Undertaker shall carry out remedial action to restore the reinstatement to a compliant condition. An interim reinstatement shall normally be made permanent within six months.

S1.1.4 The requirements and standards in this Specification apply to streets which are maintainable or prospectively maintainable at public expense. In the case of all other streets, only those relevant parts of this Specification relating to "Surround to Apparatus" and "Backfill" shall apply. Surfacing layers, if any, shall be reinstated, as far as is reasonably practicable, to match the existing construction. In all cases, reinstatement must be undertaken to the reasonable satisfaction of the Street Manager.

S1.2 Guarantee Period

S1.2.1 The Undertaker shall ensure that the interim reinstatement conforms to the prescribed standards until the permanent reinstatement is completed, and that the permanent reinstatement conforms to the prescribed standards throughout the guarantee period.

S1.2.2 The guarantee period shall begin on completion of the permanent reinstatement and shall run for two years, or three years in the case of deep openings. It should be noted that completion of the permanent reinstatement, rather than the giving of information to the Authority that the reinstatement is completed, is the event that triggers the start of the guarantee period. Failure to give this information is an offence under Section 70(6) of the Act.

S1.3 Road Categories

S1.3.1 Roads are categorised by this Specification into five types, each with a limiting capacity expressed in millions of standard axles (msa) as shown in Table S1.1.

Table S1.1 Road Categories

Road Category	Traffic Capacity
Type 0	Roads carrying over 30 to 125 msa
Type 1	Roads carrying over 10 to 30 msa
Type 2	Roads carrying over 2.5 to 10 msa
Type 3	Roads carrying over 0.5 to 2.5 msa
Type 4	Roads carrying up to 0.5 msa

S1.3.2 Roads carrying in excess of 125 msa are not included in this Specification. Reinstatement designs for such roads shall be agreed between the Undertaker and the Authority, on an individual basis.

S1.3.3 Road categories defined in Table S1.1 are based on the expected traffic to be carried by each road over the next 20 years. Each Authority shall categorise its road network on this basis and the Undertaker shall use the most current information available from the Authority. Where an Authority does not classify its roads as required by this Specification, the Undertaker shall determine the classification of these roads, as necessary, and provide a copy of the classification to all parties concerned.

S1.3.4 Valid traffic flows shall be assessed by accurately monitoring commercial vehicles in excess of 1.5 tonnes unladen weight. Traffic growth rates shall be determined from the average of at least three separate assessments carried out over at least three years. Where traffic growth rates are expected to increase significantly, as a result of changing traffic patterns, only predictions generated from a recognised planning process may be used. A zero traffic growth rate shall be assumed until accurate information is available.

S1.3.5 The reinstatement shall be designed using materials specified in Appendices A1, A2, A9 and A11. The overall layer thickness shall be as specified in Appendices A3 to A7 for the various categories of road, footway, footpath, cycle track, verge or unmade ground, and shall be compacted to the requirements of Section S10 and Appendix A8.

S1.4 Footway, Footpath and Cycle Track Categories

Footways, footpaths and cycle tracks are categorised by this Specification as follows:

S1.4.1 High duty – those designated as principal routes and used by an exceptionally large number of pedestrians and/or cyclists.

S1.4.2 High amenity – routes surfaced with one of the following surfacings, and which have been constructed and maintained to a high standard:

1) Surfaces chosen specifically for decorative purposes, with special colours, textures or surface finishes.
2) Flexible surfaces with a particular texture or distinctive coloured finish. Such surfaces will usually be situated in conservation, leisure or ornamental areas, pedestrian precincts or where an Authority has maintained high quality paving.

S1.4.3 Other – those that are neither high duty nor high amenity.

S1.4.4 Where an Authority is able to demonstrate that a high amenity or high duty footway has been constructed and maintained to a standard in excess of that prescribed in Sections S2.2 and S2.3 and registered accordingly then in these instances the reinstatement shall meet the Authority's standard of maintenance and their declared intervention criteria.

S1.5 Excavation and Trench Categories

Excavations and trenches are categorised by this Specification as follows:

S1.5.1 Small Excavations – all openings with a surface area of 2 square metres or less. For the purposes of this Specification, test holes up to 150 mm diameter are not excavations and shall be reinstated in accordance with the requirements of Section S11.

S1.5.2 Narrow Trenches – all trenches of 300 mm surface width or less, with a surface area greater than 2 square metres.

S1.5.3 Deep Openings – all excavations and trenches in which the depth of cover over the buried apparatus is greater than 1.5 metres. Trenches with a depth of cover that is intermittently more than 1.5metres for lengths of less than 5 metres are not deemed to be deep openings.

S1.5.4 Other Openings – all excavations and trenches with a surface area greater than 2 square metres.

S1.6 Alternative Options

S1.6.1 (i) Subject to the provisions of Appendix A9, an Undertaker may adopt an alternative Specification for materials, layer thickness and compaction methods to take advantage of new or local materials and/or alternative compaction equipment, subject to the prior agreement of the Authority, which shall not be unreasonably withheld. There shall be no departure from the performance requirements during the guarantee period.

(ii) An undertaker may use alternative excavation processes and equipment e.g. large diameter coring, subject to the prior agreement of the Authority.

S1.6.2 Recycled, secondary or virgin materials, or any combination thereof, are permitted by this Specification, provided they meet the performance requirements and any compositional requirements detailed in this Specification for the relevant material layer.

S1.6.3 Stabilised materials shall be permitted for use as surround to apparatus, and at backfill and sub-base layers, provided they meet the relevant performance requirements of this Specification.

S1.6.4 Alternative Reinstatement Materials are described in Appendix A9.

S1.7 Immediate Works

S1.7.1 There are circumstances when it is necessary to immediately reinstate an excavation, regardless of the material availability etc., purely to enable traffic or pedestrian movement to occur on a traffic sensitive route. In such circumstances, reinstatements may be completed using excavated or other materials, properly compacted in 100 mm layers, with a minimum surfacing thickness of 40 mm of bituminous material.

S1.7.2 All materials so placed which do not comply with the requirements of this Specification shall be re-excavated and reinstated, to the appropriate interim or permanent standard as specified, as soon as practicable, but within 10 working days, or as agreed with the Authority following the completion of the immediate works.

S1.8 Apparatus within Road, Footway and Cycletrack Structures

S1.8.1 Undertakers apparatus greater than 20mm external diameter will not be permitted within road, footway or cycletrack structures unless special circumstances exist (for example shallow cover over culverted watercourses, utility apparatus, etc). In these special circumstances the utility must consult with the Authority whose approval shall not be unreasonably withheld.

S1.8.2 Apparatus of 20 mm external diameter or less shall not be permitted above or within 20 mm of the following levels within a road structure, see Figure S1.1:

1) The Base/binder course interface in a flexible structure.

2) The underside of the concrete slab in a rigid structure.

3) The underside of the complete construction (formation layer) in a modular structure (refer to Appendices A6.1 to A6.3).

Figure S1.1 Apparatus within the Road Structure

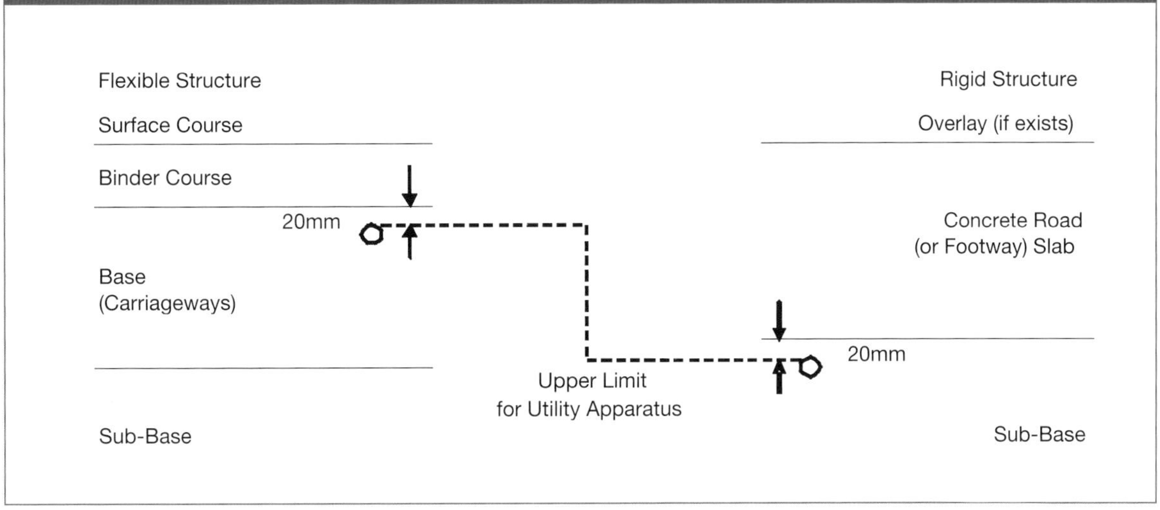

S1.8.3 Where other existing apparatus or surrounds occur within the road structure, the method of reinstatement shall be determined by agreement.

S1.9 Geosynthetic Materials, Geotextiles and Reinforcement Grids

S1.9.1 Where the Authority knows of the existence of any of the above materials in areas likely to be affected by an Undertaker's work, they should inform the Undertaker, prior to the commencement of works, so that an appropriate reinstatement method can be agreed.

S1.9.2 If the Undertaker is not informed of the existence of any of the above materials prior to the commencement of his works, but encounters them during the works, he should inform the Authority immediately so that an appropriate reinstatement method can be mutually agreed. In these circumstances, the Undertaker shall not be liable for the repair of any damage caused to geosynthetic materials, geotextiles or reinforcement grids if their existence was not known.

S1.10 Trees

S1.10.1 When working near trees, the National Joint Utilities Group publication Volume 4 "NJUG Guidelines for the Planning, Installation and Maintenance of Utility Apparatus in Proximity to Trees" should be followed. The publication gives comprehensive advice and should be followed in its entirety. Relevant extracts are reproduced in Notes for Guidance NG1.10.

S1.10.2 In addition to the recommendations of the NJUG guidelines, the use of tree root barriers may be considered. Specialist advice from an Arboriculturist should be sought.

S1.11 Conciliation and Arbitration

S1.11.1 This Specification is intended to provide sufficiently detailed guidance to enable agreement on its operation and implementation to be reached at local level. Authorities and Undertakers should always use their best endeavours to achieve a solution to disputes without having to refer them to conciliation. This might be achieved by referring the issue to management for settlement.

S1.11.2 If, however, agreement cannot be reached, the provisions set out in the Code of Practice for the Co-ordination of Street Works and Works for Road Purposes and Related Matters should be followed.

S2 Performance Requirements

S2.1 General

S2.1.1 The performance requirements of this Specification shall apply to streets that are maintainable or prospectively maintainable at public expense. In all other cases, the performance should match that of the existing construction, as far as reasonably practicable.

S2.1.2 Performance requirements shall apply to the immediate, interim and permanent reinstatements of Undertakers' excavations.

1) For all interim reinstatements, the main consideration as to meeting the performance requirements generally set out in Section S2 is primarily one of maintaining highway safety. This is particularly important where Deferred Set Mixtures (DSMs) are used in Roads, especially the higher Road Categories.
2) If the surface profile of a reinstatement exceeds any intervention limit during any guarantee period, remedial action shall be carried out to return the surface profile of the reinstatement to the as-laid condition defined in Section S2.2.1.

S2.1.3 No new guarantee period shall be required unless the cumulative settlement intervention limit is exceeded and an engineering investigation has been completed in accordance with Section S2.5. Requirements for the re-excavation and subsequent reinstatement, as determined from the results of an engineering investigation, shall be agreed and completed in accordance with Section S2.5.

S2.1.4 Reinstatement of Modular Surface Layers is described in Appendix A12. For all modular surfaces the effective width of a reinstatement shall be as follows:

1) For modular surfaces where all sides of the module are 300mm or less (or the nearest imperial equivalent), the effective width of a reinstatement (W) shall be the distance between two parallel lines drawn 150mm outside the edges of the excavation (see Fig S2.1A).

Figure S2.1A Effective Width of Reinstatement – Modules ≤ 300 mm

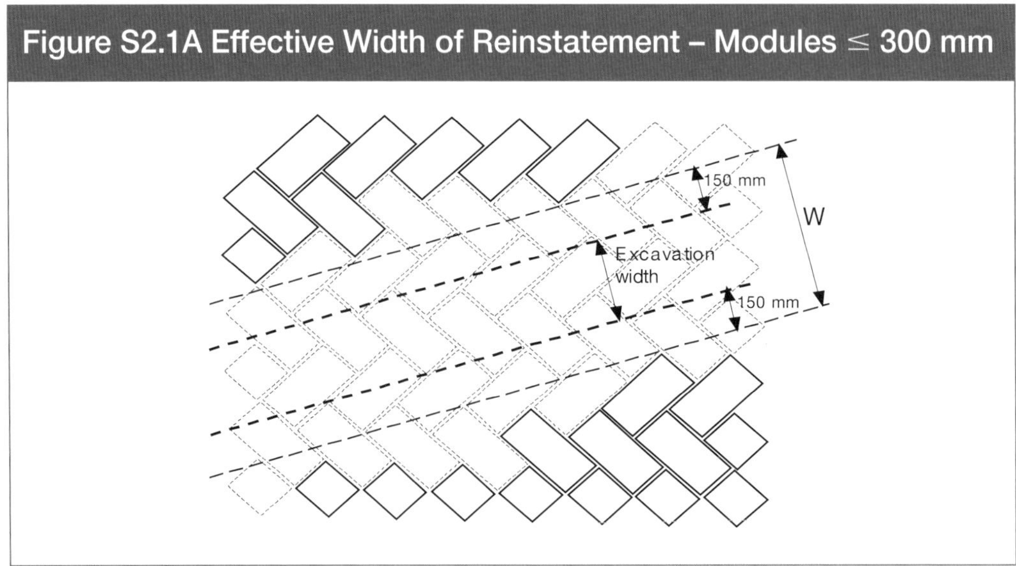

2) For modular surfaces where one side of the module is greater than 300mm, the effective width of a reinstatement (W) shall be the distance between the outer extremities of any modules that overlap the edge of the excavation (see Fig S2.1B).

3) Where there is evidence of further adjoining modules being affected by the excavation, the effective width shall be extended to include such modules.

Figure S2.1B Effective Width of Reinstatement – Modules > 300 mm

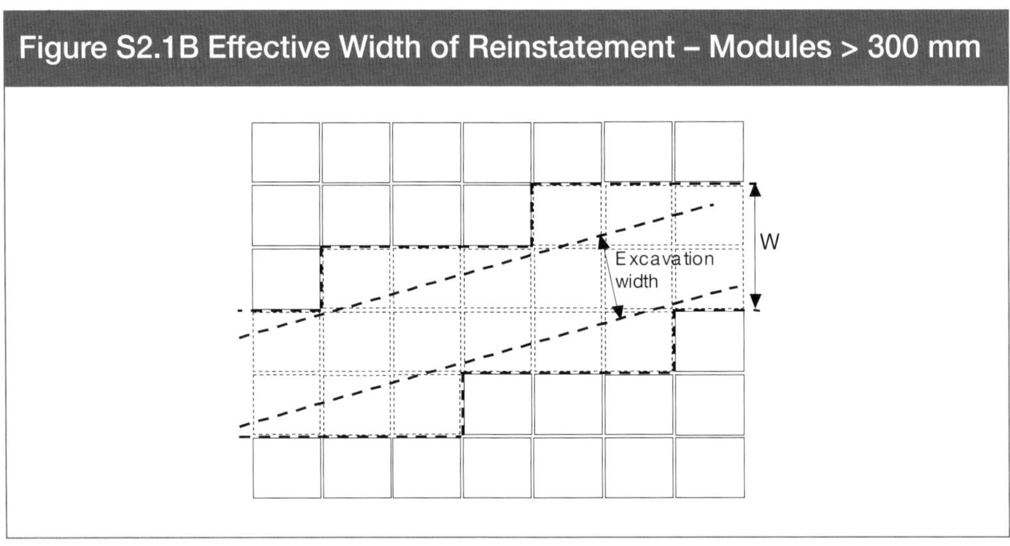

S2.1.5 Surface deformation resulting from vehicles over-running reinstatements within paved footways, including footpaths and cycle tracks, shall be excluded from all measurements carried out for the purposes of monitoring the reinstatement surface performance, unless such reinstatements have been carried out under the provisions of Section S8.4.

S2.1.6 However, properly constructed paved footways and their reinstatements may both be reasonably expected to withstand occasional overrun by non-commercial vehicles (less than 1.5 tonnes unladen). Where it can be shown that occasional over-run by non-commercial vehicles has caused surface deformation to a reinstatement within a paved footway and the adjacent surfaces do not show any associated surface deformation, the Authority may notify the Undertaker accordingly, whereupon the Undertaker shall restore the reinstatement to the as-laid profile.

S2.2 Surface Profile

S2.2.1 As-laid Profile

1) The reinstatement of any surface shall be completed so that it is as flat and flush as possible with the surrounding adjacent surfaces. There should be no significant depression or crowning in the surface. Construction tolerances at the edges of the reinstatement shall not exceed ± 6mm.

2) Once the reinstatement is registered as completed and opened to traffic, the Intervention Limits specified in Sections S 2.2.2 to S 2.2.5 shall apply.

3) At the end of the guarantee period, where the profile of the existing surfaces adjacent to the reinstatement is uniform and the surface of the reinstatement is outside the intervention limits, the Undertaker shall carry out remedial works to restore the surface profile of the reinstatement to a condition consistent with the adjacent surfaces.

4) It should be recognised that the surface profile of reinstatements carried out in restricted areas (for example, around surface boxes and fixed features) using hand tools may be difficult to match with adjacent machine-laid surface profiles. In these cases, localised variations in the hand-laid surface profile should be acceptable to the Authority provided that they are within the specified tolerances.

S2.2.2 Edge Depression – Intervention

1) An edge depression is a vertical step or trip at the interface of the reinstatement and the existing surface or a trip at the junction between ironwork and reinstatement.

2) Intervention shall be required where the depth of any edge depression exceeds 10 mm over a continuous length of more than 100 mm in any direction; see Figure S2.2.

Figure S2.2 Edge Depression Limits

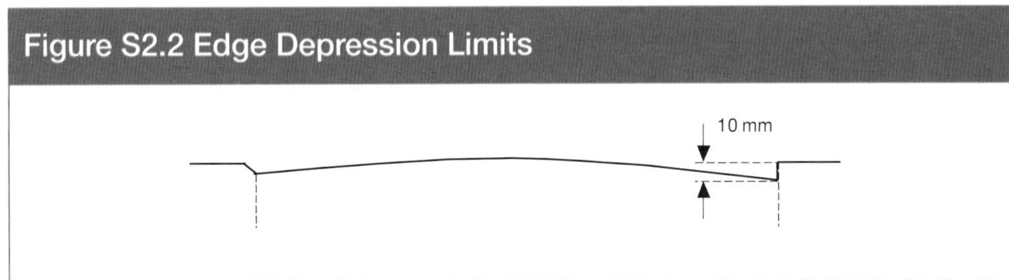

S2.2.3 Surface Depression – Intervention

1) A surface depression is a depressed area within the reinstatement having generally smooth edges and gently sloping sides, forming a shallow dish; see Figure S2.3.

2) Intervention shall be required where the depth of any area of surface depression spanning more than 100 mm in any plan dimension exceeds the intervention limit X shown in Table S2.1.

Figure S2.3 Surface Depression Limits

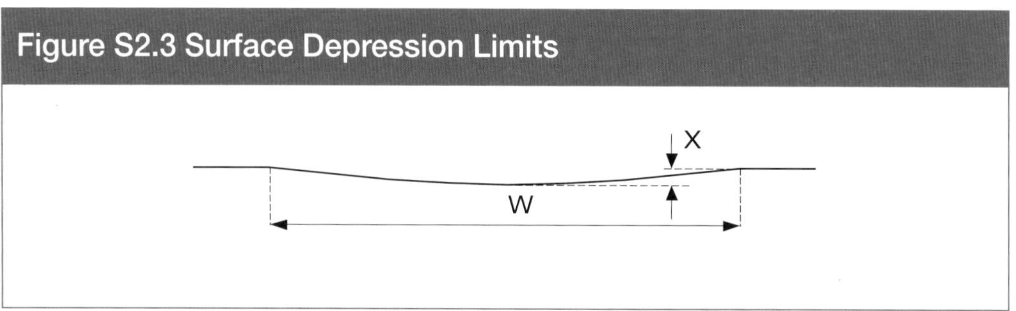

Table S2.1 Intervention Limits – Surface Depression

Reinstatement Width W (mm)	Intervention Limit X (mm)	Combined Defect Intervention Limit (mm)
Up to 400	10	10
Over 400 to 500	12	10
Over 500 to 600	14	12
Over 600 to 700	17	14
Over 700 to 800	19	16
Over 800 to 900	22	18
Over 900	25	20

3) Earlier intervention shall be required if the depression alone results in standing water wider than 500 mm or exceeding one square metre in area, at 2 hours after the cessation of rainfall.

S2.2.4 Surface Crowning – Intervention

1) Surface crowning is where the reinstatement is above the mean level of the existing adjacent surfaces; see Figure S2.4.

2) Intervention shall be required where the height of any area of surface crowning spanning more than 100 mm in any plan dimension exceeds the intervention limit Z shown in Table S2.2.

Figure S2.4 Surface Crowning Limits

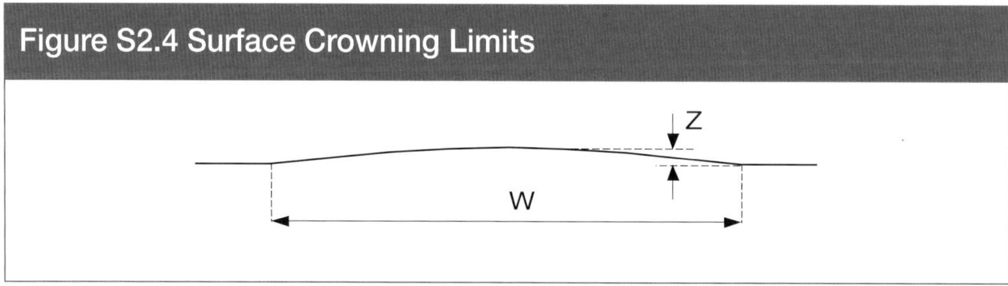

Table S2.2 Intervention Limits - Surface Crowning

Reinstatement Width W (mm)	Intervention Limit Z (mm)	Combined Defect Intervention Limit (mm)
Up to 400	10	10
Over 400 to 500	12	10
Over 500 to 600	14	12
Over 600 to 700	17	14
Over 700 to 800	19	16
Over 800 to 900	22	18
Over 900	25	20

3) Earlier intervention shall be required if crowning alone results in standing water wider than 500 mm or exceeding one square metre in area, at 2 hours after the cessation of rainfall.

S2.2.5 Combined Defect – Intervention

1) A combined defect is an area within the reinstatement where any combination of edge depression, surface depression or surface crowning overlap exists.

2) Where combined defects occur, the intervention limits for surface depression and surface crowning, shown in Section S2.2 and Tables S2.1 and Table S2.2 as intervention limits X and Z respectively, shall be reduced by 20% and rounded up to the nearest whole number, subject to a minimum of 10 mm.

3) Intervention shall be required where the extent of any individual defect, spanning more than 100 mm in any plan dimension, exceeds the combined defect intervention limit for the relevant defect, as defined in Section S2.2.2 (2), Table S2.1 and Table S2.2. The individual defects shall be measured, and the 20% reduction in intervention limits applied, as shown in Section NG2.2.5.

S2.2.6 Condition at End of Guarantee Period

1) At the end of the guarantee period the condition of the reinstatement shall not be required to be superior, in any respect, to the condition of the adjacent surfaces.

2) Where the profile of the existing surfaces adjacent to the reinstatement is uniform and substantially superior to the surface of the reinstatement, the Undertaker shall carry out remedial work to restore the surface profile of the reinstatement to a condition consistent with the adjacent surfaces.

S2.3 Fixed Features

S2.3.1 As-Laid Profile

All fixed features, such as edgings, channel blocks, drainage fixtures, surface boxes and ironware etc., should be as level and flush as possible with the adjacent surfaces and shall be installed to meet the following level criteria:

1) Fixed features shall be laid to coincide with the mean level of immediately adjacent surfaces.
2) The construction tolerance between the levels of the fixed feature (excluding drainage features) and immediately adjacent surfaces shall not exceed +/- 6mm.
3) Drainage features shall be set flush with the adjacent surface and subject to a construction tolerance of not more than 6mm below the level of the adjacent surface.
4) At a pedestrian crossing point that is flush with the adjacent surfaces, the kerbs shall be relaid flush with the adjacent surfaces to a tolerance of 0 to +6mm.

Figure S2.5 illustrates the relationship between immediately adjacent surfaces and the surround reinstatement to newly constructed Undertaker's Apparatus when setting the level of access covers and frames to the Apparatus.

Figure S2.5 As-Laid Profile of Fixed Features and Relationships with Immediately Adjacent Surfaces – Examples

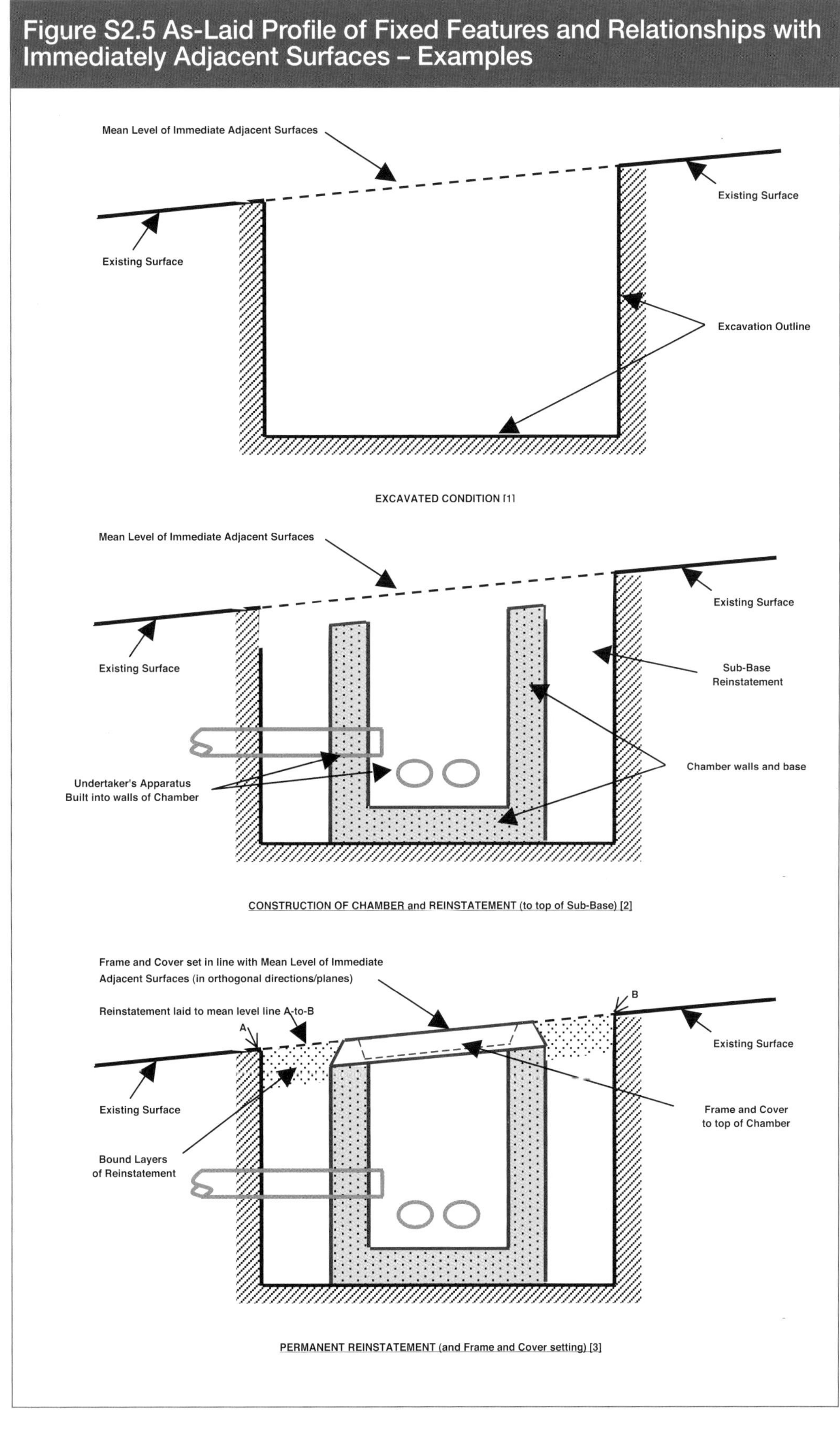

Figure S2.5 continued

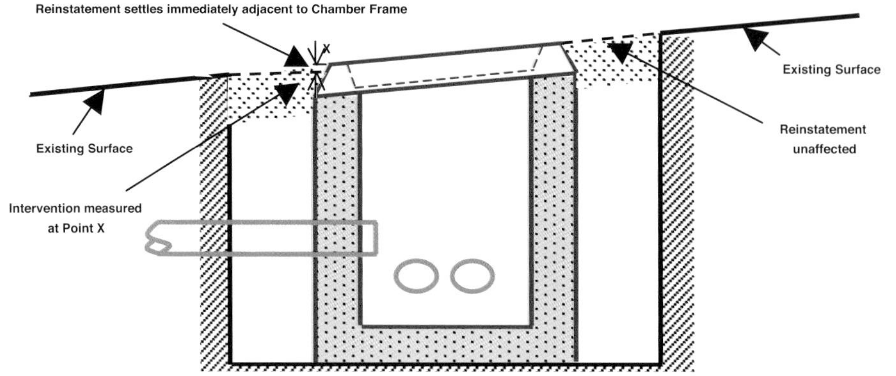

DEPRESSION OF SURROUND REINSTATEMENT (Surface Levels of Chamber Unchanged) [4]

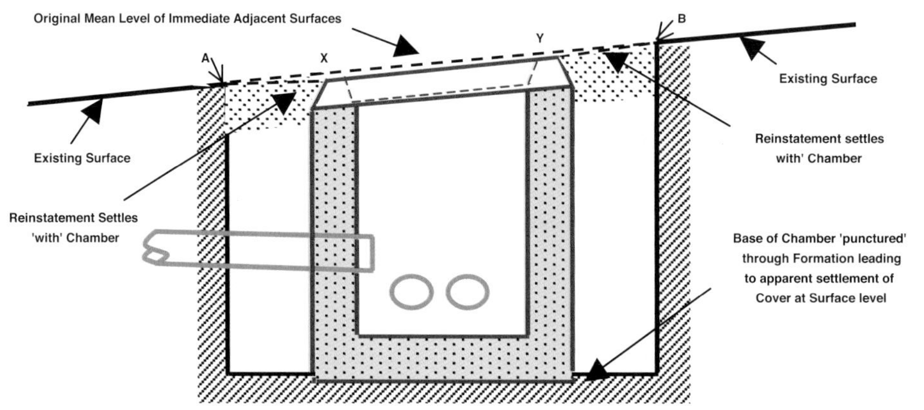

SETTLEMENT OF CHAMBER BUT NO INTERVENTION TO REINSTATEMENT AT POINTS X AND Y [5]
(Measure Depression across Mean Level of Immediate Adjacent Surfaces between Points A and B to S2.2.3)

Figure S2.5 - Individual sub-figures Sequencing:

[1] EXCAVATED CONDITION

[2] CONSTRUCTION OF CHAMBER and REINSTATEMENT (to top of Sub-Base)

[3] PERMANENT REINSTATEMENT (and Frame and Cover setting)

[4] DEPRESSION OF SURROUND REINSTATEMENT (Surface Levels of Chamber Unchanged)

[5] SETTLEMENT OF CHAMBER BUT NO INTERVENTION TO REINSTATEMENT

S2.3.2 Intervention

1) Intervention is required where the mean level of edgings, channel blocks, surface boxes and ironware etc., does not coincide with the mean level of the immediately adjacent surfaces, within a tolerance of ± 10 mm.

2) In the case of drainage fixtures, intervention is required where the mean level does not coincide with the mean level of the immediately adjacent surfaces, within a tolerance of 0 mm to -15 mm.

3) In the case of a pedestrian crossing point, intervention is required where the depth of any edge depression at the interface between the paving (which can include tactile units) and the dropped kerb exceeds 6mm over a continuous length of more than 100mm in any direction.

S2.4 Surface Regularity

S2.4.1 Requirements

At any time during the guarantee period, the longitudinal regularity in the direction of traffic flow at the surface of the permanent reinstatement in the road and the adjacent wheel track shall comply with the following requirements:

1) The number of longitudinal surface irregularities along a permanent reinstatement should not exceed the lower limit shown in Table S2.3.

Table S2.3 Surface Regularity

Surface Irregularities not less than (mm)	Irregularities per section		
	Lower Limit	Multiplier	Upper Limit
4	11	1.2	22
7	2	1.2	4
10	1	1.2	2

2) Where the number of longitudinal surface irregularities along a permanent reinstatement exceeds the lower limit shown in Table S2.3, the number of irregularities along the adjacent wheel track shall be recorded, in the same direction of traffic flow, for comparison.

3) Where the number of surface irregularities along a permanent reinstatement and the adjacent road both exceed the lower limit shown in Table S2.3, the number of longitudinal surface irregularities recorded along the reinstatement should not exceed the product of the number measured along the adjacent road and the multiplier shown in Table S2.3.

S2.4.2 Measurement

1) Surface irregularities may be measured using the TRL rolling straightedge. However, the rolling straightedge shall not be used to determine surface regularity where:

a) The line of a trench is parallel to the centreline of the road for less than 30 metres length.

or

b) The line of a trench is parallel to the line of traffic flow for less than 30 metres length.

or

c) The line of a road and/or the trench follows a bend with a radius of less than 250 metres.

or

d) The number of surface irregularities recorded along the adjacent road exceeds the upper limit shown in Table S2.3.

2) Where the rolling straight edge cannot be used, the surface regularity shall be assessed by another agreed method.

S2.4.3 Monitoring

For the purposes of monitoring the surface regularity of road reinstatements, relevant lengths of the trench should be divided into test sections of 30 metres length. The upper and lower limit values for surface irregularities, for each 30 metre section length, are shown in Table S2.3. For the final section length, which may exceed 30 metres but will be less than 60 metres, the limits should be calculated pro rata, and rounded up to the nearest whole number.

S2.5 Structural Integrity

The requirements for structural integrity are applicable to both paved and unpaved surfaces.

S2.5.1 Cumulative Settlement

1) The cumulative settlement of any reinstatement is the perpendicular distance, from the level of the adjacent surfaces, to the original surface of the reinstatement; see Figure S2.6. This measurement will effectively include the thickness of any additional materials added during any preceding remedial work.

Figure S2.6 Cumulative Settlement

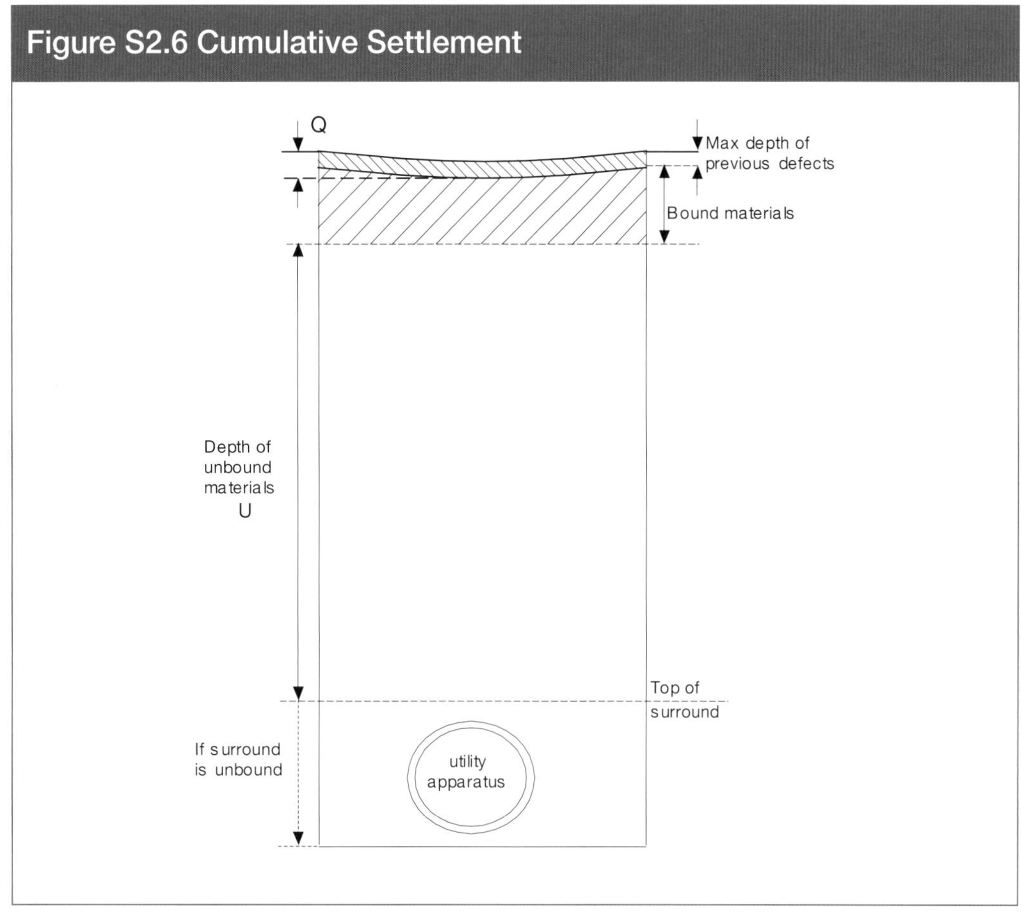

2) If the cumulative settlement of a reinstatement exceeds the limits shown in Table S2.4 at any time within the guarantee period, an agreed engineering investigation shall be carried out, jointly with the Authority. The investigation should establish whether settlement is likely to continue and determine the extent of remedial action required.

Table S2.4 Structural Integrity

Reinstatement Width (mm)	Intervention Limit Q	
	Normal Ground Conditions	Bad Ground Conditions
Up to 1000	1.5% U) whichever or 30 mm) is greater	2.5% U) whichever or 30 mm) is greater
Over 1000	1.5% U) whichever or 35 mm) is greater	2.5% U) whichever or 35 mm) is greater

3) Where it is necessary to re-excavate a reinstatement to carry out an engineering investigation, the subsequent permanent reinstatement shall be deemed to be new and the guarantee period shall begin again.

4) Where very deep excavation work is carried out in bad ground, consideration should be given to an agreed extension of the interim

reinstatement period. An appropriate extension will allow the reinstatement and surrounding ground to achieve an acceptable degree of stability before permanent reinstatement is required. The performance requirements of Section S2 shall apply throughout the extended interim period.

S2.5.2 Bad Ground

Bad ground is deemed to be natural or made-up ground between the base of the excavation and the binder course level, which contains any of the following:

a) Class E Unacceptable Materials, as specified in Appendix A1.

b) Materials that are loose or friable in their natural state and are not self-supporting at an exposed face.

c) An excessive amount of rocks or boulders, loose random rubble, penning, setts or cobbles etc, at any depth where their removal during excavation could cause loosening of the ground adjacent to the excavation.

d) Materials that are saturated, regardless of whether free or running water is present.

S2.6 Skid Resistance

S2.6.1 General

The texture depth, Polished Stone Value (PSV) and Aggregate Abrasion Value (AAV) at the running surface of all interim and permanent reinstatements in all roads shall comply with the following requirements:

1) There is no requirement to provide a texture depth, PSV or AAV that is superior to that existing at the running surfaces adjacent to the reinstatement.

2) For rigid roads, where the surface of the concrete road slab is the running surface of the road and has been randomly grooved, a brushed surface finish to the requirements of Table S2.5 shall be permitted for small excavations, narrow trenches and other openings less than 1 metre wide.

S2.6.2 Texture Depth

1) Subject to the requirements of Section S2.6.1, for all bituminous surface course materials permitted in Appendix A2 and for rigid roads where the surface of the concrete road slab is the running surface of the road, the texture depth shall comply with the requirements of Table S2.5.

Table S2.5 Texture depth

Reinstatement Location	Texture Depth (mm)			
	Chipped HRA & Surface Dressings	**SMA & Thin Surface Course Systems**	**All other Bituminous Surfaces**	**Concrete Carriageways**
Roads where speed limit > 56 mph (90 kph)	1.5 average 1.2 minimum	1.3 average 1.0 minimum	0.6 minimum	1.25 maximum 0.6 minimum
All other roads	1.0 average 0.8 minimum	1.0 average 0.8 minimum	0.6 minimum	

2) The average depth of carriageway surface macrotexture shall be measured using a volumetric patch technique described in SHW Clause 921 for bituminous surfacings and Clause 1026 for concrete surfacings. For concrete or narrow reinstatements a modified version using 50% of the test medium (eg sand or glass beads) may be used.

3) For the purposes of monitoring texture depth, the entire reinstatement shall be divided into notional units of 18 square metres and tested at evenly spaced intervals as follows:

- Reinstatement of small excavations – single measurement centred within the reinstatement
- Reinstatement of >2m^2 to 18m^2 – 3 measurements
- Reinstatement >18m^2 – 3 measurements per 18m^2
- Trenches 300mm wide or less – as above but centred along the centreline of the trench

Figure S2.7 illustrates the requirements of Section S2.6.2 (3) apart from small excavations.

4) Where the test patch extends beyond the edge of the reinstatement the test shall be repeated using half the volume of test medium. Any comparison tests on the existing road should be carried out adjacent to the test locations in the reinstatement, as close to the reinstatement edge as practicable.

5) The TRL mini texture meter may be used by agreement.

Figure S2.7 Sand Patch Testing – Typical Locations within Reinstatements

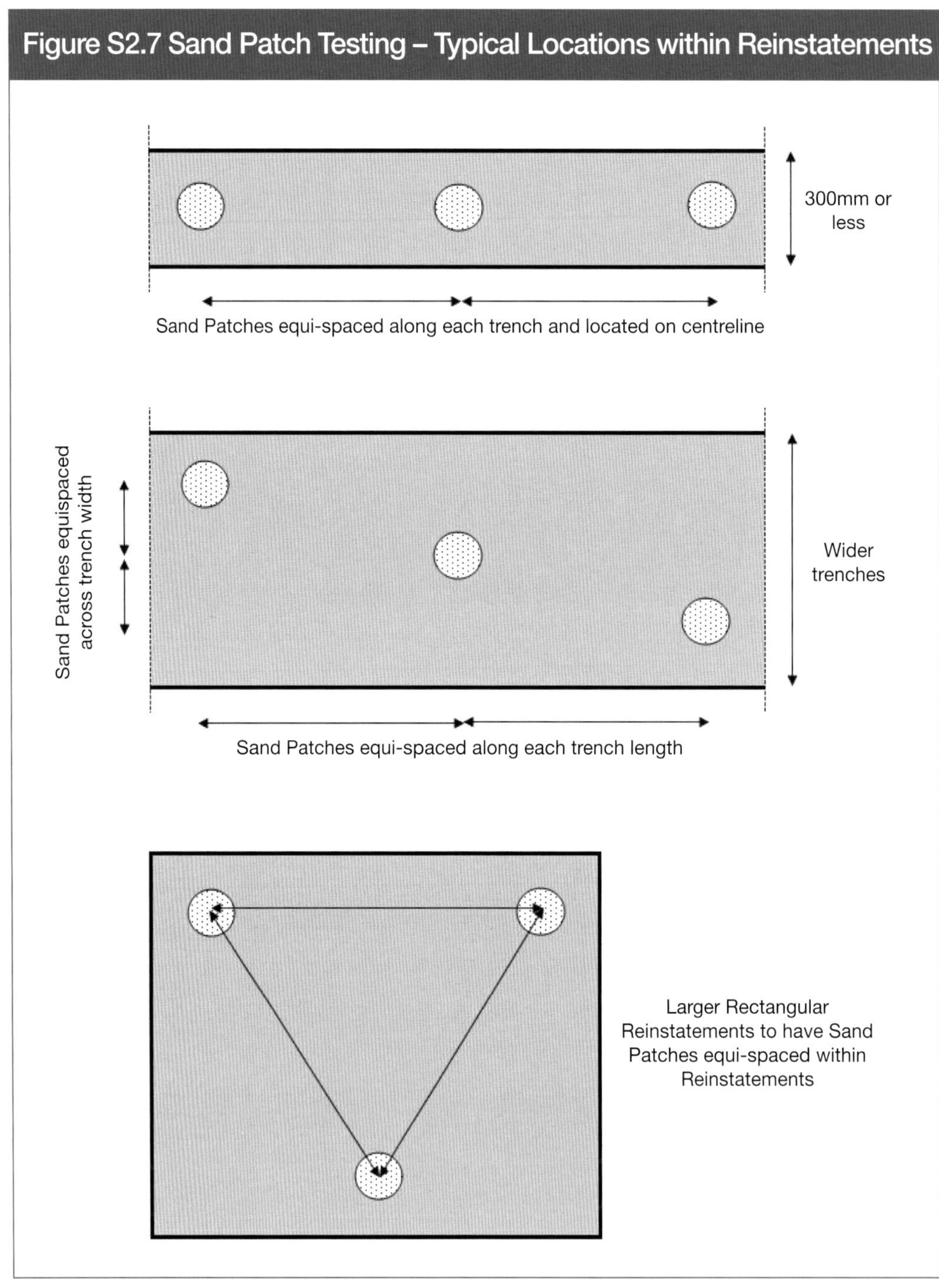

S2.6.3 Polished Stone Value (PSV)

1) To simplify the determination of the PSV requirements for aggregates in asphalt surface courses, reinstatements in roads are classified into two site categories, according to the apparent degree of risk associated with the site location, as follows:

a) Site A – Potentially High Risk

Includes:

Traffic signals, pedestrian crossings, railway level crossings – including 50 m approaches

Roundabouts and their exits - including 50 m approaches

Bends < 100 m radius where the speed limit > 40 mph (65 kph) – including 50 m approaches

Downhill gradients > 10% for more than 50 m (single or dual carriageway)

Uphill gradients > 10% for more than 50 m (single carriageway only)

or

b) Site B – Average or Low Risk

All other situations on single and dual carriageways, including the following:

Generally straight sections of carriageway

Approaches to and across major/minor road junctions

Bends of 100 m radius or greater, at any speed limit

Downhill/Uphill sections of 10% gradient or less

2) Subject to the requirements of Section S2.6.1, for all bituminous surface course materials permitted in Appendix A2, the PSV of all pre-coated chippings and the coarse aggregate in all mixes used without pre-coated chippings at the running surface shall comply with the requirements of Table S2.7. The coarse aggregate in all mixes used with pre-coated chippings at the running surface shall have a minimum PSV of 45. The PSV shall be tested in accordance with BS EN 1097-8.

Table S2.7 Bituminous Roads – Polished Stone Value

Road Type	Reinstatement Minimum PSV	
	Site A Potentially High Risk	Site B Average or Low Risk
0	68	68
1	68	65
2	65	60
3	65	55
4	65	55

3) The past use of these site categories and Table S2.7 has indicated that the minimum values noted are appropriate in most cases. However, where an Authority has alternative requirements for aggregate properties (e.g. Design Manual for Roads and Bridges HD36 or a published policy) then this information shall be supplied to the Undertaker. Where this is the case the Undertaker shall specify aggregate properties in accordance with this information subject to Section S2.6.1 (1).

4) Where an interim surface course contains an aggregate that may not comply with the requirements of Table S2.7, a surface treatment may become necessary before the reinstatement is made permanent. In this event, the requirements of Table S2.7 are applicable only to the coarse aggregate contained within the surface treatment and not to the underlying aggregate within the interim surface course.

5) Where a high friction coating is to be applied to a reinstatement to match an existing coating, an alternative PSV may be specified by agreement, in place of the requirements of Table S2.7, depending upon the nature of the site and the period over which the friction coating will be absent.

6) Where a permanent surface course contains more than one type of aggregate or aggregates from more than one source, all coarse aggregates within the mixture shall comply with the PSV requirements of Table S2.7.

S2.6.4 Aggregate Abrasion Value (AAV)

1) Subject to the requirements of Section S2.6.1, for all bituminous surface course materials permitted in Appendix A2, the AAV of all pre-coated chippings and the coarse aggregate in all mixes used without pre-coated chippings at the running surface shall comply with the requirements of Table S2.8.

Table S2.8 Bituminous Roads – Aggregate Abrasion Value

Road Type	Reinstatement Maximum AAV	
	All Pre-coated Chippings	SMA, Material to PD6691 Surface Courses
0	10	12
1	12	14
2	12	14
3	14	16
4	14	16

(See also Section S6.4 for permitted surface course options)

2) The AAV shall be measured in accordance with BS 812: Part 113.

3) Where an interim surface course material contains an aggregate that may not comply with the requirements of Table S2.8, a surface treatment may become necessary before the reinstatement is made permanent. In this event, the requirements of Table S2.8 are applicable only to the coarse aggregate contained within the surface treatment and not to the underlying aggregate within the interim surface course.

4) The past use of Table S2.8 has indicated that the minimum values noted are appropriate in most cases. However, where an Authority has alternative requirements for aggregate properties then this information shall be supplied to the Undertaker. Where this is the case the Undertaker shall specify aggregate properties in accordance with this information subject to Section S2.6.1 (1).

S2.7 Sampling and Testing

S2.7.1 All sampling and testing shall be carried out by a laboratory holding current UKAS accreditation covering the specified method of testing, unless otherwise agreed.

S2.7.2 The Authority may carry out sampling and testing at its discretion. If there is no agreement between the Authority and Undertaker on the test results and findings, further testing may be undertaken by a UKAS accredited laboratory to reconcile the matter.

S3 Excavation

S3.1 Breaking the Surface

S3.1.1 Care must be taken when cutting surface layers to avoid undue damage to the running surface or to the bond between the surface course and binder course materials. Cutting by machine, e.g. road saw, coring equipment or planer, is preferred. All loose materials shall be removed to ensure that the trench edge is in a safe and stable condition.

S3.1.2 When excavating in modular construction, the existing modules shall be lifted carefully, and stored for re-use. Where pre-existing damage has resulted in fragmentation or breakage of modules made out of natural materials the fragments shall be removed and stored, unless agreed otherwise with the Authority.

S3.1.3 The Authority shall be informed of any material, natural material, cobbles or setts encountered that may be of historical or archaeological interest and shall be afforded the opportunity to inspect the material prior to it being excavated.

S3.1.4 Modules shall be reinstated in accordance with Appendix A12.

S3.2 Excavation

S3.2.1 All excavations in the road should be carried out in a manner that avoids undue damage.

S3.2.2 The trench width should be such that adequate access is available for compaction of the surround to apparatus.

S3.2.3 The trench walls should be even and vertical with no undercutting of the running surface. If undercutting occurs and compaction is impossible, measures should be taken to fill any voids as soon as practicable or immediately after trench support has been provided.

S3.2.4 Excavations shall be protected, as far as is reasonably practicable, from the ingress of water, and water running into them shall be drained or pumped to an approved disposal point. Any drainage sumps shall be sited so as to prevent damage to the excavation.

S3.3 Excavated Material

S3.3.1 All excavated materials that are to be re-used should be protected from excessive drying or wetting during storage. Additionally, these materials should be excavated, stored, handled and laid so as to avoid contamination and loss of fines.

S3.3.2 Excavated material unsuitable for re-use shall be removed from site as soon as practicable. Excavated material retained on site shall be stockpiled within the confines of site barriers, at a safe distance from the trench edge and prevented, so far as is practicable, from entering any drainage system or water course.

S3.4 Side Support

S3.4.1 The sides of all excavations in soft or loose ground shall, ordinarily, be provided with a side support system. The support system shall be properly designed and installed to restrain lateral movement of the sidewalls, and should be installed without delay.

S3.4.2 Supports shall be progressively withdrawn as backfilling and compaction progresses, and all voids carefully filled.

S3.5 Drainage

S3.5.1 The Undertaker shall take all reasonably practicable measures to prevent the permanent disturbance of artificial or natural drainage systems/paths. Where disturbance does occur it shall be notified immediately to the owners of the system and any landowners who are affected. Disturbed systems shall be restored to the requirements of the owner; see Section S11.4.

S3.5.2 For any works site where the Authority is aware of a history of flooding or drainage problems it should inform the Undertaker in advance. In such situations the Undertaker and the Authority should liaise closely to identify a suitable method of working.

S.3.5.3 If site conditions indicate to the Undertaker that the use of some sub-base materials may be detrimental to drainage, advice on the selection of suitable materials should be sought from the Authority.

S3.5.4 See also Section S11.4 for other water-related matters.

S3.6 Shallow or Aborted Excavations

S3.6.1 No shallow or aborted excavation shall be permitted to undermine the integrity of the remaining road structure. Any excavation terminated at an incomplete stage or depth for whatever reason shall, depending on the layer at which the excavation was terminated, be reinstated in accordance with the following requirements:

1) Where reinstatement can be achieved by laying a thicker surface course in accordance with the thickness requirements of Appendix A2 and, in the case of small excavations and narrow trenches, in accordance with Section S6.4.10, no further excavation is required.

2) In all other cases, the binder course shall be excavated to allow a binder course layer to be reinstated in accordance with Appendix A2. Where the existing depth of excavation is greater than 100 mm and the additional depth is less than the minimum layer thickness of Base material a thicker binder course may be laid.

3) In deeper excavations, no further excavation shall be required. Reinstatement shall be carried out in accordance with the relevant requirements of Sections S5 to S9 inclusive, as appropriate.

S3.7 Trenchless Pipelaying

S3.7.1 Moleploughing uses a ploughing machine to pull a flexible pipe or cable below ground. It is employed in unmade ground and may be used in the verges of streets. The moleplough creates a slit in the surface of the ground, which should not require reinstating provided that the surface profile is restored in accordance with Section S9. However, where connections are made to apparatus installed by moleploughing techniques, excavations shall be carried out and reinstated in accordance with this Specification.

S3.7.2 Soil Displacement moling and other trenchless methods do not create an excavation and, when carried out in a proper manner, do not require reinstatement. However, reinstatement shall be carried out in accordance with this Specification at the launch and receive pits and at any intermediate excavations where connections are made to apparatus installed by soil displacement moling and other trenchless techniques.

S3.7.3 Where, as a result of the use of trenchless methods for the installation of apparatus under a street, the Authority has reasonable cause to believe that damage may have been caused to the structure of the street, the Investigatory Works Procedure described in the HAUC Code of Practice for Inspections should be commenced as if the defect was associated with a reinstatement defect for the purposes of that Code. Any remedial work agreed between the Authority and the Undertaker to be necessary, if carried out by the Undertaker, shall be in accordance with this Specification at the Undertaker's expense.

S3.7.4 If the agreed remedial work is carried out by the Authority at the Undertaker's expense the provisions of this Specification shall not apply.

S3.7.5 In the absence of agreement between the Authority and the Undertaker, liability for any damage shall be determined in accordance with section 82 of the Act (Liability for any damage or loss caused).

S4 Surround to Apparatus

S4.1 General

S4.1.1 Surround to the apparatus may be laid to a maximum thickness of 250 mm above the crown of the Undertaker's apparatus. The surround to apparatus shall not intrude into the road structure. It may be necessary on occasions for the Undertaker to lay apparatus deeper, should there be a need to include surround to their apparatus.

S4.1.2 Laying and compaction procedures used for all materials laid as surround to the apparatus shall be the responsibility of the Undertakers.

S4.1.3 The selection of materials for the surround to apparatus shall be the responsibility of the relevant Undertaker. However, all materials used for the surround to apparatus shall comply with the following requirements:

1) Class E Unacceptable Materials, as defined in Appendix A1, and materials that contain particles greater than 37.5 mm nominal size shall not be used as surround to the apparatus.

2) An Alternative Reinstatement Material (ARM) may be used for the entire surround to apparatus or any part thereof, in accordance with Appendix A9.

3) Preformed modules or other protective measures may be placed within the surround to apparatus, according to the Undertaker's requirements.

S5 Backfill

S5.1 Backfill Material Classification

S5.1.1 General

Backfill materials, whether imported to site or derived on-site from excavated materials, shall be classified as follows:

S5.1.2 Class A – Graded Granular Materials

1) Materials with a maximum of 10% by mass passing a 63 micron (μm) BS sieve, and with all material passing a 425 micron (μm) BS sieve showing a plasticity index of 6 or less, determined in accordance with BS1377: Part 2: Method 5.4, are classified as Class A Graded Granular Materials.
2) Class A graded granular materials may include Granular Sub-base Material Type 2 to SHW Clause 804 (excluding natural sands and gravels) and Granular Sub-base Material Type 1 to SHW Clause 803.

S5.1.3 Class B – Granular Materials

Materials with a maximum of 10% by mass passing a 63 micron (μm) BS sieve are classified as Class B Granular Materials.

S5.1.4 Class C – Cohesive/Granular Materials

Mixtures of granular, silt and clay materials with between 10% and 80% by mass passing a 63 micron (μm) BS sieve are classified as Class C Cohesive/Granular Materials.

S5.1.5 Class D – Cohesive Materials

Clay, silt or mixtures of clay and silt with at least 80% by mass passing a 63 micron (μm) BS sieve are classified as Class D Cohesive Materials.

S5.1.6 Class E – Unacceptable Materials

Materials listed as unacceptable in paragraphs 2 ii) and 3 of SHW Clause 601 shall not be used, at any level, within the permanent structure of any reinstatement. Materials classified as unacceptable are listed in Appendix A1.

S5.1.7 The requirements of Appendix A1 shall apply to unbound backfill materials.

S5.1.8 All backfill materials Classes A to D shall be compacted in accordance with Appendix A8.

S5.2 Alternative Reinstatement Materials

S5.2.1 Alternative Reinstatement Materials (ARMs) may be used for the entire backfill layer, or any part thereof, in accordance with Appendix A9.

S5.3 Additional Requirements

S5.3.1 Frost Heave Susceptibility

1) Frost susceptible material is deemed to be material with a mean heave greater than 15 mm when tested in accordance with BS 812 – 124 (as amended by SHW Clause 801.8).
2) Where frost susceptible materials already exist within 450 mm of the surface, such materials may be reinstated to the same levels but, generally, frost susceptible material shall not be used within 450 mm of a road surface. However, 300 mm of wholly bituminous material is considered to provide adequate insulation and may be used as an alternative.
3) In the event of prior notification by the Authority, where the existing depth of non-frost susceptible materials is greater than 450 mm below the road surface and the Authority requires such a thickness of non-frost susceptible material to be maintained, then only non-frost susceptible materials shall be used for the relevant depth.
4) All frost heave susceptibility testing shall be carried out by a laboratory holding current UKAS accreditation for the specified method of testing, unless otherwise agreed.

S5.3.2 Maximum Particle Size

The maximum particle size for all granular backfill materials used as backfill shall comply with the following requirements:

1) All granular backfill materials shall pass through a 75 mm BS sieve.
2) All granular backfill materials used in the reinstatement of trenches less than 150 mm wide shall pass through a 37.5 mm BS sieve.

S5.3.3 Surround to Apparatus as Backfill

Where the excavation depth does not allow the use of a separate backfill layer, the sub-base layer shall be laid directly onto the surround to apparatus. In such cases, the surround material shall represent backfill material and shall be classified in accordance with Section S5.1, for the purposes of determining the requirements for sub-base reinstatement in accordance with Section S6.2.

S5.3.4 **Protective Measures to Apparatus**

Preformed modules or other protective measures may be placed within the backfill, according to the Undertaker's requirements.

S5.3.5 **Chalk**

1) Imported chalk materials used as backfill shall comply with the following requirements:
    a) The saturation moisture content of the chalk shall be determined prior to its use.
    b) The chalk shall be laid and compacted to an approved compaction procedure developed in accordance with Section NG1.6 (3). The compaction procedure shall be proven with chalk materials of similar saturation moisture content.
2) Excavated chalk to be re-used as backfill shall comply with the following requirements:
    a) Excavated chalk shall be stockpiled for re-use and shall not be subjected to multiple handling.
    b) During wet weather, excavated chalk shall be protected against water ingress at all times.
3) Chalk materials shall be assessed by breaking up excavated fragments by hand, or by driving a steel pin into unexcavated deposits, and classified in accordance with Table S5.1. If the classification falls between two densities, then the chalk shall be assumed to be at the lower of the two densities.

Table S5.1 Suitability of Chalk Materials for Use as Backfill

Chalk Density	Physical Assessment	Backfill Suitability
High	Very difficult/impossible to break up by hand Difficult to hammer in steel pin	Carriageways, footways & verges
Medium	Some difficulty in breaking up by hand Some effort needed to hammer in steel pin	Footways & verges only
Low	Easy to break up or crush by hand Steel pin can be pushed in by hand	Unsuitable for use in any reinstatement

Notes to Table S5.1:
1) Chalk often contains flint inclusions and care should be taken to ensure that:
    a) the steel pin does not strike a flint
    b) the hand crushing sample does not contain any flints.

4) Chalk materials shall be compacted in accordance with Appendix A8.2.

S6 Flexible and Composite Roads

S6.1 Reinstatement Methods

S6.1.1 General

1) The Undertaker shall carry out the reinstatement in accordance with one of the following methods and should endeavour to achieve the greatest degree of immediate permanent reinstatement. Reinstatement methods are listed in Appendix A2.10 Table A2.6.
2) Permitted materials and layer thickness are specified in Appendices A1 to A4, A9 and A11.
3) Where the Authority knows of any site with high sulphate levels it should advise Undertakers in advance of the works so that appropriate measures may be taken.

S6.1.2 Method A – All Permanent Reinstatement

The excavation shall be reinstated to a permanent standard at the first visit.

S6.1.3 Method B – Permanent Binder Course Reinstatement

1) The backfill, sub-base, Base and binder course shall be reinstated to a permanent standard at the first visit.
2) The permanent binder course material, or an alternative interim material, shall be extended to the surface as the interim surface course, with or without a thin separating material layer of sand at the position of the binder course/surface course interface.
3) On the second visit, all interim surfacing materials shall be removed, to the top of the binder course, typically by cold planing, and a permanent surface course shall be laid.
4) Where a sand separation layer is present, prior to the reinstatement of the permanent surface course the sand shall be removed, the surface brushed clean and a tack coat or bond coat applied.

S6.1.4 **Method C – Permanent Base Reinstatement**

1) The backfill, sub-base and Base shall be reinstated to a permanent standard at the first visit.

2) The interim surface course and part, or all, of the interim binder course, may be deferred set material. Part, or all, of the entire interim binder course may be an unbound granular material.

3) On the second visit, all interim surfacing materials shall be removed, to the top of the Base, and a permanent binder course and surface course shall be laid.

S6.1.5 **Method D – Permanent Sub-base Reinstatement**

1) The backfill and sub-base shall be reinstated to a permanent standard at the first visit

2) The interim Base shall be granular and the interim surfacing shall be in accordance with the relevant requirements of Section S6.1.4.

3) On the second visit, all interim materials shall be removed, to the top of the sub-base, and a permanent Base, binder course and surface course laid.

S6.1.6 **Method E – Permanent Reinstatement incorporating Interim Surface Overlay**

Not applicable

S6.2 Sub-base Reinstatement

S6.2.1 **General**

Permitted options are shown in Appendix A3.5, A4.4 & A4.5 – subject to the following exceptions:

a) Sub-base Equivalence: The thickness of granular sub-bases may be reduced, provided that the thickness of the bituminous binder course is increased proportionately, in accordance with S6.3.3.

b) Small Reinstatements: CBGM B sub-base of 150 mm thickness may be used in small excavations and narrow trenches regardless of whether the existing sub-base is cement bound. Where this option is utilised, the Base material shall also be a bound material.

c) Alternative Reinstatement Materials: Alternative Reinstatement Materials (ARMs) may be laid to the top of sub-base level, in accordance with Appendix A9, regardless of whether the existing sub-base is a bound material.

S6.3 Base Reinstatement

S6.3.1 General

Permitted options are shown in Appendices A3 and A4, subject to the following exceptions:

S6.3.2 CBGM B in Flexible and Composite Roads

1) In Types 0 & 1 roads, where a CBGM B Base is used, the reinstatement may either be surfaced on the same day or the CBGM B shall be allowed 7 days to cure before surfacing is undertaken. In either case, the CBGM B shall be allowed 7 days to cure before the road is opened to traffic.
2) In Types 2, 3 & 4 roads, where the reinstatement is surfaced on the same day that the CBGM B Base is placed, the road may be opened to traffic on the following day. Where the CBGM B Base is not surfaced on the same day, the reinstatement shall be allowed 3 days to cure before surfacing is undertaken.
3) All composite roads constructed with a Base of CBGM B lean-mix concrete or equivalent shall be reinstated with a CBGM B Base.
4) In composite roads, the reinstated CBGM B Base shall be laid flush with the top of the existing cement-bound Base.
5) Continuously reinforced concrete bases that have been connected with dowel bars are not covered by this clause S6.3.2. Special conditions will apply to the reinstatement and shall be agreed with the Authority.

S6.3.3 Base Equivalence

In Type 3 and 4 flexible roads, the thickness of granular bases may be reduced provided that the thickness of the bituminous binder course is increased proportionately, in accordance with the following requirements:

1) Each 10 mm increase in bituminous binder course thickness is equivalent to a 35 mm decrease in thickness of Type 1 Granular Sub-Base at Base and/or sub-base levels and vice versa.
2) This equivalence rule may be applied to include the total replacement of all granular materials at both sub-base and Base levels, subject to the following restrictions:
    a) Binder course and surface course thickness in Type 3 and 4 roads are minimum values and shall not be reduced by application of the 10:35 equivalence of bituminous/granular materials; and
    b) Where part of a granular Base and/or sub-base is to be replaced by additional binder course material, the remaining total thickness of granular material at Base and/or sub-base level shall not be less than 150 mm.

S6.3.4 Modular Materials within the Excavation

1) Where cobbles or setts are encountered during excavation, they may be recovered and re-used for reinstatement of the relevant layer. Alternatively, at the discretion of the Undertaker, the layer may be reinstated using CBGM B laid to a thickness of 100 mm, or to match the original thickness, whichever is greater.

2) Layers of modules, cobbles/setts, stones, rocks, or other large aggregate particles laid upright, in an interlocking fashion, often termed 'penning', will exhibit a greater stiffness than an equivalent layer of cobbles/setts laid horizontally. Where such upright interlocking modules are encountered, the layer shall be reinstated using CBGM B laid to a thickness of 100 mm, or to match the original thickness, whichever is greater.

3) Where surplus modules, cobbles or setts are removed from site, they shall remain the property of the Authority. The Undertaker shall notify the Authority and retain them for 10 days following such notification. Thereafter, the Undertaker shall be free to dispose of all remaining modules, cobbles and setts.

4) Where CBGM B is used at base level, it shall be used in accordance with Section S6.3.2.

S6.3.5 Alternative Reinstatement Materials

Alternative Reinstatement Materials (ARMs) may be laid to the top of Base level, in accordance with Appendix A9, regardless of whether the existing Base is a bound material.

S6.4 Surface Reinstatement

Permitted options are shown in Appendices A2 to A4 inclusive, subject to the following exceptions:

S6.4.1 Hot Rolled Asphalt (HRA) Surface

1) Type 0, 1 & 2 roads, where the existing surface course is HRA, shall be reinstated with HRA surface course, regardless of whether the running surface has a surface dressing or other surface treatment.

2) Type 3 & 4 roads, where the existing surface course is HRA and does not have a surface dressing or other surface treatment, shall be reinstated with HRA surface course.

S6.4.2 Stone Mastic Asphalt (SMA) and Thin Surface Course Systems

1) Where the existing surface course material is SMA or a thin surface course (TS) system the road shall be reinstated either with SMA surface course or, at the Authority's request, with thin surface course, subject to the following requirements:

   a) Generic SMA or thin surface course mixtures shall match the existing nominal aggregate size of the existing surface course material.

Reduction in nominal aggregate size shall only be where agreed with the Authority and shall take into account texture depth requirements.

b) The standard combined thickness of binder course and SMA surface course shown in Appendices A3.0 to A3.4 shall be 100mm.

2) Edge and base preparation for permanent SMA reinstatements shall be as follows:

a) All edges shall be saw cut or trimmed by saw, to a depth of 40 mm or the thickness of the surface course, prior to permanent reinstatement.

b) A K1-40 tack coat or BBA HAPAS certified bond coat shall be applied in accordance with Section S6.5.1. In the event that no such approvals have been issued they shall not be used without approval of the Authority. Approval shall not unreasonably be withheld.

c) An edge sealant shall be applied in accordance with Section S6.5.2.2.

3) Where the existing surface is a thin surface course material and the Authority does not want the reinstatement to be completed using SMA, the Authority shall contact the Undertaker in accordance with Section S6.4.5.5.

4) Where the Authority has a policy to grit or otherwise treat newly laid Stone Mastic Asphalt surfacings, it should advise the Undertaker of the required method and materials and the Undertaker shall comply.

S6.4.3 Asphalt Concrete Surface Course Materials

Where the existing surface course material is asphalt concrete it may be reinstated with any of the surface course options in Appendix A2 to A4.

Where used, asphalt concrete surface course materials shall be AC 10 close surf, laid 40 mm thick.

S6.4.4 Asphalt Concrete Binder Course Materials

Where Asphalt concrete binder course is to be used as the running surface for a period in excess of 6 months the usual supplier declared target binder content shall be increased by 0.5%.

S6.4.5 Other Bituminous Materials

Where it is necessary to use bituminous materials not included in Appendix A2, they shall be used in accordance with the following:

S6.4.5.1 *General Requirements*

1) Where existing road surfaces have been treated or constructed with high friction surfacings, porous asphalt or coloured surfacings and local custom and practice has been to complete all previous resurfacing with like materials, their permanent reinstatement shall be carried out in accordance with the following requirements:

a) High friction surfacings shall be permanently reinstated with like materials, or an agreed alternative material, in accordance with Section S6.4.5.2.

b) In the event of notification by the Authority the reinstatement of any existing porous asphalt surface course (excluding small reinstatements) shall be carried out in accordance with the Authority's requirements. Small reinstatements shall be reinstated as detailed in Section S6.4.5.3.

c) Coloured surfacings shall be permanently reinstated with like materials, or an agreed alternative material, in accordance with Section S6.4.5.4.

2) When requested by the Undertaker, the Authority shall identify an appropriate source of suitable like or alternative materials, wherever possible. Where the Authority is unable to identify an appropriate source of suitable material, the Undertaker shall provide a suitable material on the basis of best reasonable endeavours.

3) Where existing road surfaces have been treated or constructed with high friction surfacings, porous asphalt or coloured surfacings and local custom and practice has not been to complete all previous resurfacing with like materials, the Undertaker shall consult with the Authority to determine appropriate reinstatement requirements.

4) Where other specialist surfacing materials not included in Appendix A2 or Section S6.4.5.1 (1) above have been used, they may generally be permanently reinstated in accordance with Section S6.4.5.5.

S6.4.5.2 *High Friction Surfacings*

1) High friction surfacings shall be permanently reinstated with a like material within 15 working days following the date of completion of the reinstatement, unless the prevailing weather conditions or other site circumstances mitigate against the successful application of the high friction surfacing. Where this occurs, the permanent reinstatement shall be deferred until such time as the unfavourable weather conditions or other site circumstances abate. Site circumstances justifying delaying the reinstatement of the High Friction Surfacing include the need for the new surface course material to be trafficked and/or aged prior to the application of a cold-applied material if this is specified by the system supplier.

2) Prior to the application of the permanent, or any interim, friction surfacing, warning signs shall be displayed indicating a potential slippery road surface.

3) All High Friction Surfacing applied to any roads shall have a current Type 1 BBA/HAPAS Roads and Bridges certificate. These materials shall be laid by a contractor certificated by the BBA, and being a Certificate holder for the application of that material, with the exception of small or narrow excavations in Types 2, 3 & 4 roads where the material shall have a current Type 1 BBA/HAPAS Roads and Bridges certificate, but may be applied by a contractor not approved by the BBA/HAPAS, but

with experience in applying such materials strictly in accordance with the manufacturer's instructions.

4) Some high friction surfacing materials have a limited manufacturer's guarantee and may be subject to wear and abrasion during the guarantee period. However, the reinstated area shall not be inferior to the adjoining surface during the guarantee period.

S6.4.5.3 *Porous Asphalt (small reinstatements)*

Small reinstatements which do not adversely affect the overall drainage characteristics of the site, may be reinstated using SMA subject to the following:

a) Multiple small reinstatements using SMA shall not be closer than 3 m to each other in the principal direction of fall or surface drainage flow.

b) Porous asphalt surface courses shall be reinstated to nominally match the thickness of the existing layer.

c) The binder course of porous asphalt reinstatements shall be hot rolled asphalt.

d) All edges shall be saw cut, or trimmed by saw, to a minimum depth of 50 mm (or the thickness of the surface course, if greater), prior to permanent reinstatement.

e) For permanent reinstatements using porous asphalt, all edges shall be cleared of all contamination and treated with a light application of tack coat material, not edge sealant. A K1-40 tack coat shall be applied at a minimum rate of 0.5 to 0.7 l/m^2, in accordance with Section S6.5.1.

f) For permanent reinstatements using SMA, all edges shall be treated with edge sealant, preferably a non-rubberised sealant applied by spray. A K1-40 tack coat material shall be applied to the base of the reinstatement in accordance with Section S6.5.1.

S6.4.5.4 *Coloured Surfacings*

Coloured surfacings used to highlight highway features such as speed warnings, bus or cycle lanes, 'gateways' etc. shall be permanently reinstated using like materials of equivalent type and similar colour, subject to the following requirements:

a) Where the coloured surfacing is overlaid onto a road surface, a coloured overlay shall be applied to the same thickness.

b) Where the coloured surfacing is laid full depth, a coloured material shall be laid to the same thickness, wherever possible and practical. Where it is not possible or practical, the coloured surfacing material shall be reinstated by agreement.

c) Some high friction surfacing materials that are coloured have a limited manufacturer's guarantee and may be subject to wear and abrasion during the guarantee period. However, the reinstated area shall not be inferior to the adjoining surface during the guarantee period.

S6.4.5.5 *Other Specialist Surfacing Materials*

1) Specialist surfacings not included in Appendix A2 or Section S6.4.5.1 (1) shall generally be reinstated with SMA.
2) Where the overall area is sufficiently large to facilitate machine laying and the local custom and practice has been to complete all previous resurfacing with like materials and the Authority wishes to request the use of like materials, the Authority shall:
   a) Notify the Undertaker accordingly at the planning or notice stage, or in the case of immediate works, before the permanent reinstatement.
   b) Identify an appropriate source of suitable like or equivalent materials.
3) All other surfacing materials not covered above, including grouted bituminous materials, traffic calming materials, surface treatments etc., shall be permanently reinstated by agreement.

S6.4.6 Surface Treatments

1) In Types 0, 1 & 2 roads, where an existing surface dressing or other surface treatment is readily apparent, the Undertaker shall apply an equivalent surface treatment. If requested by the Authority, an appropriate timing and methodology for the works shall be jointly agreed in accordance with national specifications and Codes of Practice (e.g. Road Note 39).
2) In Types 3 & 4 roads either:
   a) Surface dressing or other surface treatment is not required when any binder course and surface course option permitted by Section S6.4 is laid, or
   b) The surfacing layers and equivalent surface dressing or other surface treatment shall be reinstated by agreement.

S6.4.7 Coated Chippings

1) All pre-coated chippings shall be as specified in Appendix A2.
2) Where pre-coated chippings are to be embedded into a road surface, they shall be spread to give a chipping density reasonably matching that of the existing surface, notwithstanding the requirements for surface texture specified in Section S2.6.

S6.4.8 Composite Roads

The total combined thickness of the reinstated binder course and surface course shall match the existing bituminous thickness. Wherever practicable, the required surface course thickness should be maintained by adjustment of the binder course thickness.

S6.4.9 Single Course Construction

NOT USED

S6.4.10 Small Excavations, Narrow Trenches and Access Chamber Covers

1) A permanent surface course material in accordance with Appendix A2 may be laid in place of a permanent binder course material at Base and/or binder course level in:

   i) small excavations and narrow trenches (as defined in Sections S1.5.1 & S1.5.2);

   ii) within 350mm of access chamber covers

2) Where this option is used there shall be no substitution of bitumen binder equivalence, as permitted under Appendix A11.

S6.4.11 Large Diameter Cores (>150 mm diameter for Undertaking Works)

Undertakers may extract large diameter cores of bound layers and reinsert the core into the opening as part of the reinstatement. This is a new procedure within the UK and the Undertaker shall obtain the prior agreement of the Authority before proceeding. There shall be no departure from the performance requirements during the guarantee period.

S6.5 Base and Edge Preparation

S6.5.1 Base Preparation

1) All surfaces shall be free of contamination prior to the application of a tack coat or bond coat. This is especially important after the removal of a sand separation layer.

2) A tack coat or bond coat shall be applied to the surface of all bound layers prior to overlaying in all circumstances.

3) The tack coat or bond coat shall be applied at a rate to ensure a residual bitumen content of 0.15 kg/m^2.

4) Multiple lifts of the same material laid during a single visit on the same day do not require treatment between lifts. However, a tack coat or bond coat shall be applied prior to placement of the permanent surface course layer in work carried out under Section S6.4.10.

5) A bitumen emulsion edge sealant may be used as a tack coat or bond coat in small excavations and narrow trenches.

S6.5.2 Edge Preparation

S6.5.2.1 *Edge Regularity*

The edges of excavations may need to be trimmed, at binder course and/or surface course level, to meet the following requirements:

1) All bound edges shall be essentially straight, smooth and vertical.

   Edge regularity requirements are intended to provide a shape that will not hinder the compaction of material adjacent to the reinstatement edge. Overlapping edge cuts and corner cut outs should be minimal and all cuts extending into the existing surface shall be filled with flexible bituminous sealant. A circular excavation shall be considered a regular shape.

2) The internal corners and edges of a reinstatement shall be as square as possible. Internal angles less than 90° are acceptable and, where this is the case, appropriate compaction equipment shall be used to achieve the specified compaction.

3) There shall be no requirement to trim the sides of trench excavations solely to provide a uniform width, provided that individual projections are not less than 250 mm length, measured parallel to the nominal centreline of the trench. See also Figure S6.1 (Example 1).

4) There shall be no requirement to trim a small excavation solely in order to provide a square or rectangular shape. Any shape, in any excavation, with included angles which may be less than 90°, with no projection less than 250 mm length, may be considered to be regular. See also Figure S6.1 (Example 2).

5) Where the existing surfacing material is sound at the corners of an excavation, there shall be no necessity to cut out to a corner; a regular chamfer may be preferable.

The final shape of the excavation when viewed from above should be governed by the above principles rather than by aesthetic considerations (see Figure S6.1).

Figure S6.1 Examples of Prepared Edge (Example 1)

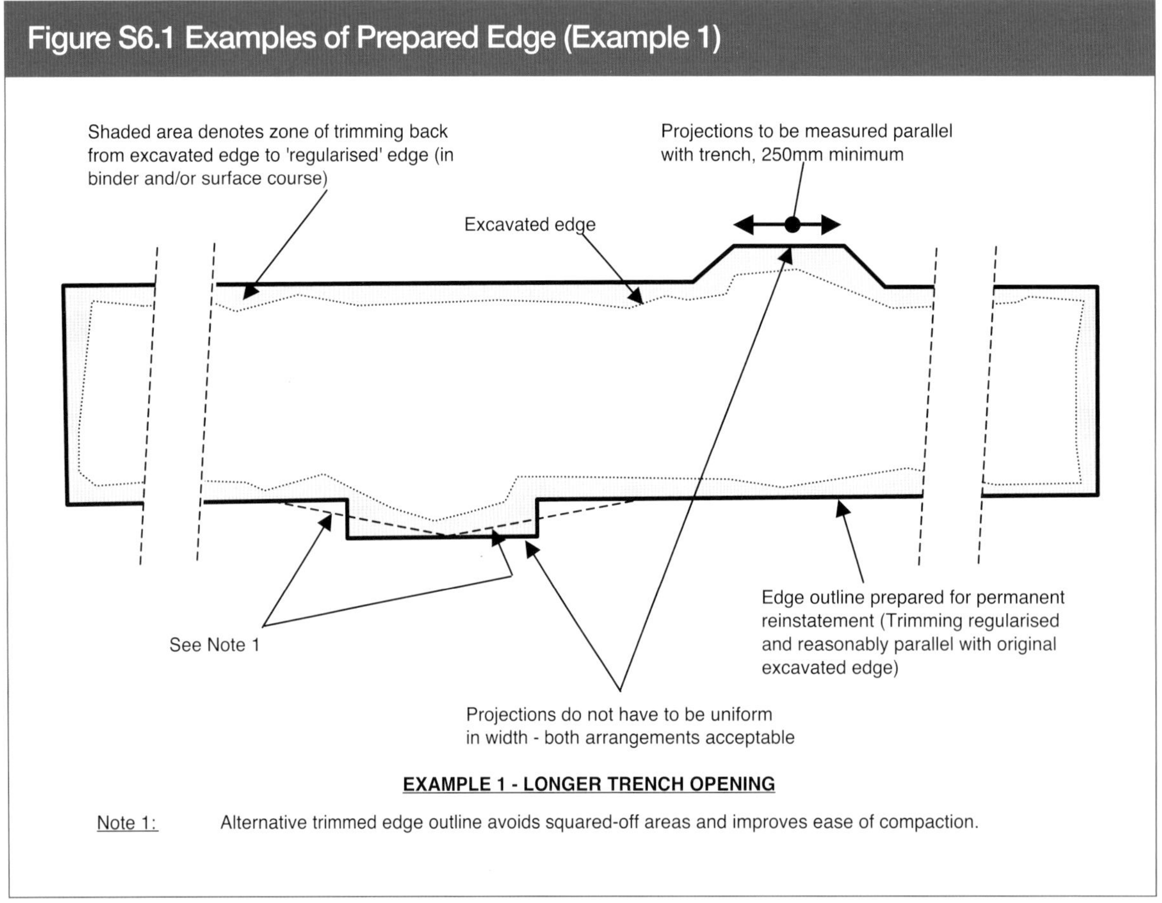

Note 1: Alternative trimmed edge outline avoids squared-off areas and improves ease of compaction.

Figure S6.1 Examples of Prepared Edge (Example 2)

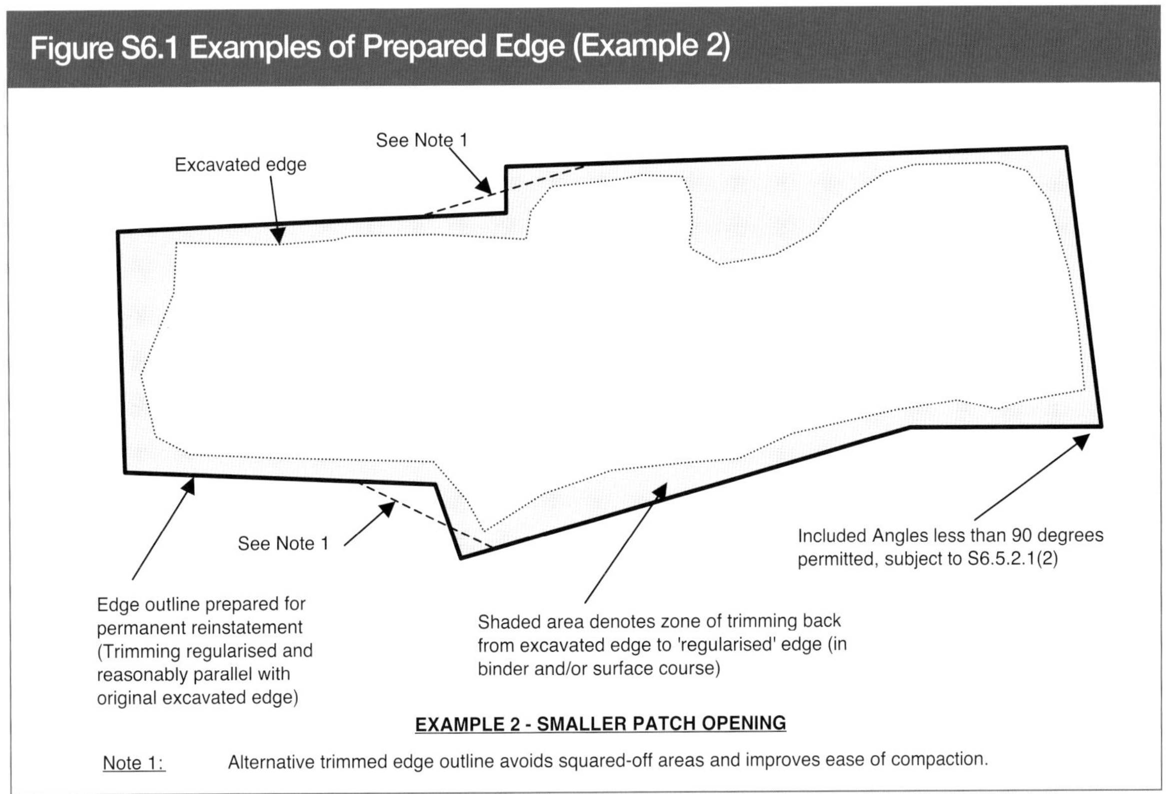

S6.5.2.2 *Edge Sealing*

1) All edges shall be adequately prepared prior to application of edge sealant e.g. free of contamination, loose material, and the like. In all cases the manufacturer's instructions shall be followed.

2) At any interim stage and at the time of permanent reinstatement, the top 100 mm, at least, of all bound vertical edges at surface course and binder course levels, and the equivalent area on kerbs and exposed fixed features, shall be painted with a bitumen based edge sealant or otherwise prepared with an edge sealing system or equivalent material There shall be no significant splashing, spillage or any deliberate over painting of the adjacent road surface, subject to the requirements of Section S11.7.

3) Tack coat, bond coat or overbanding material shall not be used as an edge sealant unless otherwise specified in Section S6.4.5.3.

4) There should be visible evidence of the use of sealant. The fact that a core may separate is not, on its own, evidence that no edge sealant has been used.

S6.5.2.3 *Proximity to Road Edges, and Fixed Features*

1) Where the "trimmed" edge of any excavation is within 250 mm of the road edge, kerbing, other fixed features or another reinstatement, the trim-line shall be extended to the interface with the road edge, kerbing etc. See Figure S6.2

2) The additional reinstatement area required by extending the trim-line may be confined to the surface course, provided the lower layers have not been damaged.

3) Where an existing fixed feature is immediately adjacent to another fixed feature (e.g. road gully, stop-cock valve cover, etc.) material selection shall be appropriate to ensure adequate compaction and surface profile – Section S2.2.1 (4) refers.

Figure S6.2 Edge Requirements and Trim Lines in Carriageways

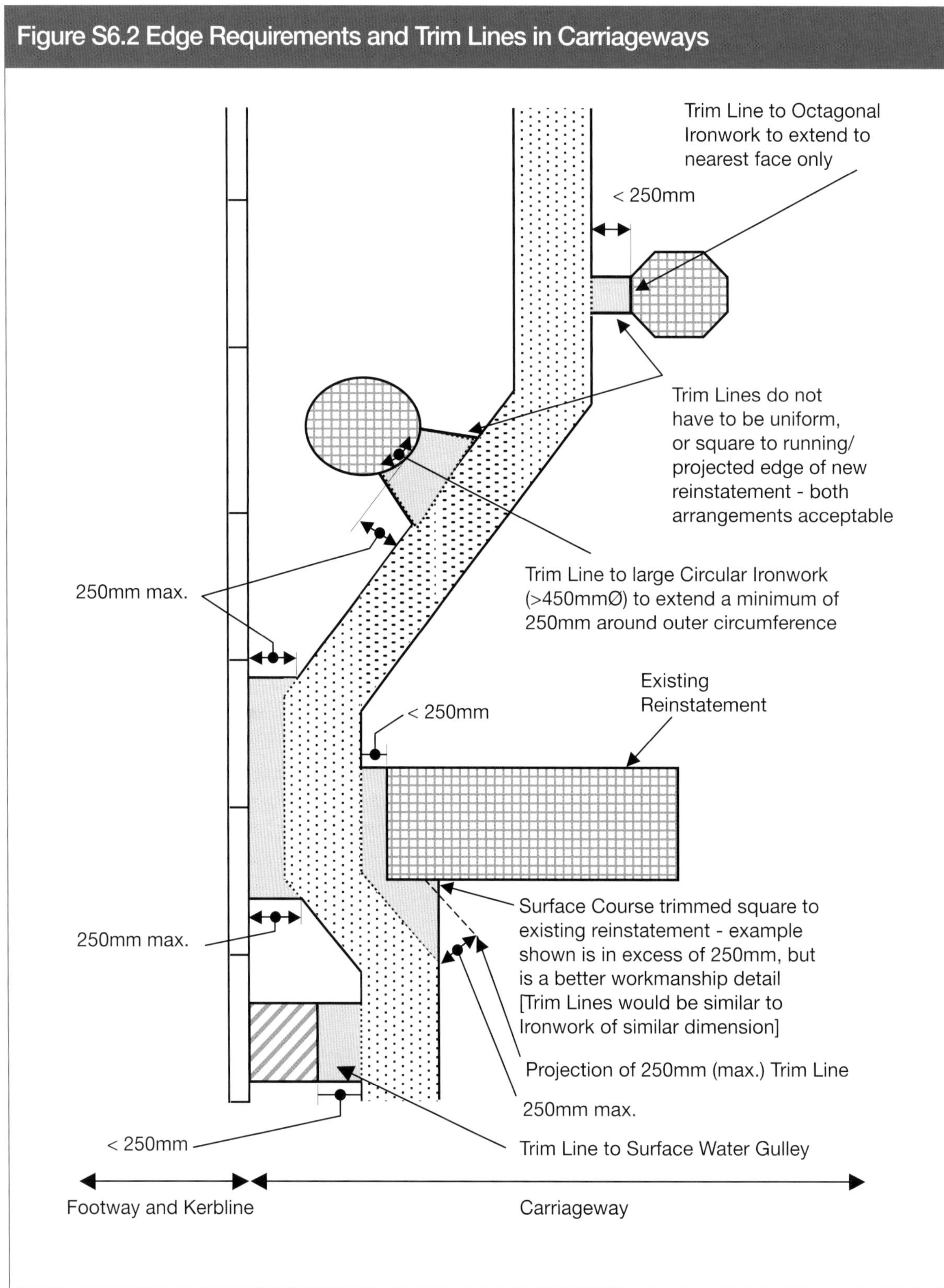

S6.5.2.4 *Undercutting*

1) All bound edges shall be essentially smooth and vertical with no significant undercutting, as shown in Figure S6.3.

Figure S6.3 Example of Need for Trimback due to Undercutting

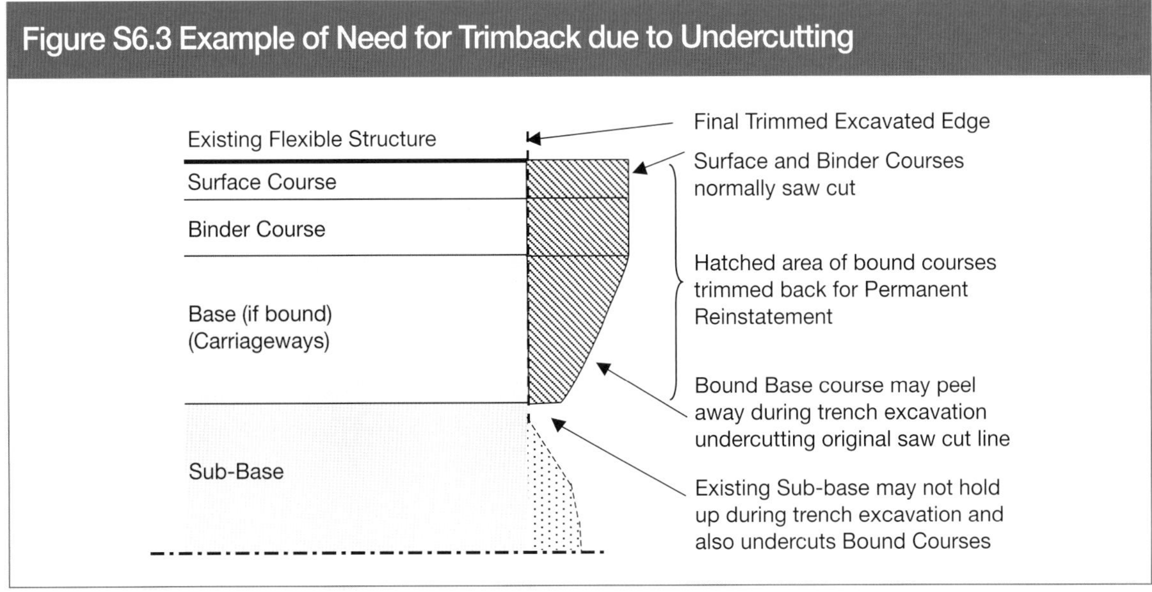

S6.5.2.5 *Stepped Joints*

On Type 0 and 1 roads where it is the custom and practice of an Authority to cut-back the surface and/or binder course to provide a stepped profile then this shall be notified to the Undertaker. Subject to the agreement of the Authority the stepped joint shall be applied to reinstatements in Type 0 and 1 roads subject to the following:

i) Small reinstatements and narrow transverse trenches shall be excluded

ii) The stepped profile shall match the Authority's policy subject to a maximum of 75mm step – see Figure S6.4

Figure S6.4 Stepped Joint in Flexible Carriageway Types 0 and 1

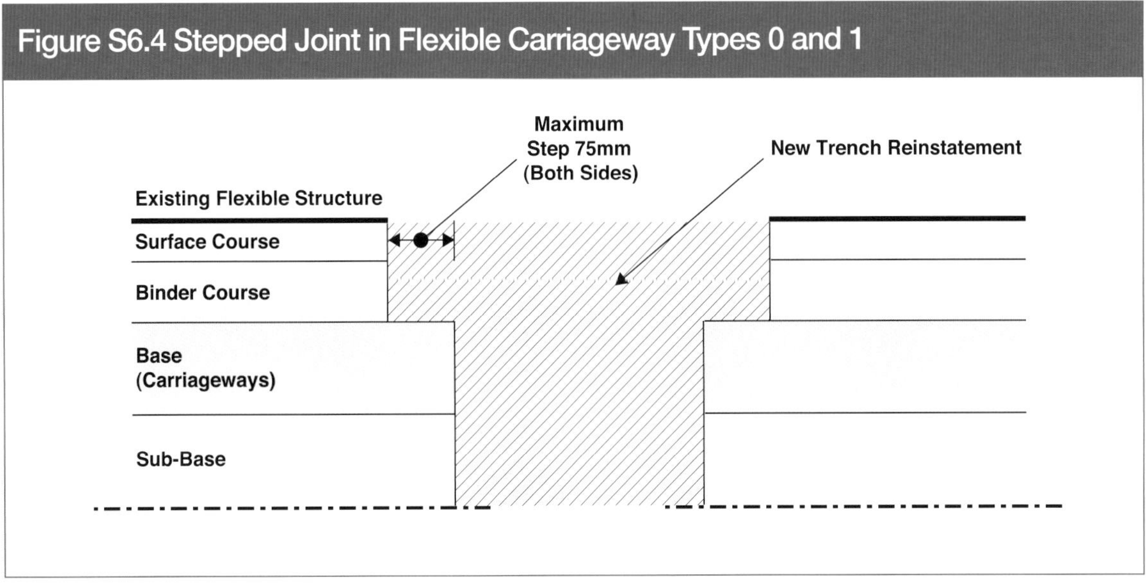

S6.6 Tolerances

1) All tolerances for all bituminous materials permitted in Appendix A2 in the reinstatement of flexible and composite roads, shall be in accordance with the requirements of Appendix A2.

2) Tolerances permitted for all other bituminous materials shall be by agreement.

S7 Rigid and Modular Roads

S7.1 Reinstatement Methods

S7.1.1 General

1) When the total thickness of any bituminous overlay is 100mm or more, it shall be reinstated as a composite road in accordance with Section S6.
2) Some modern road constructions incorporating special design philosophies are outside the scope of this Specification and reference should be made to Section NG 7.1.
3) The Undertaker shall carry out the reinstatement in accordance with one of the following methods and should endeavour to achieve the greatest degree of immediate permanent reinstatement. Reinstatement methods are listed in Appendix A2.10 Table A2.6.
4) Permitted materials and layer thickness are specified in Appendices A1, A2, A5, A9, A11 and A12.
5) Where the Authority knows of any site with high sulphate levels, it should advise Undertakers in advance of the works so that appropriate measures may be taken.

S7.1.2 Method A – All Permanent Reinstatement

The excavation and concrete road slab shall be reinstated to a permanent standard at the first visit. The bituminous overlay shall not be laid until the cured road slab has achieved a crushing strength of $25N/mm^2$.

S7.1.3 Method B – Permanent Binder Course Reinstatement

Not applicable

S7.1.4 Method C – Permanent Base Reinstatement

Not applicable

S7.1.5 Method D – Permanent Sub-base Reinstatement

1) The backfill and sub-base shall be reinstated to a permanent standard at the first visit.
2) The concrete road slab and overlay (if existing) shall be reinstated, for the interim period only, with a bound material. The interim surfacing shall be a bound material to a thickness of 100mm or 50mm as shown in Appendices A5.0 to A6.3.
3) On the second visit, all interim materials shall be removed to the top of the sub-base and a permanent concrete road slab reinstated. The road slab shall be in accordance with Sections S7.3.2 and S7.3.5. Any overlay may be reinstated, to an interim standard, in accordance with the relevant requirements of Section S6.1.4.
4) Any interim overlay shall be removed at a later date, to the top of the concrete road slab, and a permanent overlay reinstated.

S7.1.6 Method E – Permanent Reinstatement incorporating Interim Surface Overlay

1) Any bituminous surface overlay may be reinstated, to an interim standard, in accordance with the relevant requirements of Section S6.1.4.
2) Any interim bituminous overlay shall be removed at a later date, to the top of the concrete road slab, and a permanent bituminous overlay reinstated.

S7.2 Sub-base Reinstatement

S7.2.1 General

1) In a rigid road, the sub-base is deemed to be any layer of imported granular or cement bound material existing immediately below the base of the concrete road slab. Where such a sub-base layer exists, a similar or equivalent material shall be laid to match the existing thickness subject to a minimum thickness of 150mm.
2) Permitted options are shown in Appendix A5, subject to the following exceptions:

S7.2.2 Small Reinstatements

A CBGM B sub-base of 150 mm thickness may be used in small excavations and narrow trenches regardless of whether the existing sub-base is cement bound.

S7.2.3 Alternative Reinstatement Materials

Alternative Reinstatement Materials may be laid at sub-base level, in accordance with Appendix A9.

S7.3 Concrete Road Slab Reinstatement

S7.3.1 General

Permitted options are shown in Appendix A5, subject to the following exceptions:

S7.3.2 Concrete Specification

1) The concrete road slab shall be reinstated using C32/40 concrete mixed in accordance with SHW Clause 1001, with an air entrainment admixture used in at least the top 50 mm of the road slab.

   Exceptionally, where agreed, the concrete road slab may be reinstated using an alternative material, to suit site conditions, e.g. a high early strength mix may be agreed to allow an earlier re-opening of a heavily trafficked road.

2) Where concrete is mixed off site, Quality Assurance Certificates detailing the Specifications against which the concrete has been ordered and supplied should be obtained by the Undertaker for confirmation of material quality. Where possible, the concrete should be obtained from a plant which holds a valid Quality Assurance Certificate.

3) In the case of small excavations, a site-batched equivalent to C32/40 concrete may be used.

S7.3.3 Joints

All expansion, contraction and warping joints removed or otherwise damaged during the excavation must be replaced or reconstructed to a similar design, using equivalent materials, at the time of permanent reinstatement.

S7.3.4 Membranes

1) Any slip membrane shall be reinstated beneath the road slab and a curing membrane shall be used above the road slab.

2) Impermeable polythene or similar sheeting may be used for both the slip and curing membranes.

3) Sprayed plastic film may be used as a curing membrane by agreement.

S7.3.5 Texture Depth

1) For small excavations, narrow trenches and other openings less than 1.0m wide, reference shall be made to Section S2.6.1(2) and Table S2.5.

2) For all other excavations the highway authority shall be consulted and a method agreed. The finished surface shall comply with Table S2.5.

S7.3.6 Opening to Traffic

The cured road slab may be opened to traffic as soon as a crushing strength of 25 N/mm^2 has been achieved.

S7.4 Edge Support and Preparation

The edges of all excavations in rigid roads shall comply with the following requirements:

S7.4.1 Edge Support

Support for the edges of the reinstatement shall comply with one of the following options:

1) Edge Taper Support

a) Where the surface of the road slab is the running surface of the road, the excavation shall be delineated by sawing the pavement to a depth of 30 mm ±10 mm. The remainder of the exposed faces should be rough cut, at an angle of 27° ± 18° to the vertical; see Figure S7.1.

b) In all other cases, the exposed faces should be rough cut, at an angle of 27° ± 18° to the vertical. Delineation by pavement saw, to a depth of 30 mm ± 10 mm, may also be applied.

Figure S7.1 Slab Edge Taper Options

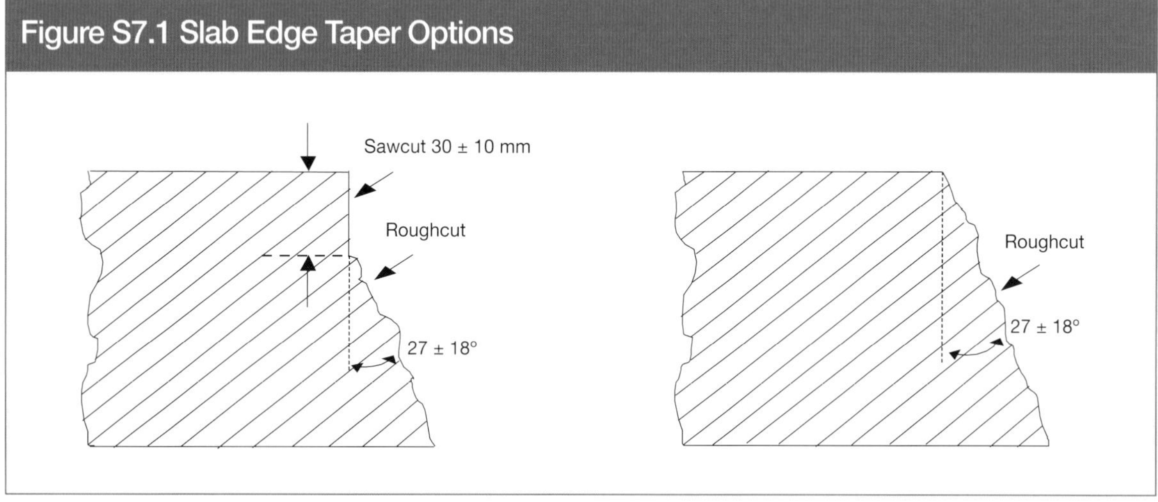

2) Dowel Bar Support

a) Where the surface of the road slab is the running surface of the road, the excavation shall be delineated by pavement saw, to a minimum depth of 20 mm. Any unsawn section of the slab shall be left roughcut to give an essentially vertical surface; see Figure S7.2.

b) Where the road is of composite construction or has been overlaid, the exposed faces should be prepared as detailed in Figure S7.1.

c) In all excavations, a row of horizontal holes shall be drilled along the centreline of the exposed faces, to provide a sliding fit for 20 mm or 25 mm nominal diameter steel dowel bars.

d) All holes shall be drilled at 600 mm ± 100 mm centres, with the holes along one face offset or staggered, relative to the opposite face, by at least 200 mm when viewed from above; see Figure S7.2. The nominal hole depth shall be equal to 50% of the dowel bar length ± 50 mm.

The maximum dowel bar length shall be 400 mm; minimum dowel bar length shall be equal to the width of the reinstatement less 50 mm.

Figure S7.2 Dowel Bar Arrangement – Plan View

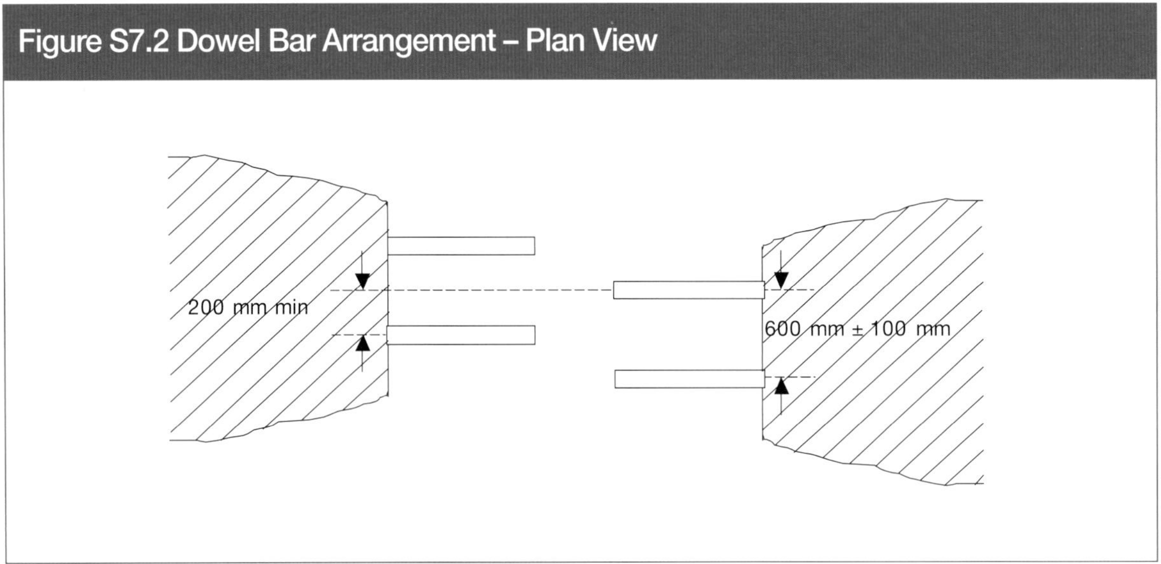

S7.4.2 Edge Preparation

The edges of the reinstatement shall be trimmed, where necessary over part or all of the thickness of the concrete road slab, to comply with the following requirements:

1) The edge regularity shall comply with the requirements of Section S6.5.2.
2) Any undercutting shall comply with the requirements of Section S6.5.2.4.
3) Cracking within the adjacent road slab, resulting from the excavation operation, shall require the relevant area of the slab to be removed and included within the area to be reinstated.
4) Where, following trimming, the excavation extends to within 300 mm of the road slab edge, joint, other reinstatement or ironwork, the relevant area of the slab shall be removed and included within the area to be reinstated.
5) All edges shall be cleaned and wetted prior to the placement of the concrete.

S7.5 Reinforcement

Where steel reinforcement within the concrete road slab has been cut, new steel reinforcing of equivalent weight shall be provided, in accordance with the following requirements:

1) The new reinforcement shall be lapped and wired or welded to the existing reinforcement.
2) A minimum of 150 mm of the existing reinforcement shall be exposed to allow adequate attachment of the new reinforcement.

3) Where 150 mm of the exposed reinforcement cannot be preserved during the excavation, the concrete road slab shall be trimmed, as necessary, to expose additional reinforcement. This additional trimming shall not supersede the requirement to provide a slab edge taper or dowel bars.

S7.6 Overlays

S7.6.1 General

1) Where the surface of the concrete road slab or the modular surface layer is overlaid with a bituminous material or surface treatment, a matching thickness of a similar or equivalent material shall be laid.

2) Wherever practicable, the required surface course thickness should be maintained, by adjustment of the binder course thickness. The surface course and binder course materials shall not be laid to a thickness less than that required by Appendices A2 and A3 for the nominal size of each material laid.

3) Where the surface of the concrete road slab or modular surface has had a surface treatment including overlay, an equivalent surface treatment or overlay shall be applied.

S7.6.2 Surface Reinstatement

Permitted options are shown in Appendices A4 and A5, subject to the following exceptions:

1) Edge preparation shall be carried out in accordance with Section S6.5, except that the existing edge of the overlay shall be trimmed by a distance equal to the nominal thickness of the surface course, or 40 mm, whichever is the greater.

2) Surface reinstatement shall be carried out in accordance with the requirements of Section S6.4.

S7.7 Modular Roads

S7.7.1 General

1) Types 0, 1 and 2 modular roads are not included in this Specification and reinstatement designs shall be in accordance with BS 7533:Part 3, BS 6717:Part 1 & BS 6667:Part 1.

2) The Undertaker shall carry out the reinstatement of Types 3 and 4 modular roads in accordance with one of the following methods and should endeavour to achieve greatest degree of immediate permanent reinstatement.

3) Permitted materials and layer thickness are specified in Appendices A1, A2, A6, A9, A11 and A12, subject to the following requirements.

4) Where modules of natural stone material are present in trafficked roads refer to Appendix A12.

S7.7.2 **Method A – All Permanent Reinstatement**

The backfill, sub-base (if existing), bedding and modular surface layer shall all be reinstated to a permanent standard at the first visit.

S7.7.3 **Method B – Permanent Sub-base Reinstatement**

1) The backfill and sub-base shall all be reinstated to a permanent standard at the first visit, together with an interim granular Base and interim bituminous surface course, as per Section S6.1.5.
2) On the second visit, the interim reinstatement shall be removed to the top of the sub-base and a permanent Base, bedding and modular surface layer reinstated.

S7.7.4 **Sub-base Reinstatement**

1) Permitted options are shown in Appendix A6, subject to the requirements of Section S6.2.
2) The sub-base shall be reinstated to match the existing, or its structural equivalent.

S7.7.5 **Base Reinstatement**

1) Permitted options are shown in Appendix A6, subject to the requirements of Section S6.3.
2) The Base shall be reinstated to match the existing, or its structural equivalent.

S7.7.6 **Surface Reinstatement**

The modular surface layer shall be reinstated in accordance with Appendices A6 and A12. The requirements and recommendations for the provision of replacement modules are given in Appendix A12.

S7.8 Tolerances

All performance requirements and tolerances permitted in the reinstatement of rigid and modular roads shall be in accordance with the requirements of Section S2 and Appendix A2.

S8 Footways, Footpaths and Cycle Tracks

S8.1 Reinstatement Methods

S8.1.1 General

1) The Undertaker shall carry out reinstatement in accordance with one of the following methods and should endeavour to achieve the greatest degree of immediate permanent reinstatement. Reinstatement methods are listed in Appendix A2.10 Table A2.6.

2) In the event of prior notification by the Authority, where local custom and practice has been to surface footways, footpaths and cycle tracks with aggregates of a certain colour and/or minimum PSV, then the Undertaker shall provide equivalent aggregate, at the time of permanent reinstatement, subject to the requirements of Section S2.6.1.

3) Permitted materials and layer thickness are specified in Appendices A1, A2, A7, A9, A11 and A12. In all flexible reinstatements, the Surface Course material may also be used at Binder Course level, as shown in Appendix A7.1.

4) Cycle tracks that are part of the carriageway shall be reinstated to carriageway standards.

S8.1.2 Method A – All Permanent Reinstatement

The excavation shall be reinstated to a permanent standard at the first visit.

S8.1.3 Method B – Permanent Binder Course Reinstatement

1) In flexible structures, the backfill, sub-base and the binder course shall be reinstated to permanent standard at the first visit.

2) The permanent binder course material, or an alternative interim material, shall be extended to the running surface, with or without a thin separating medium at the binder course/surface course interface. The alternative interim material may be a bituminous mixture.

3) On the second visit, all interim surfacing materials shall be removed, to the top of the binder course, and an appropriate permanent surface course laid.

4) Where a sand separation layer is present, prior to the reinstatement of the permanent surface course, the sand shall be removed, to the top of the binder course, the surface brushed clean and a tack coat or bond coat applied.

S8.1.4 Method C – Permanent Base Reinstatement

Not applicable

S8.1.5 Method D – Permanent Sub-base Reinstatement

1) The backfill and sub-base shall be reinstated to a permanent standard at the first visit, with an interim surfacing.
2) For flexible or rigid structures, the interim surface course and some, or all, of the interim binder course may be a bituminous mixture. The lower portion of the interim binder course may be an unbound granular material.
3) For modular structures, the interim surfacing may be a bituminous mixture, paving modules or any combination thereof.
4) On the second visit, all interim surfacing materials shall be removed, to the top of the sub-base, and an appropriate permanent surfacing shall be laid.

S8.1.6 Method E – Permanent Reinstatement incorporating Interim Surface Overlay

Not applicable

S8.2 Sub-base and Binder Course Reinstatement

S8.2.1 General

1) In a footway, footpath or cycle track, the sub-base is any layer of imported granular or cement bound material existing immediately below the surfacing materials. Where such a sub-base layer exists, a similar or equivalent material shall be laid to a thickness of 150 mm, or to match the existing, whichever is less, subject to a minimum of 100 mm of Class A Graded Granular Material.
2) Permitted options are shown in Appendix A7, subject to the exceptions described in Sections S8.2.2, S8.2.3 and S8.2.4.

S8.2.2 Small Reinstatements

1) In small excavations and narrow trenches, the following options shall be permitted, regardless of whether the existing sub-base is a bound material:
   a) A CBGM B sub-base of 100 mm thickness.
   b) A 50/20 HRABC or 20mm DBC material of 40 mm thickness, laid in place of the granular sub-base layer.
   c) Three equal layers of 15/10 HRASC, 6mm DSC or 6mm SMA material may be laid to a total thickness of 100 mm, as a combined sub-base, binder course and surface course.

S8.2.3 Alternative Reinstatement Materials

Alternative Reinstatement Materials may be laid at sub-base level, in accordance with Appendix A9.

S8.2.4 Reinstatements Adjacent to Roads

Where road construction layers, foundation platforms, structural courses, kerb beams and/or backing providing the edge support to the road structure are found to extend below an adjacent footway, footpath, cycle track or verge, any reinstatement therein shall take account of such provisions.

In such cases, the sub-structure of the footway, footpath, cycle track or verge shall be reinstated to match the existing layer thickness with similar or equivalent materials.

S8.3 Surface Reinstatement

S8.3.1 General

Surface reinstatement options are shown in Appendix A7, subject to the following exceptions:

S8.3.2 High Duty and High Amenity Areas

1) The Authority shall register all high duty and/or high amenity footways, footpaths or cycle tracks and shall identify a suitable source or supplier of reinstatement materials.
2) The Undertaker shall reinstate all registered High Duty/High Amenity footways, footpaths or cycle tracks with matching materials from the identified source or supplier.
3) Where aggregates of an especially distinctive colour are encountered and the local custom and practice has been to complete all previous surfacing in a similarly matching material, the reinstatement shall be in accordance with S6.4.5.4.

S8.3.3 Areas Surfaced with Asphalt Concrete

Footways, footpaths or cycle tracks surfaced with Asphalt Concrete shall be reinstated with an AC6 dense surf, unless the existing surface is an asphalt that is significantly finer than 6mm nominal size, in which case it may be regarded by the Undertaker as either Asphalt Concrete or Hot Rolled Asphalt and reinstated accordingly.

S8.3.4 Other Asphalt Areas

1) Where the Authority has maintained a policy of using and reinstating with a specific type of asphalt surfacing on footways (e.g. mastic asphalt, sand asphalt, etc.), unless otherwise agreed with the Authority, the Undertaker shall take all reasonable measures to reinstate excavations with such material.

2) The Authority, when requested, shall provide any details they have on suitable suppliers and specifications. In the absence of such a policy or where no practicable source of supply can be found the reinstatement shall be undertaken in accordance with Section S8.3.3.

3) All other asphalt footways, footpaths or cycle tracks shall be reinstated with 15/10 Hot Rolled Asphalt, chipped as necessary to match the existing surface.

S8.3.5 Areas Constructed in Concrete

1) Concrete footways, footpaths or cycle tracks shall be reinstated with C25/30 minimum strength concrete, to match the existing thickness. For small excavations, a site-batched concrete of equivalent strength may be used.

2) Where the Authority knows of any site where air entrained concrete has been used it should advise Undertakers in advance of the works.

3) Where the existing concrete has been air entrained, then air-entrained concrete, to SHW Clause 1001, shall be used. Air-entrained concrete may be used elsewhere, at the discretion of the Undertaker.

S8.3.6 Modular Footways, Footpaths and Cycle Tracks

1) Modular footways, footpaths and cycle tracks shall be reinstated in accordance with the permitted materials and layer thickness specified in Appendix A7.3.

2) The modular surface layer shall be reinstated in accordance with Appendix A12. The requirements and recommendations for the provision of replacement modules are shown in Appendix A12.

3) Specific to the reinstatement of natural stone modular surfaces, the following shall apply:

   (i) Natural stone modules within the area to be excavated shall be removed and stored by the Undertaker for reuse.

   (ii) Modules shall be reinstated in accordance with Appendix A12.

   (iii) Pre-existing damage may have resulted in fragmentation or breakage of modules. Where the Authority has a policy which seeks to reuse damaged modules, the parts or fragments shall also be removed and stored by the Undertaker for reuse. The Undertaker shall notify the Authority and the method of reinstatement of these materials shall be agreed, including any limitation on the size of the fragments.

   (iv) Where it has been agreed that damaged modules are to be reused as part of the permanent reinstatement, the surface profile at the end of the guarantee period is not required to be superior to that existing at the time of excavation.

   (v) The Undertaker shall use its best endeavours to match existing profiles and meet the tolerances specified in Section S2, but subject also to the limitations outlined in Appendix A12.

S8.3.7 Edge Requirements

1) For all footways, footpaths and cycle tracks, the edge regularity and any undercutting shall comply with the requirements specified in Sections S6.5.2.1 and S6.5.2.4, respectively.

2) For all flexible footways, footpaths and cycle tracks, the edge sealing shall comply with the requirements specified in Section S6.5.2.2 and any overbanding shall comply with the requirements specified in Section S11.7.

3) For all concrete footways, footpaths and cycle tracks, the treatment of any cracking shall comply with the requirements specified in Section S7.4.2 (3).

4) For all footways, footpaths and cycle tracks, where trim-lines for the reinstatement edges are within 150 mm of an edge, kerb, ironwork or other reinstatements, the trim-lines shall be extended to the interface of the edge, kerb etc. This additional reinstatement may be confined to the surface course provided lower courses have not been damaged. See Figure S8.1.

5) Fixed features in the footway such as sign posts, lamp columns, stop-cock valve boxes, etc. that are less than 250mm diameter or 250 mm width on the side facing the reinstatement are exempt from the trim-line extension.

Figure S8.1 Edge Requirements and Trim Lines in Footways

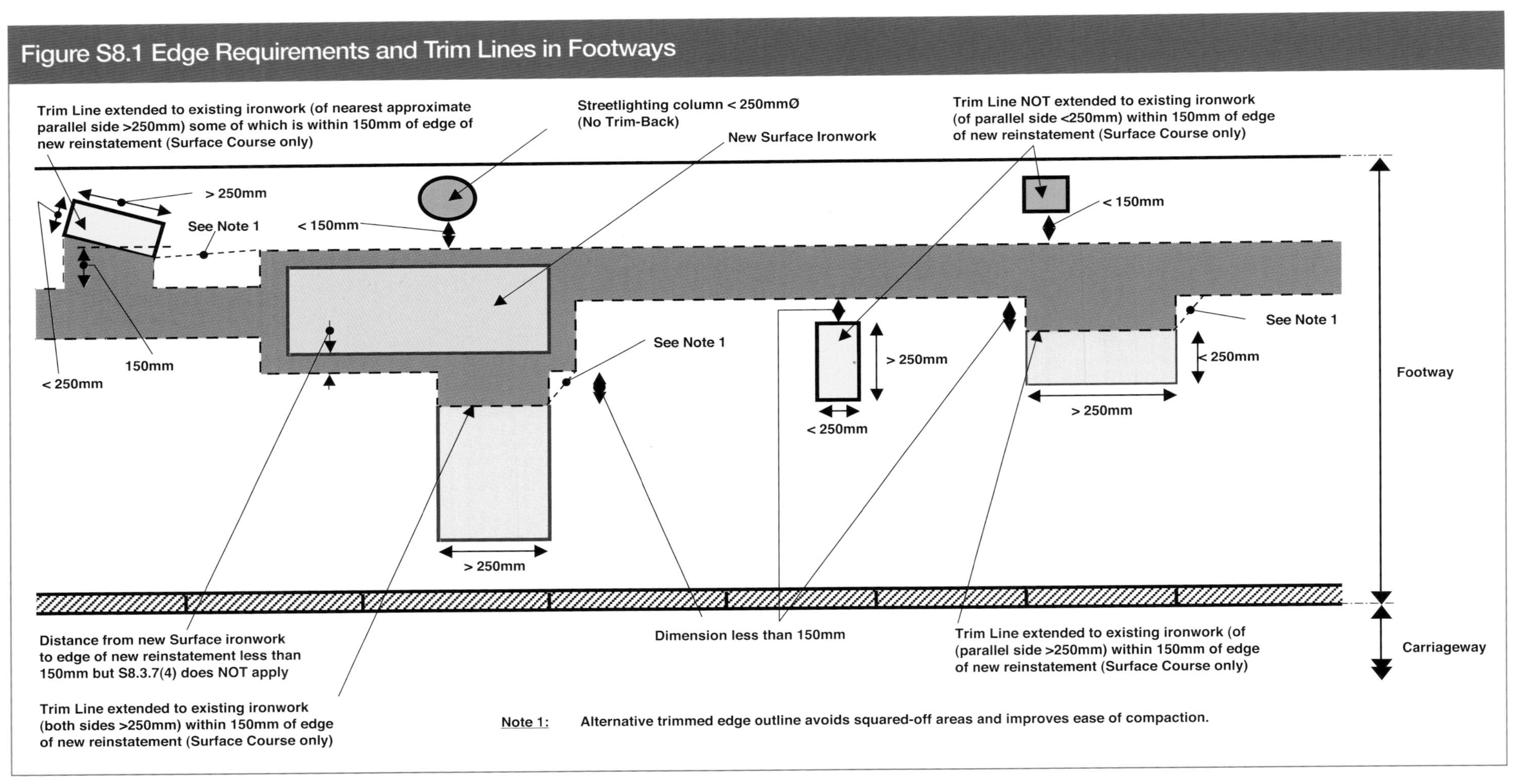

S8.3.8 Special Materials

1) Other specialist surfacing materials shall be reinstated in accordance with Section S6.4.5.5.
2) In high duty footways, footpaths and cycle tracks where local custom and practice has been to complete previous surface restoration of excavations with overbanding or other coating of a certain minimum skid resistance value, the Undertaker shall provide a similar minimum skid resistance value for the material used to overband reinstatement edges.

S8.4 Vehicular Trafficking

S8.4.1 Commercial Access

1) Where a recognised route for commercial vehicles crosses a footway, footpath or cycle track, including specified pedestrian areas and precincts, it shall be assumed that provisions for commercial vehicle loading were incorporated in the original design. The relevant area of footway, footpath or cycle track shall be deemed to be a Type 4 road, of flexible, composite, rigid or modular construction, depending on the existing structure.
2) The reinstatement of such areas shall comply with the relevant requirements of Sections S6 or S7, as appropriate.
3) Where a special construction has been incorporated within the original design to cater for expected traffic greater than the Type 4 limiting capacity, the Undertaker should consult the Authority.

S8.4.2 Domestic Access

1) Where a recognised domestic vehicle crossing or occasional emergency service vehicle access route crosses a footway, footpath or cycle track, including specified pedestrian areas or precincts, the existing structure may include thicker layers, higher quality materials or other strengthening measures.
2) The reinstatement of such areas shall match the existing layer thickness, with similar or equivalent materials.

S8.4.3 Other Trafficking

1) Where a footway, footpath or cycle track, including specified pedestrian areas or precincts, is subjected to regular vehicle overrunning or parking, the existing structure may include thicker layers, higher quality materials or other strengthening measures.
2) The reinstatement of such areas shall match the existing layer thickness, with similar or equivalent materials.

S8.5 Tolerances

S8.5.1 Performance requirements and tolerances permitted in the reinstatement of footways, footpaths and cycle tracks shall be in accordance with the requirements of Section S2 and Appendix A2.

S9 Verges and Unmade Ground

S9.1 General

All backfill materials shall comply with the requirements of Section S5.

1) Topsoil within 200mm of the surface of the verge shall be stored and reused. Where insufficient topsoil is available from the excavation, imported topsoil may be used to a depth of 100mm or to match the existing depth, whichever is the less.

2) Care shall be taken to ensure that imported topsoil is not contaminated with non-organic material or noxious weeds.

3) The re-use of excavated materials as backfill material in verges and unmade ground is to be encouraged as part of a policy of environmentally sustainable construction.

4) Where invasive plant species are identified within the excavated materials, these materials shall not be re-used in the reinstatement. Appropriate advice may be sought from the Highway Authority or DEFRA as to the means of permissible disposal.

S9.2 Adjacent Road Structures

1) Where road construction layers, that may include structural courses, foundations, kerbs and/or backing that provides edge support to road structures, extend below adjacent verges or unmade ground, any reinstatement therein shall take account of such provisions. The reinstatement of such areas shall match the existing layer thicknesses, with similar or equivalent materials.

2) Where there is no such edge support within adjacent verges or unmade ground, any part of the reinstatement of an excavation that comes within 600 mm of the edge of a road, shall include sub-base materials at backfill level, up to a level where a 45° fall line extending downwards from the road surface intersects the side of the trench nearest the road, as shown in Figure S9.1.

Figure S9.1 Verge Reinstatement Adjacent to Edge of Road

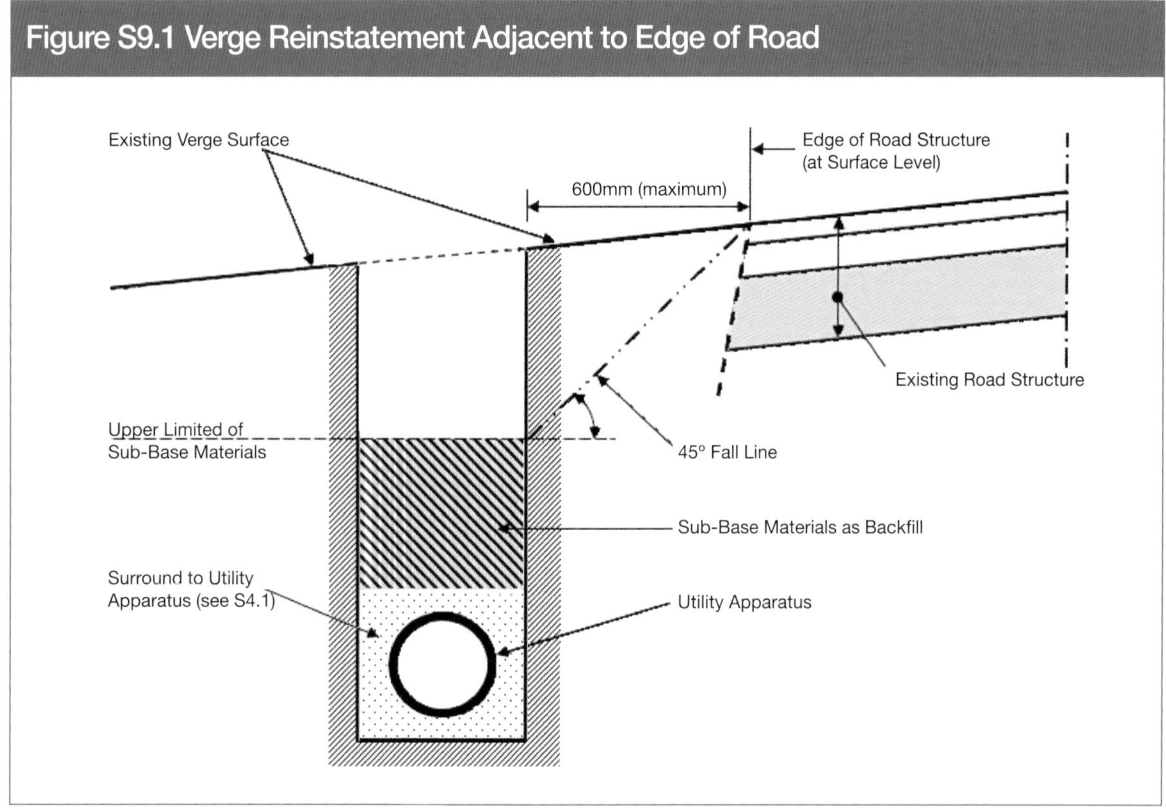

S9.3 ## Cultivated Areas

Unless otherwise agreed, cultivated areas containing shrubs, plants or bulbs shall be reinstated using the same or similar species. Thereafter, a reasonable growth shall be established within the following 12 months. Where the Authority knows of special features in verges (e.g. orchid sites etc.) it should inform the Undertaker in order to agree the best means of conserving the special features.

S9.4 ## Grassed Areas

1) Grassed areas shall be reinstated using the original turf, replacement turf or an equivalent seed, depending on weather and growing season. In all cases, a reasonable growth shall be established within the following 12 months.

2) Where grassed areas have previously been mown, the reinstated surface shall be demonstrably left free from stones greater than 20mm nominal size. All other debris arising from the works shall be removed from the site. It should be recognised that stones in grassed areas tend to migrate to the surface over a period of time and this should not lead to repeated intervention.

S9.5 ## Verges, Ditches and Drainage Courses

Verges, ditches and drainage courses shall be restored to their original profile, unless otherwise agreed.

S10 Compaction Requirements

S10.1 Introduction

1) All compaction equipment covered by this Specification shall be checked, adjusted, maintained and operated in accordance with working practices, maintenance schedules, operating procedures and vibrating frequencies recommended by the equipment manufacturer. Relevant records shall, where available, be provided on request within a reasonable period of time to the Authority.

2) If available, records can demonstrate to the Authority that the Undertaker is using calibrated equipment. If data is not available the Authority may monitor more closely to check on compaction.

3) All equipment and operating procedures used for the compaction of all reinstatement materials laid above the surround to apparatus shall comply with the following requirements:

S10.2 Compaction of Materials

For all materials, compaction shall be carried out in accordance with the requirements of Appendix A2 and/or Appendix A8, immediately after the material has been placed.

S10.2.1 Unbound Granular and Cohesive Materials

1) All Class A Graded Granular Materials, Class B Granular Materials and Class C Cohesive/Granular Materials shall be compacted in accordance with the relevant requirements of Appendix A8, Table A8.1.

2) All Class D Cohesive Materials shall be compacted in accordance with the relevant requirements and restrictions of Appendix A8, Table A8.1.

3) Where access is restricted, including small excavations and trenches less than 200 mm wide, compaction shall be in accordance with the restricted access provisions of Appendix A8, Table A8.1.

S10.2.2 Alternative Reinstatement Materials

1) Certain Structural Materials for Reinstatements (SMRs) and Stabilised Materials for Fill (SMFs) may not require the full compaction specified in Appendix A8, Table A8.1 and may be damaged if compaction is continued. Such materials should be placed and compacted in

accordance with the manufacturer's recommendations and with due regard to the requirements of Appendix A9.

2) Foamed concretes (FCRs) shall not be compacted or tamped unless specifically required by the manufacturer. Thereafter, such FCR materials shall be placed and compacted in accordance with the manufacturer's recommendations and with due regard to the requirements of Appendix A9.

S10.2.3 Bituminous Materials

1) All bituminous materials permitted by Appendix A2 shall be laid and compacted in accordance with the relevant requirements of Appendix A2, Tables A2.1, 2.3 and A2.4, and Appendix A8, Section A8.3.

2) The in-situ air voids content for all bituminous materials as permitted in Appendix A2 shall comply with the requirements shown in Table S10.1. The in-situ air voids content shall be calculated as the average from all results obtained. The maximum density shall be determined in accordance with EN 12697 – 5 Procedure A, in water. For reference purposes and in the event of dispute the bulk density shall be determined in accordance with EN12697 – 6 Procedure C sealed specimen. The maximum density and core bulk density shall be used to determine air void content in accordance with EN12697-8.

Table S10.1 In-Situ Air Voids Content Requirements

Bituminous Materials	Permitted Air Voids			
	Carriageways		Footways	
	Max %	Min %	Max %	Min %
AC 6 dense Surface Course	NP	NP	13	2
AC 10 close Surface Course	11	2	NP	NP
HRA Surface Course	7	2	10	2
SMA Surface Course	8	2	10	2
AC Binder Course	10	2	12	2
HRA Binder Course	9	2	12	2
SMA Binder Course	6	2	NP	NP
Permanent Cold-Lay Surfacing Materials (PCSM)	10	2	13	2
Any other bituminous materials within the Specification	No air-voids limits apply. Guidance on compaction contained in NG A8.3			
Note to Table S10.1 – **NP** = not permitted				

3) All surface course materials used at binder course level shall comply with the in-situ air voids content requirement for the relevant surface course material.

4) To determine the in-situ air void content core samples shall be taken at a rate of 1 per 6 m^2 or part thereof. The average void content shall be calculated for each reinstatement covered by a single notice. All core samples shall be 100 mm minimum diameter with no part of any core being within 100 mm of any surface apparatus within the reinstatement. Where there is a potential to encounter the edge of the frame or apparatus then this distance should be increased accordingly.

5) Unless agreed otherwise, all air voids testing shall be carried out by a laboratory holding current UKAS accreditation for the specified test methods.

6) Where the prevailing weather conditions or other site circumstances are considered likely to mitigate against the successful laying and compaction of any surfacing materials and the achievement of the required in-situ air voids content, consideration should be given to deferring the permanent surface reinstatement and, if necessary, to an agreed extension of the interim reinstatement period.

S10.2.4 Cementitious Materials

1) Pavement quality concrete, laid as the surface slab of road, footway, footpath or cycle track reinstatements, shall be compacted using a proprietary vibrator, selected and operated in accordance with the manufacturer's recommendations. However, proprietary vibrators may be unsuitable for concrete sections less than 100 mm wide or less than 0.5 square metres in area. In such cases, as a minimum requirement, all concrete shall be thoroughly tamped by hand.

2) Cement-bound granular materials, including CBGM B shall be compacted in accordance with the relevant requirements of Appendix A8, Table A8.1.

S10.2.5 Modular Surfacing Materials

Compaction equipment shall be operated in accordance with the manufacturer's instructions.

S10.3 Equipment Operation and Restrictions

1) All compaction equipment shall be used in accordance with the requirements of Appendix A8.

2) Additional guidance on compaction procedures is included in Section NG10.3.

S10.3.1 Hand Rammers

Except as permitted in Sections S2.2.1 (4), S10.2.2 and S10.2.4 (1), hand rammers shall be permitted to assist the initial placement of material only.

For all materials, full compaction shall be applied, in accordance with the relevant requirements of Appendix A8.

S10.3.2 **Percussive Rammers**

Percussive rammers shall be permitted for the compaction of reinstatement materials, in accordance with the following requirements:

a) The nominal mass shall not be less than 10 kg.

b) The width of the foot shall not exceed 200 mm.

c) The contact length of the foot shall not exceed 200 mm.

S10.3.3 **Vibrotampers**

Vibrotampers shall be permitted for the compaction of reinstatement materials, in accordance with the following requirements:

1) 50 kg Minimum Nominal Mass

a) The width of the foot shall not exceed 5 mm per kg of the nominal mass.

b) The contact length of the foot shall not exceed 350 mm nor be less than 175 mm.

c) The foot contact area shall not exceed 1000 sq. mm per kg of the nominal mass.

d) The mass of any extension leg shall not exceed 10% of the nominal mass.

2) 25 to 50 kg Nominal Mass – permitted in areas of restricted access only

a) The width of the foot shall not exceed 150 mm.

b) The contact length of the foot shall not exceed 200 mm.

S10.3.4 **Vibrating Rollers**

Vibrating rollers shall be permitted for the compaction of reinstatement materials, in accordance with the following requirements:

1) Single-Drum Vibrating Rollers

a) Single drum vibrating rollers shall include a mechanical means of applying vibration to the roll. Single-drum rollers without a specific vibration unit shall be considered to be single-drum deadweight rollers and shall not be permitted for reinstatement purposes.

b) The minimum mass of a single-drum vibrating roller shall be 600kg per metre (kg/m) width.

2) Twin-Drum Vibrating Rollers

a) Twin-drum vibrating rollers shall include two vibrating rolls. Twin-drum rollers in which only one roll vibrates shall be considered to be single-drum vibrating rollers.

b) The minimum mass of a twin-drum vibrating roller shall be 600 kg/m width.

3) All Vibrating Rollers

a) The mass per metre width of a vibrating roller shall be calculated by dividing the total mass supported by the roll(s) by the total width of the roll(s).

b) A minimum mass of 600 kg/m width is required for vibrating rollers for the compaction of bituminous material. Where existing roads, footways, footpaths or cycle tracks may be marked or otherwise damaged by the use of 600 to 1000 kg/m vibrating rollers, the Authority shall notify the Undertaker accordingly, whereupon the use of lower weight vibrating rollers shall be agreed.

S10.3.5 Vibrating Plate Compactors

Vibrating plate compactors of 1400 kg/m^2 minimum mass shall be permitted for the compaction of reinstatement materials.

S10.3.6 Other Compaction Equipment

Other compaction equipment, including machine-mounted compactors and all other compaction devices not specifically referenced within Appendix A8, may be permitted for the compaction of reinstatement materials, subject to the requirements of Section NG10.

S11 Ancillary Activities

S11.1 Traffic signs, road markings, studs and verge markers

S11.1.1 General

1) Prior to the opening of any works to traffic, all traffic signs, road markings, studs and verge markers removed during the works shall be reinstated to a permanent or temporary standard. Temporary traffic signs, road markings, studs and verge markers shall be permitted for a maximum of 15 working days following completion of the permanent reinstatement.

2) All traffic signs, road markings, studs and verge markers removed during works shall be reinstated at their original location, wherever possible. Where any traffic signs, road markings, studs or verge markers cannot be reinstated at their original locations, they shall be permanently reinstated to a new layout in accordance with the Traffic Signs Manual: Chapter 5 and the Traffic Signs Regulations & General Directions.

3) Where the layout of existing traffic signs, road markings, studs or verge markers is not in accordance with the Traffic Signs Manual: Chapter 5 and the Traffic Signs Regulations & General Directions, and the Authority notifies the Undertaker prior to the commencement of works, the layout of all traffic signs, road markings, studs or verge markers to be reinstated following the works shall be determined by agreement. In this event, if the Authority provides any new traffic signs, studs or verge markers, to replace obsolete or previously damaged items removed during the works, then the Undertaker shall install such items as part of the permanent reinstatement of the works.

S11.1.2 Traffic Signs, Studs and Verge Markers

Wherever possible, all traffic signs, studs and verge markers removed during the works shall be re-erected or re-installed on completion. Where the original items cannot be re-erected or re-installed, they shall be replaced using items of equivalent type, colour, performance and dimensions.

S11.1.3 Road Markings – General

1) Prior to permanent reinstatement, temporary road markings may be made using quick drying, durable paint, adhesive strip or like materials of similar colour and dimensions to the original markings.

2) Road markings removed during the works shall be permanently reinstated using materials of equivalent colour and dimensions.

3) Except where otherwise specified by the Authority, the retro-reflectivity and skid resistance of all yellow and white lines shall comply with BS EN 1436, as follows:

   a) Dry retro-reflectivity to Table 3:

      Yellow – Class R0

      White – Class R2

   b) Wet skid resistance to Table 7:

      Yellow – Class S1

      White – Class S3

4) Unless otherwise agreed by the Authority, all white thermoplastic road markings shall be treated with surface-applied glass beads so as to achieve the performance requirements in 3) a) & b) above.

5) Hot-applied thermoplastic road marking materials with synthetic resin binder shall be laid to the following thickness:

   a) Screed lines – 3.5 mm ± 1.5 mm

   b) Sprayed yellow edge lines (No Waiting, etc.) – 0.8 mm minimum

   c) Sprayed lines, other than yellow – 1.5 mm minimum

   d) Extruded lines – 3.0 mm ± 0.5 mm

6) Cold applied road markings (e.g. Methylmethacrylate) may be used as an alternative to hot-applied thermoplastic materials provided that they at least match the appropriate BS EN 1824 durability and BS EN 1436 performance requirements as set out in this Section.

7) The performance requirements for permanent road marking materials shall have been established from road trials in accordance with BS EN 1824. The material used to reinstate road markings shall be in accordance with Table S11.1.

Table S11.1 Performance Requirements for Road Markings

Road Type	Required Roll-over Class (BS EN 1824 Table 1)
0	P5
1 to 4 & f'ways/cycletracks	P4

S11.1.4 Road Markings – Small Reinstatements

Road markings for small excavations (as defined in Section S1.5.1) shall meet the criteria in Section S11.1.3. Alternative materials may be used, subject to the following:

1) Road marking tape may be used in place of thermoplastic markings or marking paint – individual tape lengths shall be no more than 2.5 m in length.
2) Pre-formed thermoplastic markings may be used in place of hot applied thermoplastic materials – individual lengths shall be no more than 2.5 m in length.
3) No alternatives may be used in place of specialist materials such as rib markings without the prior approval of the Authority.

S11.2 Street Furniture and Special Features

Street furniture and other special features, such as tactile paving removed to facilitate street works, shall be replaced in the same position and layout before opening the highway to traffic and pedestrians. Items removed to facilitate street works must be carefully stored and maintained during the works. Advice on replacement may be provided by the Authority.

S11.3 Traffic Sensors, etc.

Where excavation is planned at or near to traffic sensors etc, advice regarding precautions to avoid damage shall be sought from the relevant Authority before work commences.

S11.4 Water-related Matters

S11.4.1 Sewers, Drains and Tunnels

1) An Undertaker executing street works that involve breaking up or opening a sewer, drain or tunnel that is vested in or owned by another responsible Authority shall obtain the approval of the responsible Authority before executing the works to the reasonable requirements and satisfaction of the responsible Authority.
2) In the case of a public sewer, the "responsible Authority" shall mean the sewerage Undertaker (i.e. the water service company for the relevant area).
3) In the case of any other sewer, drain or tunnel, the "responsible Authority" shall mean the owner (or the Authority, body or person) responsible for the management or control of the sewer, drain or tunnel.
4) Where the responsible Authority knows of the existence of sustainable drainage systems (SuDS) in areas likely to be affected by the Undertaker's work, they shall inform the undertaker, so that an appropriate excavation and subsequent reinstatement method can be agreed.

S11.4.2 **Water Egress (Reinstatements)**

1) If water issues from a reinstatement, the street authority shall initiate an investigatory works procedure to determine the cause and source of the water egress. Prior to commencement of the investigatory work, the Authority should contact any Undertaker or Undertakers which it believes may be responsible for the egress of water. Undertakers shall cooperate with the Authority in its investigation and may take trial holes.

2) If following the investigation, the Authority has reasonable cause to believe that water egress has been caused by an Undertaker's operations, remedial measures shall be agreed between the Authority and the Undertaker and shall be at the Undertaker's cost.

S11.4.3 **Water Egress (Street Surface and Utility Apparatus)**

Notes for Guidance are provided to cover situations where water issues from the street surface or an Undertaker's apparatus.

S11.5 Ironwork and Apparatus

S11.5.1 Access Covers, Frames and Surround

The installation, construction and maintenance of apparatus such as access covers and frames are an integral part of street works. Works undertaken to apparatus shall be to the standard and specification of the owner of the apparatus.

The sub-structure of an underground chamber supporting an access cover and frame is constructed in such a way that it is not usually possible to achieve a full depth reinstatement in the area defined as the 'access surround'. The access surround is the width between the fixed feature (access frame) and the point at which a full depth reinstatement can be achieved with a full load transfer. The 'access surround' width will vary depending on the size of the access frame and cover.

Figures S11.1 (Example 1) and S11.1 (Example 2) show a typical construction detail relating to a large road access cover and frame of a minimum 600 mm dimension with the access surround constructed in flowable and asphaltic material.

Figure S11.1 Reinstatement adjacent to Undertaker's Apparatus (Carriageway)

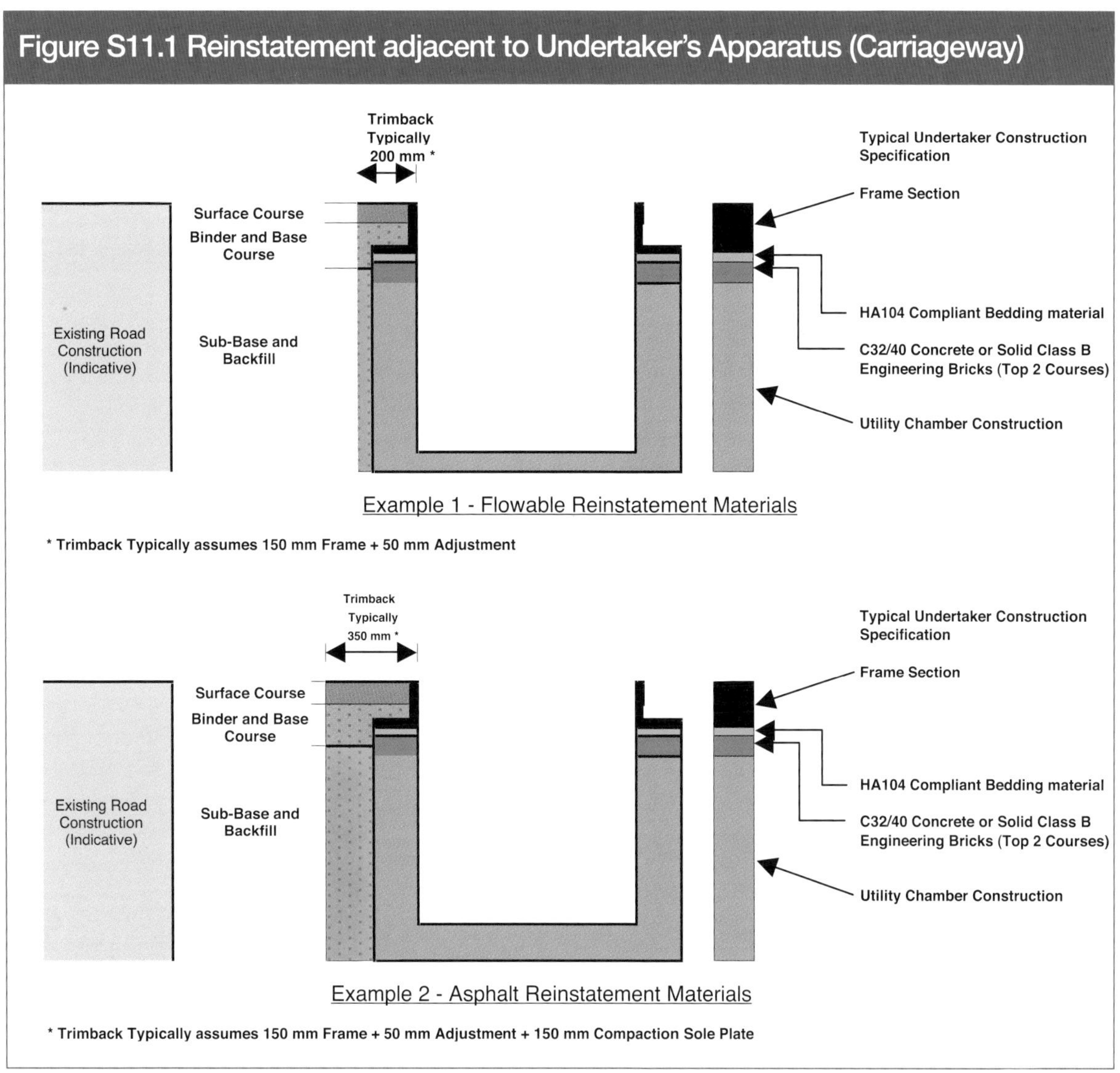

S11.5.1.1 *Trimback*

The width of trimback shall be dependent on the reinstatement materials used.

S11.5.1.2 *Reinstatement Materials which do not require compaction*

If reinstatement materials are being used which do not require compaction e.g. rapid cure concrete, flowable mastic asphalt, etc. then a minimum width of trimback will be required. Typically, it will be 50mm in excess of the flange width e.g. a frame which has a 150 mm base will require 200 mm width of trimback.

S11.5.1.3 *Reinstatement Materials which require compaction*

If reinstatement materials are being used that require compaction e.g. granular sub base, hot rolled asphalt, etc. then the width of trimback required will be the width of the frame base plus the width of the compaction tool sole plate plus 50 mm. Typically, a frame which has a 150 mm flange will require 350 mm width of trimback to accommodate a compaction tool sole plate of 150 mm.

S11.5.1.4 *Excavation*

1) Edge preparation of the excavation shall comply with section S6.5.2 for flexible roads and Section S7.4.2 for rigid and modular roads.

2) All loose excavation material and the existing frame shall be removed and the structure prepared to receive the new frame.

3) All loose supporting materials e.g. proprietary packing materials, engineering bricks etc., shall be removed.

S11.5.1.5 *Reinstatement Materials*

1) Bedding material, including C32/40 strength concrete may be used to fill the excavation to within 100 mm of the road surface within 350mm of the edge of the access chamber frame cover.

2) A suitable edge sealant shall be applied, and where necessary a primer applied to the frame and bedding materials.

3) All bedding materials shall be allowed to cure prior to the application of the surfacing.

4) To provide longevity of service life in high stress areas such as braking and turning areas, consideration should be given to the use of proprietary flowable mastic asphalt.

S11.6 Test Holes

Test holes greater than 150 mm diameter are regarded as excavations and shall be reinstated to comply with this Specification. Test holes of nominal 150 mm diameter or less are not excavations for the purposes of this Specification and shall be reinstated to a permanent standard within 10 working days of completion of all associated work on the site.

1) *General*

   a) Prior to reinstatement, all test holes should be made safe and maintained in a safe condition.

   b) Test holes up to 25 mm diameter shall be reinstated to an immediate permanent standard.

   c) Test holes larger than 25 mm diameter may be reinstated to an interim standard, if required.

   d) In modular surfaces, preference should be given to the lifting of individual modules prior to the drilling of test holes, whenever reasonably practical.

   e) In unmade ground, test holes shall be tamped closed or filled with appropriate materials.

2) *50 mm Diameter or Less*

   Test holes shall be reinstated to finish flush with the surface by any of the following methods:

   a) Using a fine aggregate, bound with cement or bitumen for the upper layers, as appropriate, and compacted in layers of 100 mm thickness, or less.

b) Using a self compacting proprietary product.

c) Using a flexible sealing plug. The void beneath the flexible sealing plug shall be reinstated using sand and cement mix or a proprietary product.

   i. In bituminous surfaces, all sealing plugs shall be coloured black (or dark grey).

   ii. In modular or concrete surfaces, sealing plugs shall be coloured white (or light grey) or black (or dark grey) as appropriate.

d) If a flexible sealing plug should become dislodged during the guarantee period, the Undertaker shall replace the plug.

3) *50 to 150 mm Diameter*

In paved surfaces, test holes shall be reinstated using a fine aggregate, appropriately compacted in layers of 100mm thickness, or less, and surfaced with appropriate cementitious, cold or hot-lay bituminous materials to finish flush with the surface.

S11.7 Overbanding

Overbanding or coating of the road surface at the interface between the existing road and the reinstatement edge is not mandatory, but where carried out it should be undertaken in accordance with the following requirements:

1) The minimum skid resistance value (SRV), or Pendulum Test Value (PTV), for all overbanding materials shall be 55.

2) The SRV/PTV shall be measured in accordance with BS EN 13036: Part 4 except that the narrow slider shall be used over the full 126mm sliding length utilising the normal slider scale C.

3) Overbanding shall not exceed 3 mm thickness nor 40 mm width. Properly applied overbanding may be subject to spreading and may eventually wear away under trafficking. Overbanding which displays these characteristics shall not require intervention.

4) Overbanding shall not be used as a substitute for any edge sealing required in accordance with Section S6.5.2.2.

5) All materials used for overbanding shall have a current HAPAS Approval Certificate. In the event that no such approvals have been issued, then it shall not be used without the approval of the Authority, which shall not be unreasonably withheld. There shall be no departure from the performance requirements at the time of application.

S12 Remedial Works

S12.1 General

S12.1.1 The Undertaker shall be responsible for ensuring that reinstatements comply with the required performance criteria throughout the interim reinstatement and guarantee periods.

S12.1.2 When determining whether a reinstatement requires any remedial action, the quality of the reinstatement shall be assessed relative to the condition of the adjacent surfaces.

S12.2 Safety Requirements

Should a reinstatement fail any safety requirements of this Specification, the surface shall be restored to comply with such requirements, in accordance with section 71 (for England and Wales) or section 130 (for Scotland) of the New Roads and Street Works Act 1991.

S12.3 Repair of Cracking

S12.3.1 Interface Cracking

Cracking along the reinstatement interface, greater than 2.5 mm open width at the surface for more than the maximum permitted length shown in Table S12.1, shall require remedial action in accordance with the requirements of Section S12.3.3.

Table S12.1 – Interface Cracking

Reinstatement	Surface	Maximum Crack Length	
Small Excavations to S1.5.1	All Surfaces	500 mm total cumulative length	
Narrow Trenches to S1.5.2 and All Other Openings to S1.5.4	Footway	1000mm maximum Crack Length,) Or 10% of Reinstatement Perimeter)	Whichever is greater
	All Carriageway Types	500mm maximum Crack Length,) Or 10% of Reinstatement Perimeter)	Whichever is greater

S12.3.2 **Cracking Beyond Reinstatement Limits**

Cracks remote from the reinstatement interface, greater than 2.5 mm open width at the surface for more than 2 metres of continuous length, shall also require remedial action in accordance with the requirements of Section S12.3.3, provided it can reasonably be shown that such cracks occurred directly as a result of the Undertakers' works (see also Section S10.3.4 (3) b)).

S12.3.3 **Repair of Interface Cracking**

1) Cracking along the interface of the reinstatement shall be repaired in accordance with the following methods:
   a) Cracks of between 2.5 mm and 10 mm open width at the surface shall be repaired by filling with a flexible bituminous sealant, subject to the requirements of Section S11.7.
   b) Cracks between 10 mm and 15 mm open width at the surface shall be repaired by filling with a flexible bituminous sealant incorporating suitable fine aggregate filler, subject to the requirements of Section S11.7.
   c) Cracks of greater than 15mm open width shall be repaired using the procedure described in Section (2) a) & b) below.
2) Two re-sealing operations, excluding the original sealing, shall be permitted during the guarantee period. Further significant cracking of the third seal shall require a surface repair, as follows:
   a) The surfacing materials shall be removed to the full depth of the surface course or to 40 mm depth, whichever is less; for the full length of the crack or for 1 metre length, whichever is greater. If the crack extends into the binder course layer, the affected materials shall be removed and replaced in accordance with Section S6.4.
   b) Surfacing materials shall be removed over sufficient width to ensure that the repair patch extends beyond the edges of the crack, by a minimum distance equal to the nominal thickness of the replacement surface course. The minimum width of the repair patch shall be 100 mm.
   c) Inclusion of a geosynthetic material at the base of the repair patch could assist in limiting any reoccurrence of cracking.
   d) The replacement surface course patch shall be laid in accordance with Section S6.4.
3) Where, as a result of Undertaker's works, a crack requiring repair in accordance with Section S12.3.3 exists within 300 mm of another similar crack repair, the intermediate area shall be included in the new repair.

S12.3.4 **Cracking within High Friction Surfacings**

Where cracks appear in High Friction Surfacing provided that it is well bonded to the substrate and with the agreement of the Street Authority, the cracking may be sealed using a suitable epoxy or similar resin and the high friction surfacing made good. Guidance on this should be sought either from the system supplier or the HAPAS Certificate.

S12.4 Repair of Settlement beyond Reinstatement Limits

1) Where significant settlement of the surface beyond the edges of the reinstatement can reasonably be shown to have occurred as a direct result of the Undertaker's works, the effective width of the reinstatement shall be revised to include the actual width of the settled area. The relevant requirements of this Specification shall apply over the revised width of the reinstatement.

2) The extent of any significant settlement beyond the reinstatement limits shall be assessed, by agreement, from consideration of the following:

   a) The apparent extent of any excessive areas of standing water following heavy rainfall.

      or

   b) The apparent extent of any significant deterioration of highway shape compared with the existing profile remote from the excavation.

      or

   c) The true extent of any significant deterioration of highway shape determined by profile measurements taken before and after the Undertaker's works.

S12.5 Repair of Other Significant Defects

1) The requirement for, and extent of, any repair shall be determined, by agreement, from a consideration of the existing and adjacent surfaces.

2) Where it can reasonably be shown that a repair is required, as a direct result of the Undertaker's works, the Undertaker shall carry out remedial actions, as necessary.

Appendix A1

Backfill Materials

A1.1 Class A – Graded Granular Materials

1) Materials should be well-graded granular material with a uniformity coefficient greater than 10. Material shall, at the time of compaction, be at an appropriate moisture content between +1% and -2% of the optimum moisture content as determined by BS1377: Part 4; Vibrating Hammer Method, Method 3.7, or shall be acceptable when subjected to Field Identification Test No.3.
2) Materials shall show a Los Angeles Coefficient – maximum of LA_{60} when tested in accordance with BS EN 1097-2. The principal materials that will be excluded are sandstones, weakly cemented gritstones, argillaceous (clay derived) materials, the softer magnesium limestones, oolitic limestones and the majority of chalks.
3) Manmade aggregates, e.g. slag, PFAs, clinkers and furnace bottom ash will need individual assessment; it is possible to demonstrate satisfactory performance with some of these materials, even when they fail to meet the 10% fines value requirement.

A1.2 Class B – Granular Materials

Material at the time of compaction shall be at an appropriate moisture content between +1% and -2% of the optimum moisture content as determined by BS1377: Part 4; Vibrating Hammer, Method 3.7, or shall be acceptable when subjected to Field Identification Test No.3.

A1.3 Class C – Cohesive/Granular Materials

1) Materials with less than 50% granular content by mass shall, at the time of compaction, be at an appropriate moisture content between 0.8 and 1.2 times the plastic limit, or be acceptable when subjected to Field Identification Test No.2.

2) Materials with a minimum of 50% granular content by mass, shall at the time of compaction, be at an appropriate moisture content between +1% and -2% of the optimum moisture content as determined by BS1377: Part 4; Vibrating Hammer, Method 3.7, or shall be acceptable when subjected to Field Identification Test No.3.

A1.4 Class D – Cohesive Materials

1) Cohesive materials at the time of compaction shall be at an appropriate moisture content between 0.8 and 1.2 times the plastic limit, or be acceptable when subjected to Field Identification Test No. 2.

2) Clays that contain insufficient moisture when excavated, or have dried excessively during site storage, as defined by Field Identification Test No. 2, may only be re-used provided that they are wetted to comply with Section A1.4 (1) and compacted in accordance with Appendix A8 for Class D Cohesive Materials.

3) It may be difficult to compact cohesive materials to uniformly achieve an adequate bearing capacity. Undertakers must select a lump size for clays within the limits specified in Appendix A2 and must ensure that all compaction equipment is operated within the requirements of Appendix A8. Failure to comply with Appendix A2 and/or Appendix A8 will result in unacceptable settlement and variable bearing capacity.

4) High silt content materials, as defined by Field Identification Test No. 1, shall be compacted in accordance with Appendix A8 requirements for Class D Cohesive Materials.

A1.5 Class E – Unacceptable Materials

The following materials, listed as unacceptable in SHW Clause 601 paragraphs 2(ii) and 3, shall not be used at any level within the permanent structure of any reinstatement:

1) Peat and materials from swamps, marshes or bogs.

2) Logs, stumps and perishable materials.

3) Materials in a frozen condition. (Such materials, if otherwise suitable, shall be classified as suitable when unfrozen.)

4) Clays having a liquid limit exceeding 90, determined in accordance with BS1377: Part 2 Method 4, or a Plasticity Index exceeding 65, determined in accordance with BS1377: Part 2, Method 5.4.

5) Materials susceptible to spontaneous combustion.

6) Materials having hazardous chemical or physical properties requiring special measures for excavation, handling, storage, transportation, deposition and disposal.

A1.6 Field Identification Tests

The following identification tests must be carried out immediately prior to the placement and compaction of the backfill material.

Field Identification Test No 1 – Silt Identification

High silt content materials can usually be identified by a simple hand test:

Preparation

Select a moist sample of the fine material only.

Test – Silt Identification

With clean dry hands, rub the sample between the palms, remove the excess material by striking the palms together and wait a few minutes for body heat to dry out any material adhering to the hands. Finally, rub hands together briskly.

Result

If no significant quantity of material remains adhering to the palms, i.e. the palms are relatively clean, then the sample tested is essentially a silt.

Note: The proportion of granular material discarded to produce the fine sample must to be taken into account when estimating the approximate silt content of the bulk material.

Field Identification Test No 2 – Clay Condition

Clays suitable for compaction with pedestrian controlled compaction plant can usually be identified by a simple roll test:

Preparation

Select a sample of small lumps of the fine material only, at a moisture content representative of the bulk material.

Test – Clay Condition

With clean dry hands, take the sample and squeeze together in onc hand and release. If the sample crumbles away and mostly fails to hold together into a ‘ball’ then the sample is too dry for compaction. If not, break off part of the ball and roll between the palms or between one palm and any convenient clean dry flat surface, for example the back of a spade. Roll out the sample into a long thin cylinder until it fractures or begins to show significant transverse cracks.

Result

If the strand can be rolled into intact or uncracked lengths that are thinner or longer than a standard pencil, i.e. less than 7 mm diameter or more than 175 mm length then the sample is too wet or too plastic for compaction. Any result between the ball and the pencil is acceptable for use provided the bulk of the material consists of lumps less than 75 mm in size.

Field Identification Test No 3 – Granular Condition

All granular materials including Clause 803 Type 1 granular sub-base must be compacted near to their optimum moisture content. The optimum moisture content can vary considerably depending on the average particle size and to a much smaller extent, on the type of mineral or rock involved. However, a laboratory compaction test is invariably carried out on a sample of material from which the larger particles have been removed. The sample is always compacted in a small smooth sided steel cylinder and the standard methods of compaction bear little similarity with current compaction plant. Experience has shown that the most commonly specified laboratory compaction test i.e. BS1377: Part 4; Vibrating Hammer, Method 3.7 will produce an optimum moisture content result that is, typically, significantly wetter than the field optimum for a granular material that is to be compacted within a trench using a vibrotamper.

Granular materials suitable for compaction by pedestrian controlled plant can usually be identified by a simple visual examination. Typically, the test will identify materials within 1% to 1.5% of the field optimum moisture content depending on the mineral type. Experience has shown that compaction within this visual moisture range will not normally show any significant reduction in compaction performance. The test cannot indicate the actual moisture content of any material but this is rarely of any relevance as far as an operator is concerned.

Preparation

Depending on the size of the stockpile, dig out representative samples from beneath the outer surface, at several positions around the outside in a conical shape.

Test – Coarse Aggregate

Examine several of the medium- and larger-sized particles from each sample extracted.

Result

Material within the target moisture content range will show a dull sheen when viewed obliquely against the light, with all fines adhering to the larger particles, and no free water will be visible. Material at the dry limit will not show the characteristic sheen, fines will not be strongly adherent and many of the fines will be free. Material at the wet limit will begin to show free moisture collecting in surface grooves or amongst the fines, fines will not be strongly adherent and many of the fines will amalgamate as soggy clusters. Any result between the wet and dry limits is acceptable provided the bulk of the sample is reasonably well graded.

Sands used as finefill or as a regulating layer also need to be used near to the optimum moisture content and can be identified by a simple squeeze test.

Test – Fine Aggregate

Take a small sample of representative sand, squeeze in one hand and release.

Result

If the sample crumbles away and mostly fails to adhere together into a 'ball' then the sample is too dry. Any reasonable degree of adherence is acceptable provided no free water is squeezed out.

Field Identification Test No 4 – Granular Grading

All unbound granular materials must be reasonably well graded; i.e. must contain a range of particle sizes, from fine to coarse, with an adequate proportion of particles of intermediate sizes. A well-graded material can be compacted to give a dense and stable structure of interlocking particles with a low proportion of air voids within the structure.

Preparation

Depending on the size of the stockpile, dig out representative samples from beneath the outer surface at several positions around the outside.

Test – Granular Grading

Spread out each sample and examine under good light.

Result

Class A Graded Granular Materials – should not contain any particles greater than 75 mm nominal size and, in general, should be 50 mm or smaller. Smaller particles down to less than 5 mm nominal size should be present in gradually increasing numbers as the size decreases. Finer particles, from sand size down to dust, should be present and will usually be adhering to the larger particles. Fine particles should be visible adhering to around 30 per cent or more of the surface of the majority of the larger particles.

Class B Granular Materials – should show the same general features as described above but will usually be less well graded overall compared with Class A Graded Granular Materials.

Class C Cohesive/Granular Materials – will usually contain a much larger proportion of fine material. The granular content should still be less than 75 mm nominal size, down to less than 5 mm nominal size and should not be single sized.

Appendix A2

Key to Materials

A2.0 ## Introduction

1) This Specification covers the reinstatement of excavations made by Undertakers. Whilst the Specification captures all forms and sizes of excavations, the substantial majority of reinstatements carried out by Undertakers are small rectangular-type openings and trenches. By implication these reinstatements can be considered to be carried out in restricted or confined areas.

2) Undertakers primarily adopt hand laying operations in their reinstatements, rather than machine laying operations, which are allied to new-build and larger surface area situations, i.e. those which are not necessarily restricted or confined. In addition to the final compaction of asphalt layers, hand laying operations also include the on-site transportation and handling of the asphalt materials.

3) The preferred and permissible materials set out in this Appendix are predominantly for hand laying operations by Undertakers, and have been selected accordingly, which supports other end-performance criteria, generally set out through the Specification.

A2.0.1 **Roads – General**

1) In small excavations and narrow trenches, the preferred binder course mixture may be replaced by any surface course mixture that complies with the Specification for the respective road type, provided that the same mixture is used as the surface course, see Section S6.4.10.

A2.0.2 **Footways, Footpaths and Cycle Tracks – General**

1) In all excavations, the preferred binder course mixture may be replaced by any surface course mixture that complies with this Appendix and with Section S8. This substitution is limited solely to the binder course layer. Void contents shall meet the requirements of Table S10.1 for footways.

A2.1 Hot Rolled Asphalt (HRA) Mixtures

1) All HRA shall conform to BS EN 13108-4. Conformity shall be established in accordance with BS EN 13108-20 and BS EN 13108-21. Natural gravels are not permitted as coarse aggregate for use in Types 0, 1 and 2 roads.
2) Requirements for deformation resistance as assessed by wheel tracking performance (WTR) are in accordance with PD6691 Appendix C, Table C.3
3) Design Type C mixtures listed in this section may only be used by agreement where satisfactory local experience has been gained in their use.
4) Chippings for surface application to HRA surface course mixtures shall be coarse aggregate conforming to PD 6691 Appendix C, C.2.3 and meet the requirements of C.2.8. The size and grading of chippings shall be 14/20 as in Table C.5. Where the existing surface has 8/14 chippings these may be used In the reinstatement.

A2.1.1 Surface Course Mixtures

The following HRA surface course mixture options are permitted. The preferred HRA mixtures may be replaced by one of the other alternative permitted mixtures.

1) **Roads Type 0 and 1**

   The preferred HRA surface course mixture shall be: HRA 35/14 F surf PMB des WTR 2

   Alternative permitted mixtures are:

   a) HRA 30/14 F surf PMB des WTR 2
   b) HRA 35/14 F surf 40/60 des WTR 2
   c) HRA 30/14 C surf 40/60 des WTR 2 (before use refer to A2.1. (3))

2) **Roads Type 2, 3 and 4**

   The preferred HRA surface course mixture shall be: HRA 35/14 F surf 40/60 des WTR 1

   Alternative permitted mixtures are:

   a) HRA 30/14 F surf 40/60 rec WTR 1
   b) HRA 30/14 F surf 40/60 des WTR 1
   c) HRA 30/14 C surf 40/60 des WTR 1 (before use refer to A2.1. (3))

3) **Footways, Footpaths and Cycle Tracks**

   HRA surface course mixture shall be HRA 15/10F surf 100/150 rec or, HRA 15/10F surf 70/100 rec or HRA 15/10F surf 40/60 rec.

   Areas which exhibit signs of regular trafficking by commercial vehicles or, such sites notified to the Undertaker by the Authority, shall be reinstated in accordance with Section S8.4. In such situations 100/150 pen material shall not be used.

A2.1.2 HRA Binder Course Mixtures

1) **Road Type 0 & 1**

   The HRA binder course mixture shall be HRA 60/20 F bin 40/60 des WTR 2.

2) **Road Types 2, 3 and 4**

   The preferred HRA binder course mixture shall be HRA 50/20 F bin 40/60.

   Alternative permitted mixtures (a) and (b) below may be used by agreement where satisfactory local experience has been gained in their use.

   a) Openings up to 500 mm width – HRA 50/14 F bin 40/60.

   b) Openings over 500 mm width – HRA 60/20 F bin 40/60.

3) **Footways, Footpaths and Cycle Tracks**

   The preferred HRA binder course mixture shall be HRA 50/20 F bin 100/150 or, HRA 50/20 F bin 70/100 or HRA 50/20 F bin 40/60.

   Alternative permitted mixtures (b) and (c) below may be used by agreement where satisfactory local experience has been gained in the use of these mixtures.

   a) Openings up to 500 mm width – HRA 50/14 F bin 100/150 or, HRA 50/14 F bin 70/100 or HRA 50/14 F bin 40/60.

   b) Openings over 500 mm width – HRA 60/20 F bin 100/150 or, HRA 60/20 F bin 70/100 or HRA 60/20 F bin 40/60.

   Areas which exhibit signs of regular trafficking by commercial vehicles or, such sites notified to the Undertaker by the Authority, shall be reinstated in accordance with Section S8.4. In such situations the preferred binder course mixture may not be replaced by any carriageway surface course mixture and 100/150 pen material shall not be used.

   In areas not subject to vehicular trafficking the preferred binder course mixture may also be replaced by any permitted carriageway surface course mixture.

A2.2 Stone Mastic Asphalt (SMA) Mixtures

1) SMA shall conform to BS EN 13108-5 and PD 6691. Conformity shall be established in accordance with BS EN 13108-20 and BS EN 13108-21.The following SMA mixtures are permitted by this Specification, depending upon the detail requirements of the relevant section.

2) Requirements for deformation resistance as assessed by wheeltracking performance (WTR) are in accordance with PD6691 Appendix D, Table D.2 and the note to that table.

A2.2.1 Surface Course Mixtures

The required performance properties are to be set by agreement with the Authority. Some Authorities, e.g., Highways Agency, will generally require the use of:

HAPAS certificated Thin Surface Course Systems, e.g., TSCS 14 or TSCS 10.

Where the Authority requires the use of generic SMA mixtures the SMA surface course mixture shall match the existing nominal size unless otherwise agreed.

1) **Roads Type 0 and 1**

   The permitted mixtures are:

   a) SMA 14 surf PMB WTR 2

   b) SMA 14 surf 40/60 WTR 2

   c) SMA 10 surf PMB WTR 2

   d) SMA 10 surf 40/60 WTR 2

   Alternative permitted mixtures subject to the Authority's approval are:

   e) SMA 6 surf PMB WTR 2

   f) SMA 6 surf 40/60 WTR 2

2) **Roads Type 2, 3 and 4**

   The permitted SMA mixtures are:

   a) SMA 14 surf PMB or 40/60 or 70/100 WTR 1 or 2

   b) SMA 10 surf PMB or 40/60 or 70/100 WTR 1 or 2

   Alternative permitted mixtures subject to the Authority's approval are:

   c) SMA 6 surf PMB or 40/60 or 70/100 WTR 1 or 2

   (see Section S6.4.2)

3) **Footways, Footpaths and Cycle Tracks**

   The permitted surface course mixtures, unless advised otherwise by the Authority, shall be:

   a) SMA 6 surf 40/60

   b) SMA 6 surf 70/100

   c) SMA 6 surf 100/150

A2.2.2 SMA Binder Course Mixtures

1) **Roads Type 0 and 1**

   The preferred SMA binder course mixture shall be SMA 20 bin 40/60 WTR 2.

   Alternative permitted mixtures shall be SMA 14 bin 40/60 WTR 2.

2) **Roads Type 2, 3 and 4**

The preferred SMA binder course mixtures shall be:

a) SMA 20 bin 40/60 WTR 1 or SMA 20 bin 70/100 WTR 1.

b) Openings up to 500 mm width – as a) or SMA 14 bin 40/60 WTR 1 or SMA 14 bin 70/100 WTR 1.

A2.3 Asphalt Concrete Mixtures

1) All asphalt concrete shall conform to BS EN 13108-1. Conformity shall be established in accordance with BS EN 13108-20 and BS EN 13108-21. The following coated mixtures to BS EN 13108-1 and PD 6691 are permitted by this Specification depending upon the detailed requirements of the relevant section.

2) Where the existing mixture is HDM (Heavy Duty Macadam to the now superseded BS 4987-1) or HMB (High Modulus Base) and the Authority requires the reinstatement to be completed using a similar mixture, the Authority shall notify the Undertaker accordingly.

3) Requirements for deformation resistance as assessed by wheeltracking performance (WTR) are in accordance with PD6691 Appendix B, Table B.4 and the note to that table.

A2.3.1 Surface Course Mixtures

1) **All Road Types**

The coated surface course mixtures to PD 6691 shall be AC10 close surf 100/150.

2) **Footways, Footpaths and Cycle Tracks**

a) The preferred coated surface course mixtures shall be AC 6 dense surf 100/150 or AC 6 dense surf 160/220.

b) The preferred mixture may be replaced by other agreed, alternative materials where the existing surface is a coated mixture to the now superseded BS 4987 or current PD 6691 of aggregate size significantly finer than 6 mm nominal size, see Section S8.3 3.

A2.3.2 Binder Course Mixtures

1) **Road Type 0 & 1**

The preferred binder course mixture to PD 6691 shall be AC 20 dense bin 40/60 WTR 2.

2) **Road Types 2, 3 & 4**

The preferred binder course mixture to PD 6691 shall be AC 20 dense bin 100/150 WTR 2.

3) **Footways, Footpaths and Cycle Tracks**

The preferred binder course mixture shall be AC 20 dense bin 100/150 or AC 20 dense bin 160/220.

A2.4 Cold-lay Surfacing Materials

A2.4.1 Permanent Cold-lay Surfacing Materials (PCSMs)

1) Only PCSMs with a current HAPAS certificate shall be used for the permanent reinstatement of openings.

   PCSMs shall be stored, transported, handled and used strictly in accordance with the manufacturer's requirements contained in the HAPAS certificate for that material.

   Approved PCSMs, laid and compacted in accordance with the HAPAS certificate may be used in substitution for any permitted equivalent bituminous material type, e.g., an SMA, AC etc., at the discretion of the Undertaker, as follows:

   a) Permanent Cold-lay Surfacing Material (PCSM), at any position, in all reinstatements in footways, footpaths and cycle tracks.

   b) Permanent Cold-lay Binder Course (PCBC) in all reinstatements in Type 3 & 4 roads.

   c) Permanent Cold-lay Surface Course (PCSC) in all reinstatements in Types 3 & 4 roads.

2) The required thickness of the PCSM in a), b) & c) shall be as stated in the HAPAS certificate.

3) Whenever a potential PCSM binder has begun a HAPAS PCSM Approval Trial, regardless of aggregate or material formulation under trial, then any material manufactured using that binder shall be considered to be an approved Deferred Set Material to PD 6691 for interim use only, with immediate effect.

A2.4.2 Deferred Set Mixtures (DSMs)

1) Deferred set coated mixtures shall be in accordance with PD 6691 and shall be AC 6 dense surf 160/220 DS (6 mm Surface Course) or AC 10 close surf 160/220 DS (10 mm Surface Course) or AC 20 dense bin 160/220 DS (20 mm dense Binder Course).

   The binder grade & amount of flux oil may need to be amended as necessary to meet the performance requirements for surfacing mixtures for the duration of the interim reinstatement period. Advice on this is contained in PD 6691 Appendix B.2.3.

   The binder viscosity should be adjusted to give approximately the equivalent to 10 days deferred set.

2) Deferred set coated mixtures can be used at any position, in all interim and immediate reinstatements, but are not permitted within permanent reinstatements.

A2.5 Structural Layer Thickness Tolerances

1) Several individual layers of material, commonly termed "lifts", may be required to reinstate a structural layer.

2) The thickness of each complete structural layer is specified as a nominal value.

3) The lower tolerance for the thickness of a structural layer shall be as follows:

   a) -5 mm for the surface course

   b) -10 mm for any other structural layer comprising bound material

   c) -20 mm for any other structural layer comprising unbound material

4) The upper tolerance for a structural layer thickness is not subject to any restriction although an excessive thickness of surface course is not expected. Where large thicknesses of surface course are used:

   a) the requirements for compacted lift thicknesses under Appendix A2.6 shall be met, as shall the in-situ air-voids through the full depth of the as-laid surface course layer, as set out in Section S10.2.3.

   b) the required combined binder and base course material thickness is still required, unless the binder course mixture is replaced with surface course mixture, as permitted by Appendix A2.0.1(1) and A2.0.2(1).

   c) the surface profile performance requirements set out in Section S2.2 shall not be exceeded.

5) The combination of permitted tolerances for the thickness of each structural layer of bituminous and/or cement bound mixtures shall not result in any of the following:

   a) An overall reduction in thickness of the bound pavement, excluding the sub-base, of more than 15 mm from the specified nominal thickness in a road, subject to an absolute minimum of 100 mm of bound materials.

   b) An overall reduction in the thickness of the bound pavement, excluding the sub-base, of more than 10 mm from the specified nominal thickness in a footway, subject to an absolute minimum of 60 mm of bound materials.

   c) A non-compliance with the Specification if the combined thickness of the relevant layers equals or exceeds that of the Specification requirements, provided that each individual lift meets the thickness requirements of Tables A2.1 or A2.2 and the bituminous mixtures meet the void requirements of S10.2.3.

A2.6 Compacted Lift Thickness

The compacted thickness of all individual lifts of reinstatement mixtures, within all reinstatement structural layers, shall be in accordance with the following requirements:

A2.6.1 Bituminous Mixtures

The compacted thickness of all individual 'lifts' of bituminous mixtures shall be in accordance with Table A2.1.

Table A2.1 Compacted Lift Thickness (mm) – Bituminous Mixtures

		Compacted Lift Thickness (mm)		
Material Type	**PD 6691 Reference**	**Minimum at any point**	**Nominal Lift Thickness**	**Maximum at any point**
6mm DSC	AC 6 dense surf	15	20 – 30	40
10mm CGSC	AC 10 close surf	25	30 – 40	50
15/10 HRA	HRA 15/10 F surf	25	30	50
30/14 HRA	HRA 30/14 F surf HRA 30/14 C surf	35	40	50
35/14 HRA	HRA 35/14 F surf HRA 35/14 C surf	45	50	60
6mm SMA	SMA 6 surf	15	20 – 40	45
10mm SMA	SMA 10 surf	20	25 – 50	55
14mm SMA	SMA 14 surf	30	35 – 50	55
10mm Porous Asphalt	No reference*	25*	30 – 35*	40*
20mm Porous Asphalt	No reference*	40*	45 – 60*	65*
50/20 HRA BC	HRA 50/20 bin	40	45 – 80	100
60/20 HRA BC	HRA 60/20 bin	40	45 – 80	100
14mm SMA BC	SMA 14 bin	25	30 – 60	65
20mm SMA BC	SMA 20 bin	40	50 – 100	110
20 mm DBC	AC 20 dense bin	40	50 – 100	110

* The use of porous asphalt is now very limited in the UK except for specialist uses such as sustainable drainage systems. Where porous asphalt surfaces are encountered refer to S6.4.5.3. (BS EN 13108 – 7 contains specifications for this group of asphalts and guidance on the appropriate material should be obtained from the Authority).

A2.6.2 **Non-Bituminous Materials**

The compacted thickness of all individual 'lifts' of non-bituminous materials shall be in accordance with Table A2.2.

Table A2.2 – Compacted Lift Thickness – Non-Bituminous Materials

Material	Compacted Lift Thickness (mm)		
	Minimum at any point	Nominal Lift Thickness	Maximum at any point
CBGM B	75	100 to 150	200
C25/30 Concrete	100	As Required	As Existing
C32/40 Concrete	100	As Required	As Existing
GSB1	75	100 to 150	200
Classes A & B	75	100 to 150	200
Classes C & D	75	100 to 150	200
SMF-A & SMF-B	75	100 to 150	200
SMF-C & SMF-D	75	100 to 150	200

A2.7 Bituminous Laying Temperatures

The laying temperatures for bituminous mixtures shall be in accordance with Table A2.3.

Table A2.3 – Laying Temperatures – Bituminous Materials

Material	Binder Grade	Maximum Temperature at any Stage (°C)	Minimum Temperatures (°C)	
			Arrival ✲	Minimum Rolling#
CGSC	100/150	170	120	95
DSC	160/220	170	110	85
DBC	40/60	190	130	100
	70/100	180	125	95
	100/150	170	120	90
	160/220	170	110	80
HRA SC#	40/60	190	140	110
	70/100	180	125	90
	100/150	170	120	85
HRA BC	40/60	190	130	105
	70/100	180	125	90
	100/150	170	120	85

Table A2.3 – Laying Temperatures – Bituminous Materials

SMA SC SMA BC	40/60 70/100 100/150	200 180 170	130 125 120	100 90 85
Porous Asphalt	125 190	135 145	110	85

Notes to Table A2.3:
1 ✻ = In the lorry within 30 minutes after arrival on site.
2 For coated slag mixtures temperatures may be 10°C lower than the recommended values.
3 Greater compactive effort may be required to achieve an acceptable air voids ratio as the temperature approaches the lower limit.
4 # = See table A2.4 for the final rolling temperatures when chippings are applied to HRA surface courses.

Table A2.4 – Final Rolling Temperatures – HRA

Binder Grade	Minimum temperature (°C) at completion of rolling
40/60	85
70/100	80
100/150	75

Note: When using modified bitumen or additives, different temperatures might be applicable.

A2.8 Identification of Structural Layers

A2.8.1 Road Structures

1) For the purposes of defining permissible material options, layer thickness etc, this Specification classifies road structures as being of flexible, composite, rigid or modular design. The road structures assumed to be representative of each of these designs are shown in Figure A2.1. For each design, a typical reinstatement structure, identifying the principal structural layers, is also shown.

Figure A2.1 Typical Reinstatement Structure within recognised Road Designs

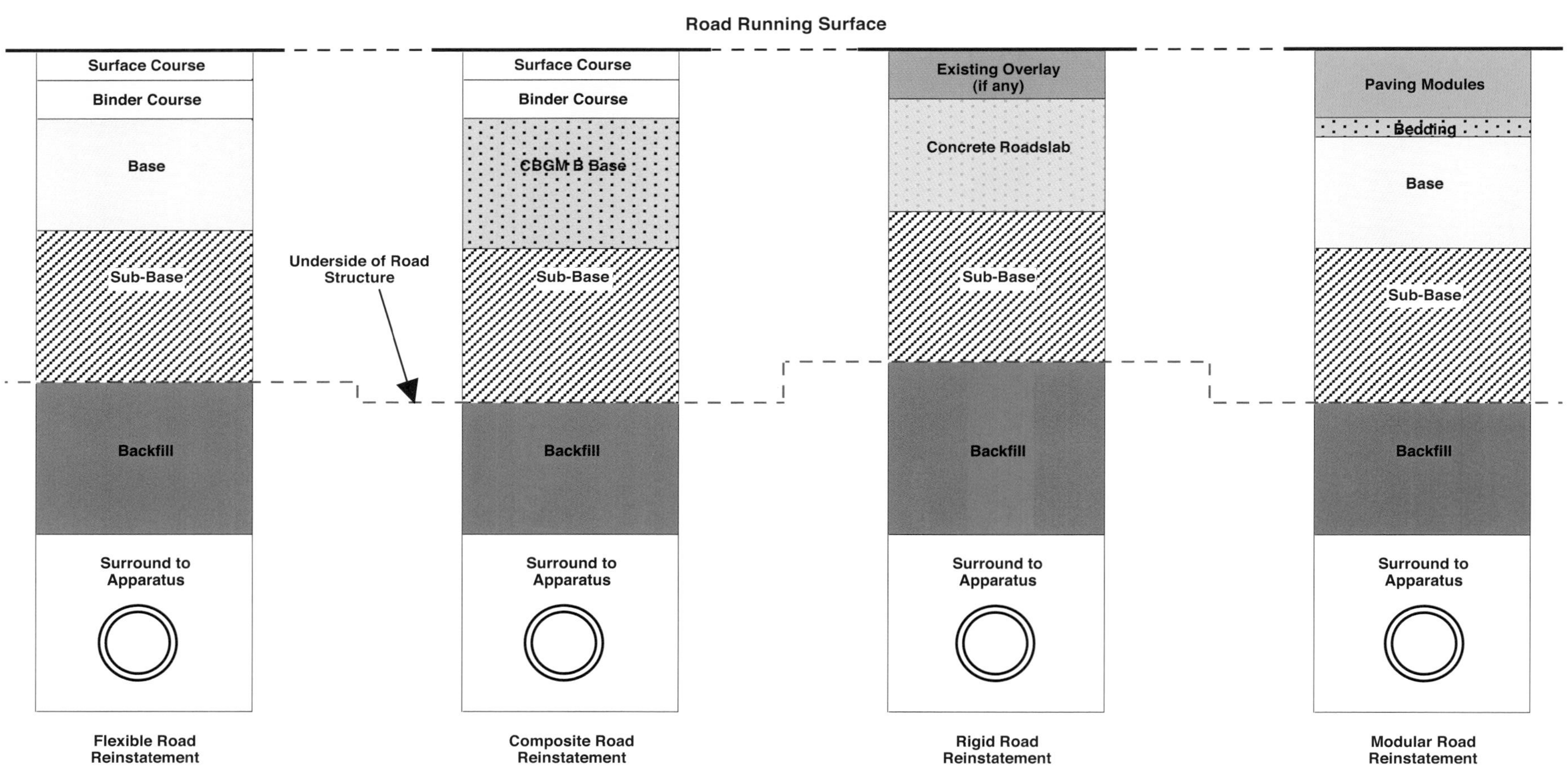

2) Permitted materials and layer thickness for road structures are specified as follows:

   a) Flexible Design – see Appendix A3.0 to A3.4

   b) Flexible Sub-structure – see Appendix A3.5

   c) Composite Design – see Appendix A4.0 to A4.3

   d) Composite Sub-structure – see Appendix A4.4 to A4.5

   e) Rigid Design – see Appendix A5.0 to A5.2

   f) Modular Design – see Appendix A6.1 to A6.3

3) All layer thicknesses are in millimetres.

A2.8.2 Footway, Footpath and Cycle Track Structures

1) For the purposes of defining permissible material options, layer thickness, etc. this Specification classifies footway, footpath and cycle track structures as being of flexible, rigid or modular design. The structures assumed to be representative of each of these designs are shown in Figure A2.2. For each design, a typical reinstatement structure, identifying the principal structural layers, is also shown.

2) Permitted materials and layer thickness for footway, footpath and cycle track structures are specified as follows:

   a) Flexible Design see Appendix A7.1

   b) Rigid Design see Appendix A7.2

   c) Modular Design see Appendix A7.3.

3) All layer thicknesses are in millimetres.

Figure A2.2 Typical Reinstatement Structure within recognised Footway Designs

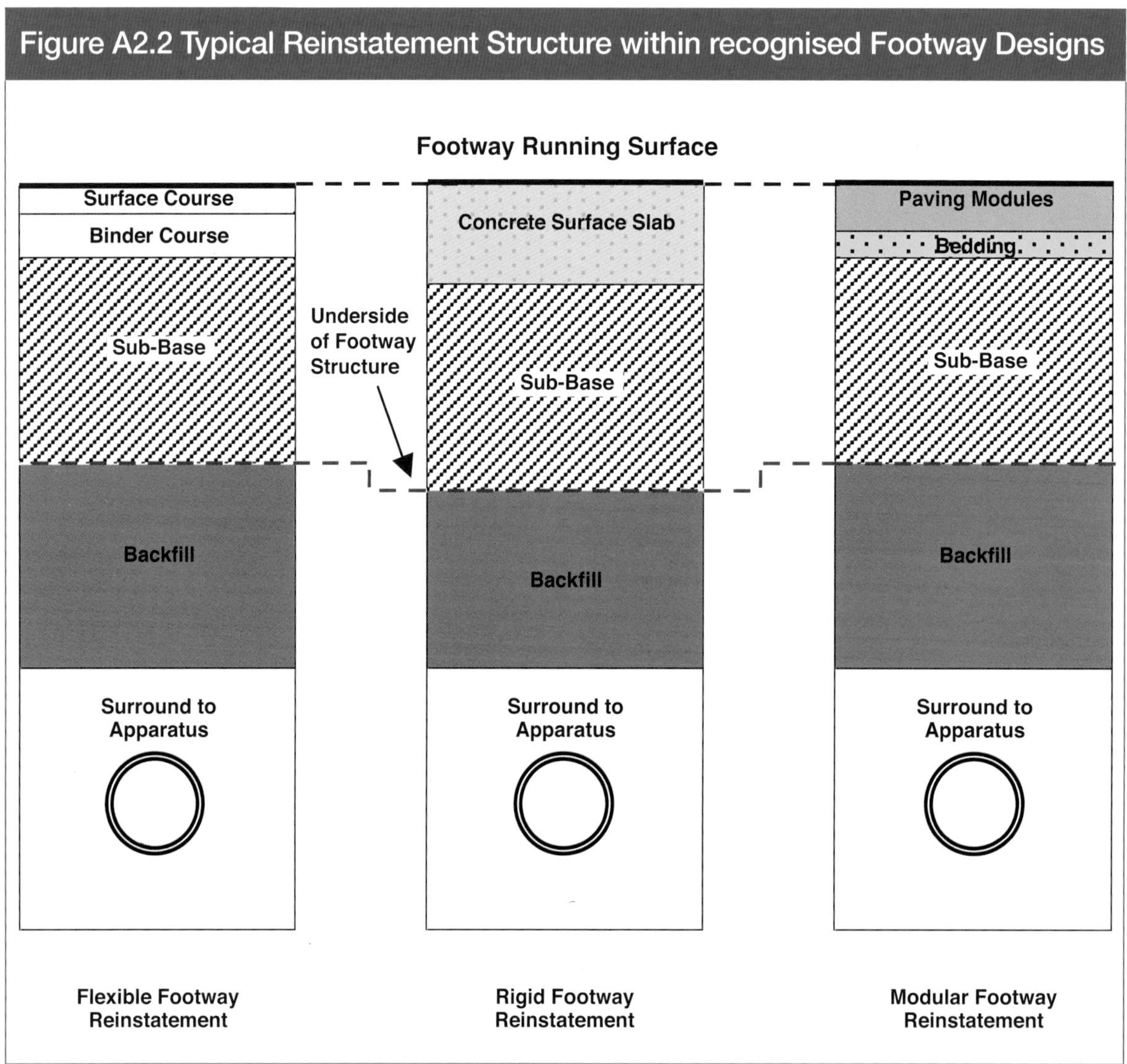

A2.9 ## Key to Materials

1) For the purposes of defining the main material options, layer thickness, etc. required by this Specification, Appendices A3 to A7, inclusive, show the principal structural layers within cross-sections of typical reinstatement designs in each of the main surface categories. Materials are denoted by the symbols in Table A2.5.

2) Proprietary asphalt materials are not included in Table A2.5, given their specialist and limited application, an example being flowable mastic asphalts, which may be used in footway surface courses and access surrounds to larger apparatus in roads.

3) ARMs are not shown, given the wide range of options and material variations.

Table A2.5 Key to Reinstatement Materials

Symbol	Materials	Key
	HRASC ACCSC SMASC HRASC ACCSC ACDSC SMASC PCSC	HRASC - Hot Rolled Asphalt Surface Course See Appendix A2.1.1 SMASC - Stone Mastic Asphalt Surface Course See Appendix A2.2.1 ACCSC - Asphalt Concrete Close Surface Course See Appendix A2.3.1 ACDSC - Asphalt Concrete Dense Surface Course See Appendix A2.3.1 PCSC - Permanent Cold-lay Surface Course See Appendix A2.4.1
	HRABC ACBC SMABC HRABC ACBC SMABC PCBC	HRABC - Hot Rolled Asphalt Binder Course See Appendix A2.1.2 SMABC - Stone Mastic Asphalt Binder Course See Appendix A2.2.2 ACBC - Asphalt Concrete Binder Course See Appendix A2.3.2 PCBC - Permanent Cold-lay Binder Course See Appendix A2.4.1
	DSM PCSM	DSM - Deferred Set Mixtures See Appendix A2.4.2 PCSM - Permanent Cold-lay Surfacing Material See Appendix A2.4.1
	Concrete	Concrete - Pavement Quality Concrete To SHW Clause 1001
	CBGM B	CBGM B - Cement Bound General Material Category B To SHW Clause 822
	GSB 1	GSB 1 - Type 1 Granular Sub-base Material To SHW Clause 803
AAA AAA	CLASS A	Class A - Graded Granular Backfill Material See Appendix A1.1
BBB BBB	CLASS B	Class B - Granular Backfill Material See Appendix A1.2
CCC CCC	CLASS C	Class C - Cohesive Granular Backfill Material See Appendix A1.3
DDD DDD	CLASS D	Class D - Cohesive Backfill Material See Appendix A1.4

A2.10 Key to Reinstatement Methods

Sections S6.1, S7.1 and S8.1 set out the permissible reinstatement methods for all of the main types of construction categories covered by the Specification. Appendices A3 to A7, inclusive, indicate different materials and material thicknesses for each permissible reinstatement method, which may also vary between different Road Categories. Table A2.6 summarises these permissible reinstatement methods.

Table A2.6 Key to Reinstatement Methods

Reinstatement Method (At First visit)	Flexible & Composite Roads Section S6		Rigid & Modular Roads Section S7				Footways, Footpaths & Cycle Tracks Section S8		
	Flexible	Composite	Rigid	Modular			Flexible	Rigid	Modular
	(Appendix A3.0-A3.4 incl.)	(Appendix A4.0-A4.3 incl.)	(Appendix A5.0-A5.2 incl.)	Bituminous Base (Roadbase) (Appendix A6.1)	Composite Base (Roadbase) (Appendix A6.2)	Granular Base (Roadbase) (Appendix A6.3)	(Appendix A7.1)	(Appendix A7.2)	(Appendix A7.3)
All Permanent	Method A (Types 0-4 incl.)	Method A (Types 0-4 incl.)	Method A (Types 0-4 incl.)	Method A (Types 3, 4 only)	Method A (Types 3, 4 only)	Method A (Types 3, 4 only)	Method A	Method A	Method A
Interim with Permanent Binder Course	Method B (Types 0-4 incl.)	Method B (Types 0-4 incl.)	N/A	N/A	N/A	N/A	Method B	N/A	N/A
Interim with Permanent Base	Method C (Types 3, 4 only)	Method C (Types 0-4 incl.)	N/A	N/A	N/A	N/A	N/A	N/A	N/A
Interim with Permanent Sub-base	Method D (Types 0-4 incl.)	Method D (Types 0-4 incl.)	Method D (Types 0-4 incl.)	Method D (Types 3, 4 only)	Method D (Types 3, 4 only)	Method D (Types 3, 4 only)	Method D	Method D	Method D
Permanent incorporating Interim Surface Overlay	N/A	N/A	Method E (Types 0-4 incl.)	N/A	N/A	N/A	N/A	N/A	N/A

A2.11 Summarised Selection Process for Hot Lay Flexible Materials

Specific to the hot-lay reinstatement of flexible roads and footways (including footpaths and cycle tracks), different parts of the Specification set out the following criteria:

- overall class, layer designation and mixture design for Hot Rolled Asphalts, Stone Mastic Asphalts and Asphalt Concretes (A2.1 to A2.3);
- different thicknesses of mixture layers (A3 and A7);
- specific requirements and limitations for surface courses (Sections S6.4 and S8.3).

The overall process for selecting the correct materials to reinstate flexible roads and footways is particularly more complex at the reinstatement design selection stage. Figure S0.1 provides a generic overview of this process, but to assist practitioners, Figures A2.3, A2.4 and A2.5 respectively set out the summarised overall processes specific to:

- Types 0 and 1 Flexible Roads
- Types 2, 3 and 4 Flexible Roads
- Flexible Footways, Footpaths and Cycle Tracks

Figure A2.3 Permanent Reinstatement Options for Hot Lay Flexible Materials (Roads Types 0 and 1)

Existing Carriageway Construction

Confirm Road Category and Select Permissible Reinstatement Appendix

Identify ALLOWABLE Bound Course Options and relevant Specification under Appendices A2 and A3

Flexible → Types 0 and 1 → Type 0 - Appendix A3.0 / Type1 - Appendix A3.1

Flexible → Types 2, 3 and 4 → Separate Table

Surface Course (Types 0 and 1):
- HRASC → 40mm → Appendix A2.1.1
- SMASC → 40mm for 14mm SMA / 30mm for 10mm SMA [S6.4.2(1)(a) & S6.4.2(1)(b)] → Appendix A2.1.1
- ACSC → 40mm → Appendix A2.3.1

Binder Course [incl. Base Course] (Types 0 and 1):
- HRABC → Type 0 - 375mm (60+315) / Type 1 - 310mm (60+250) → Appendix A2.1.2
- SMABC → Type 0 - 375mm (60+315) / Type 1 - 310mm (60+250) → Appendix A2.2.2
- ACBC → Type 0 - 375mm (60+315) / Type 1 - 310mm (60+250) → Appendix A2.3.2

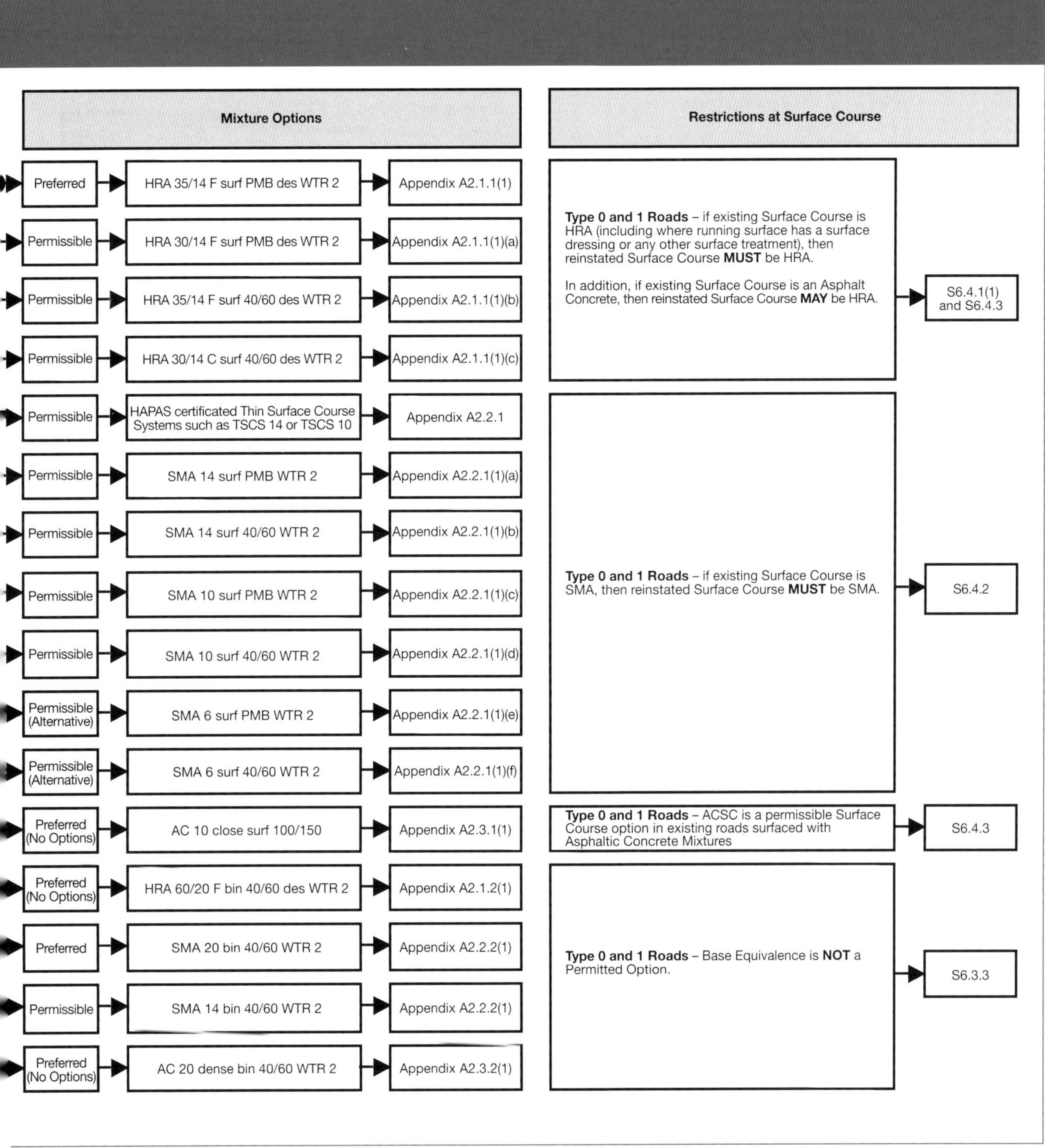
Mixture Options
Restrictions at Surface Course
Preferred
HRA 35/14 F surf PMB des WTR 2
Appendix A2.1.1(1)
Permissible
HRA 30/14 F surf PMB des WTR 2
Appendix A2.1.1(1)(a)
Permissible
HRA 35/14 F surf 40/60 des WTR 2
Appendix A2.1.1(1)(b)
Permissible
HRA 30/14 C surf 40/60 des WTR 2
Appendix A2.1.1(1)(c)
Type 0 and 1 Roads – if existing Surface Course is HRA (including where running surface has a surface dressing or any other surface treatment), then reinstated Surface Course MUST be HRA.
In addition, if existing Surface Course is an Asphalt Concrete, then reinstated Surface Course MAY be HRA.
S6.4.1(1) and S6.4.3
Permissible
HAPAS certificated Thin Surface Course Systems such as TSCS 14 or TSCS 10
Appendix A2.2.1
Permissible
SMA 14 surf PMB WTR 2
Appendix A2.2.1(1)(a)
Permissible
SMA 14 surf 40/60 WTR 2
Appendix A2.2.1(1)(b)
Permissible
SMA 10 surf PMB WTR 2
Appendix A2.2.1(1)(c)
Permissible
SMA 10 surf 40/60 WTR 2
Appendix A2.2.1(1)(d)
Permissible (Alternative)
SMA 6 surf PMB WTR 2
Appendix A2.2.1(1)(e)
Permissible (Alternative)
SMA 6 surf 40/60 WTR 2
Appendix A2.2.1(1)(f)
Type 0 and 1 Roads – if existing Surface Course is SMA, then reinstated Surface Course MUST be SMA.
S6.4.2
Preferred (No Options)
AC 10 close surf 100/150
Appendix A2.3.1(1)
Type 0 and 1 Roads – ACSC is a permissible Surface Course option in existing roads surfaced with Asphaltic Concrete Mixtures
S6.4.3
Preferred (No Options)
HRA 60/20 F bin 40/60 des WTR 2
Appendix A2.1.2(1)
Preferred
SMA 20 bin 40/60 WTR 2
Appendix A2.2.2(1)
Permissible
SMA 14 bin 40/60 WTR 2
Appendix A2.2.2(1)
Preferred (No Options)
AC 20 dense bin 40/60 WTR 2
Appendix A2.3.2(1)
Type 0 and 1 Roads – Base Equivalence is NOT a Permitted Option.
S6.3.3

Figure A2.4 Permanent Reinstatement Options for Hot Lay Flexible Materials (Road Types 2, 3 and 4)

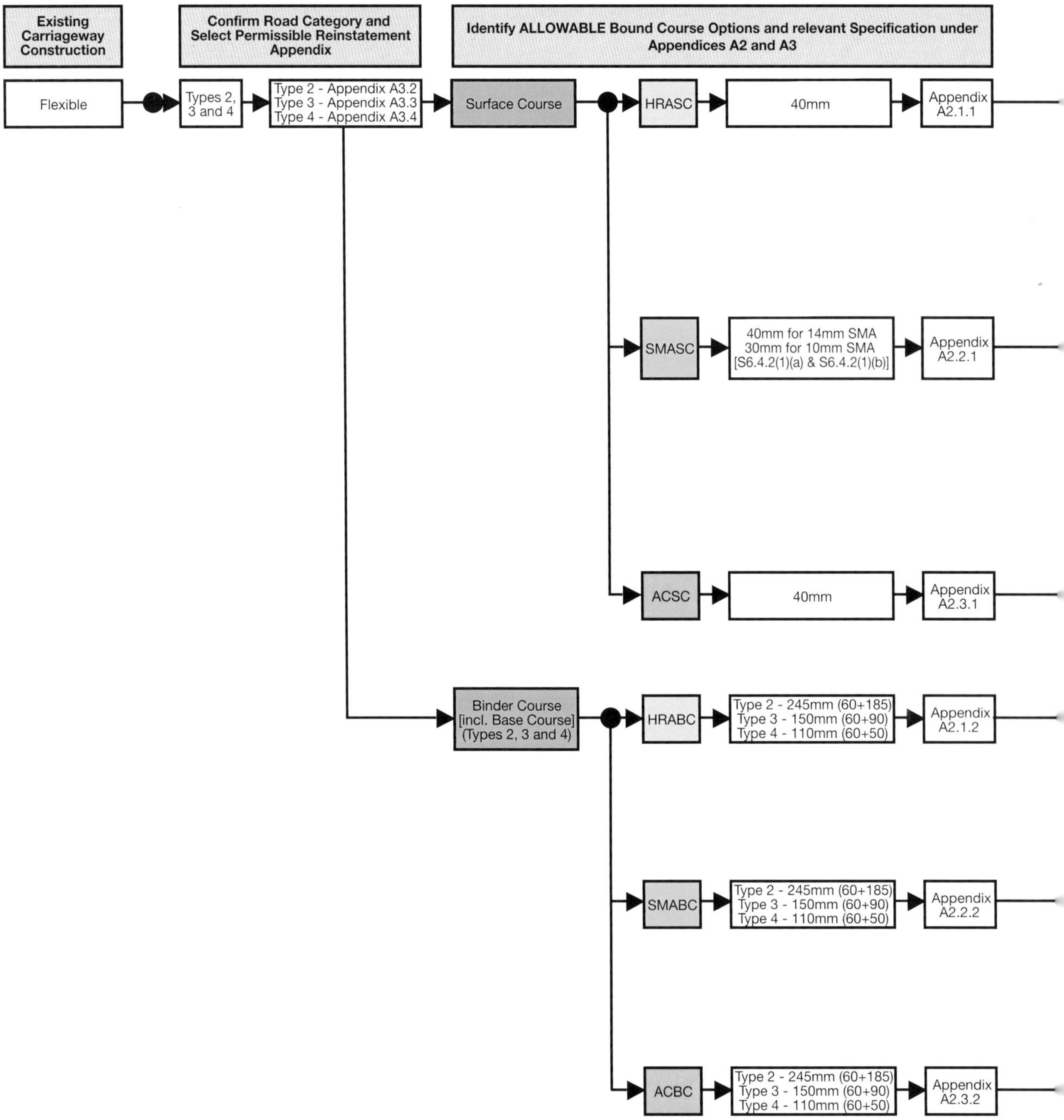

Existing Carriageway Construction

Confirm Road Category and Select Permissible Reinstatement Appendix

Identify ALLOWABLE Bound Course Options and relevant Specification under Appendices A2 and A3

Flexible → Types 2, 3 and 4 → Type 2 - Appendix A3.2, Type 3 - Appendix A3.3, Type 4 - Appendix A3.4

Surface Course
- HRASC → 40mm → Appendix A2.1.1
- SMASC → 40mm for 14mm SMA, 30mm for 10mm SMA [S6.4.2(1)(a) & S6.4.2(1)(b)] → Appendix A2.2.1
- ACSC → 40mm → Appendix A2.3.1

Binder Course [incl. Base Course] (Types 2, 3 and 4)
- HRABC → Type 2 - 245mm (60+185), Type 3 - 150mm (60+90), Type 4 - 110mm (60+50) → Appendix A2.1.2
- SMABC → Type 2 - 245mm (60+185), Type 3 - 150mm (60+90), Type 4 - 110mm (60+50) → Appendix A2.2.2
- ACBC → Type 2 - 245mm (60+185), Type 3 - 150mm (60+90), Type 4 - 110mm (60+50) → Appendix A2.3.2

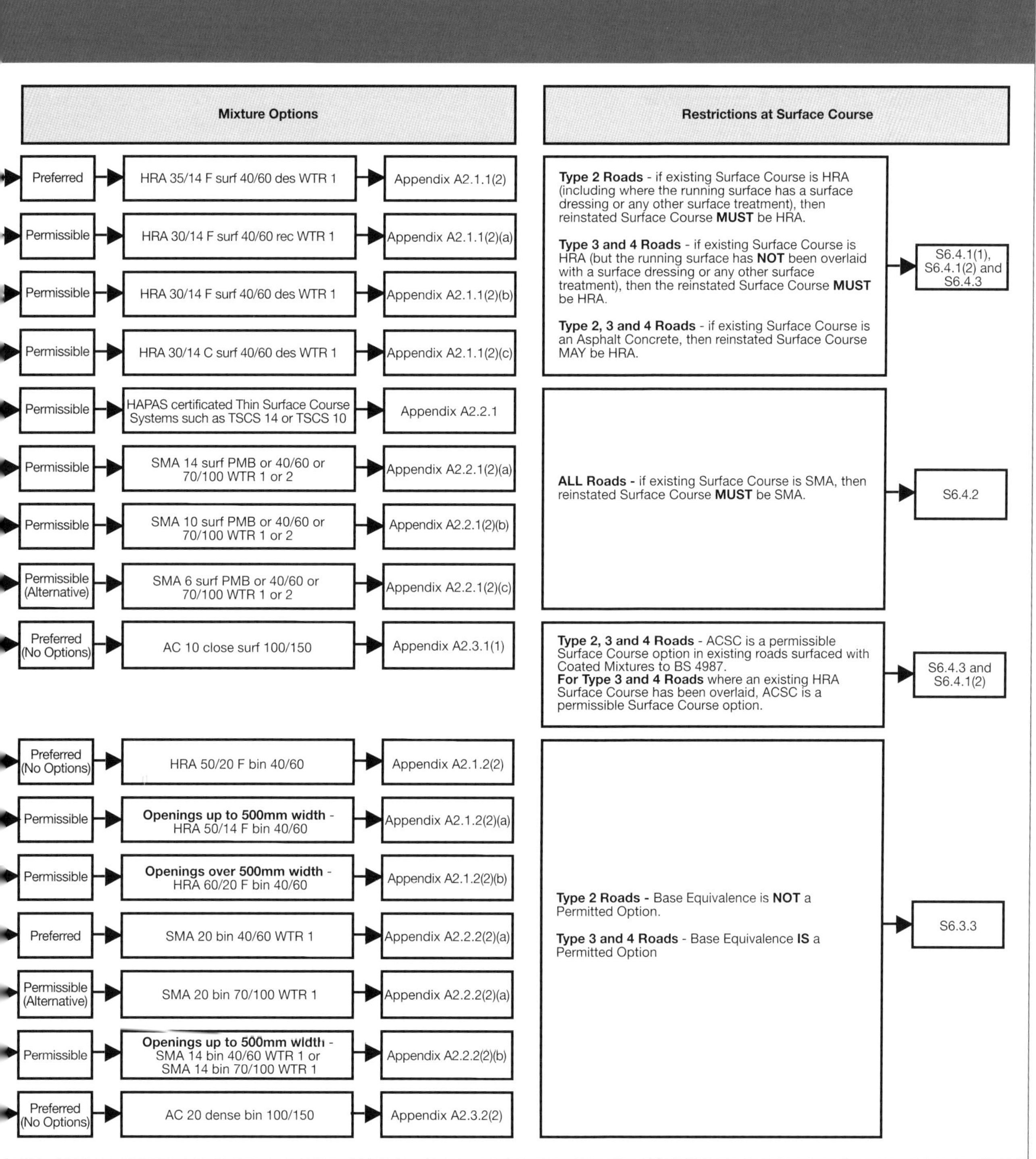
Mixture Options
Restrictions at Surface Course
Preferred
HRA 35/14 F surf 40/60 des WTR 1
Appendix A2.1.1(2)
Permissible
HRA 30/14 F surf 40/60 rec WTR 1
Appendix A2.1.1(2)(a)
Permissible
HRA 30/14 F surf 40/60 des WTR 1
Appendix A2.1.1(2)(b)
Permissible
HRA 30/14 C surf 40/60 des WTR 1
Appendix A2.1.1(2)(c)
Type 2 Roads - if existing Surface Course is HRA (including where the running surface has a surface dressing or any other surface treatment), then reinstated Surface Course MUST be HRA.
Type 3 and 4 Roads - if existing Surface Course is HRA (but the running surface has NOT been overlaid with a surface dressing or any other surface treatment), then the reinstated Surface Course MUST be HRA.
Type 2, 3 and 4 Roads - if existing Surface Course is an Asphalt Concrete, then reinstated Surface Course MAY be HRA.
S6.4.1(1), S6.4.1(2) and S6.4.3
Permissible
HAPAS certificated Thin Surface Course Systems such as TSCS 14 or TSCS 10
Appendix A2.2.1
Permissible
SMA 14 surf PMB or 40/60 or 70/100 WTR 1 or 2
Appendix A2.2.1(2)(a)
Permissible
SMA 10 surf PMB or 40/60 or 70/100 WTR 1 or 2
Appendix A2.2.1(2)(b)
Permissible (Alternative)
SMA 6 surf PMB or 40/60 or 70/100 WTR 1 or 2
Appendix A2.2.1(2)(c)
ALL Roads - if existing Surface Course is SMA, then reinstated Surface Course MUST be SMA.
S6.4.2
Preferred (No Options)
AC 10 close surf 100/150
Appendix A2.3.1(1)
Type 2, 3 and 4 Roads - ACSC is a permissible Surface Course option in existing roads surfaced with Coated Mixtures to BS 4987.
For Type 3 and 4 Roads where an existing HRA Surface Course has been overlaid, ACSC is a permissible Surface Course option.
S6.4.3 and S6.4.1(2)
Preferred (No Options)
HRA 50/20 F bin 40/60
Appendix A2.1.2(2)
Permissible
Openings up to 500mm width - HRA 50/14 F bin 40/60
Appendix A2.1.2(2)(a)
Permissible
Openings over 500mm width - HRA 60/20 F bin 40/60
Appendix A2.1.2(2)(b)
Preferred
SMA 20 bin 40/60 WTR 1
Appendix A2.2.2(2)(a)
Permissible (Alternative)
SMA 20 bin 70/100 WTR 1
Appendix A2.2.2(2)(a)
Permissible
Openings up to 500mm width - SMA 14 bin 40/60 WTR 1 or SMA 14 bin 70/100 WTR 1
Appendix A2.2.2(2)(b)
Preferred (No Options)
AC 20 dense bin 100/150
Appendix A2.3.2(2)
Type 2 Roads - Base Equivalence is NOT a Permitted Option.
Type 3 and 4 Roads - Base Equivalence IS a Permitted Option
S6.3.3

Figure A2.5 Permanent Reinstatement Options for Hot Lay Flexible Materials (Footways, Footpaths and Cycle Tracks)

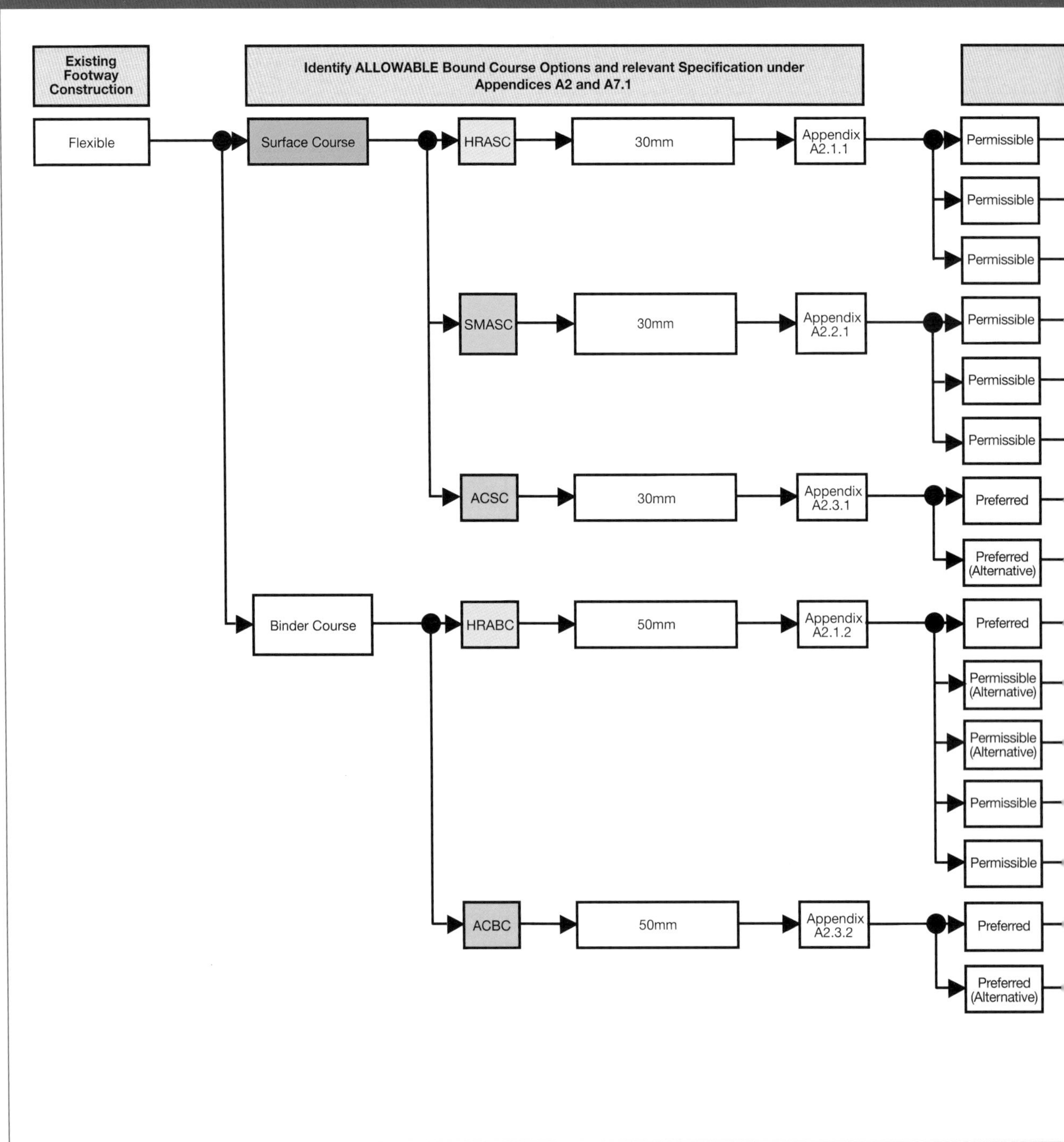

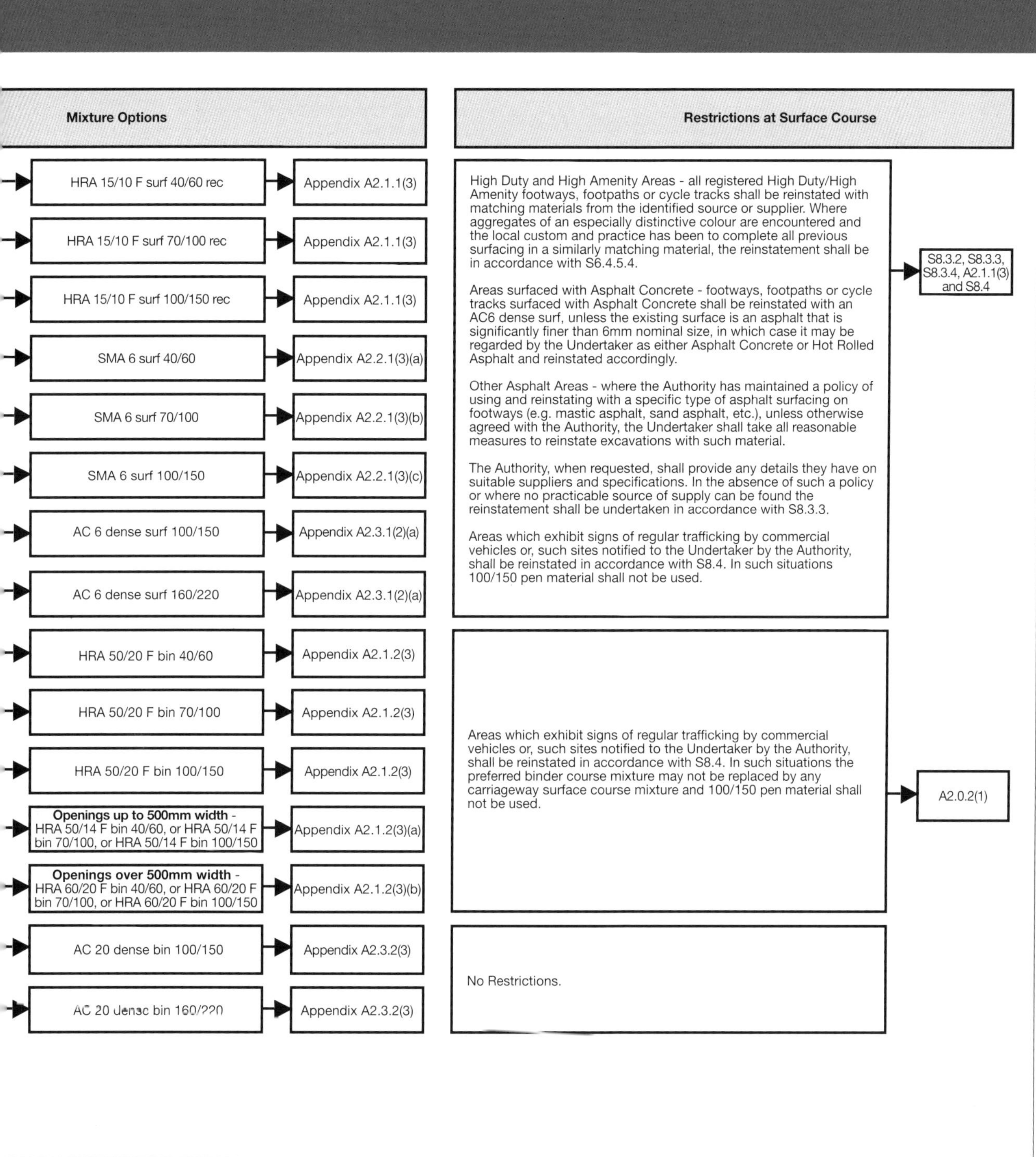
Mixture Options
Restrictions at Surface Course
HRA 15/10 F surf 40/60 rec
Appendix A2.1.1(3)
HRA 15/10 F surf 70/100 rec
Appendix A2.1.1(3)
HRA 15/10 F surf 100/150 rec
Appendix A2.1.1(3)
SMA 6 surf 40/60
Appendix A2.2.1(3)(a)
SMA 6 surf 70/100
Appendix A2.2.1(3)(b)
SMA 6 surf 100/150
Appendix A2.2.1(3)(c)
AC 6 dense surf 100/150
Appendix A2.3.1(2)(a)
AC 6 dense surf 160/220
Appendix A2.3.1(2)(a)
High Duty and High Amenity Areas - all registered High Duty/High Amenity footways, footpaths or cycle tracks shall be reinstated with matching materials from the identified source or supplier. Where aggregates of an especially distinctive colour are encountered and the local custom and practice has been to complete all previous surfacing in a similarly matching material, the reinstatement shall be in accordance with S6.4.5.4.
Areas surfaced with Asphalt Concrete - footways, footpaths or cycle tracks surfaced with Asphalt Concrete shall be reinstated with an AC6 dense surf, unless the existing surface is an asphalt that is significantly finer than 6mm nominal size, in which case it may be regarded by the Undertaker as either Asphalt Concrete or Hot Rolled Asphalt and reinstated accordingly.
Other Asphalt Areas - where the Authority has maintained a policy of using and reinstating with a specific type of asphalt surfacing on footways (e.g. mastic asphalt, sand asphalt, etc.), unless otherwise agreed with the Authority, the Undertaker shall take all reasonable measures to reinstate excavations with such material.
The Authority, when requested, shall provide any details they have on suitable suppliers and specifications. In the absence of such a policy or where no practicable source of supply can be found the reinstatement shall be undertaken in accordance with S8.3.3.
Areas which exhibit signs of regular trafficking by commercial vehicles or, such sites notified to the Undertaker by the Authority, shall be reinstated in accordance with S8.4. In such situations 100/150 pen material shall not be used.
S8.3.2, S8.3.3, S8.3.4, A2.1.1(3) and S8.4
HRA 50/20 F bin 40/60
Appendix A2.1.2(3)
HRA 50/20 F bin 70/100
Appendix A2.1.2(3)
HRA 50/20 F bin 100/150
Appendix A2.1.2(3)
Openings up to 500mm width - HRA 50/14 F bin 40/60, or HRA 50/14 F bin 70/100, or HRA 50/14 F bin 100/150
Appendix A2.1.2(3)(a)
Openings over 500mm width - HRA 60/20 F bin 40/60, or HRA 60/20 F bin 70/100, or HRA 60/20 F bin 100/150
Appendix A2.1.2(3)(b)
Areas which exhibit signs of regular trafficking by commercial vehicles or, such sites notified to the Undertaker by the Authority, shall be reinstated in accordance with S8.4. In such situations the preferred binder course mixture may not be replaced by any carriageway surface course mixture and 100/150 pen material shall not be used.
A2.0.2(1)
AC 20 dense bin 100/150
Appendix A2.3.2(3)
AC 20 dense bin 160/220
Appendix A2.3.2(3)
No Restrictions.

Figure A3.0 Flexible Roads Type – '0'

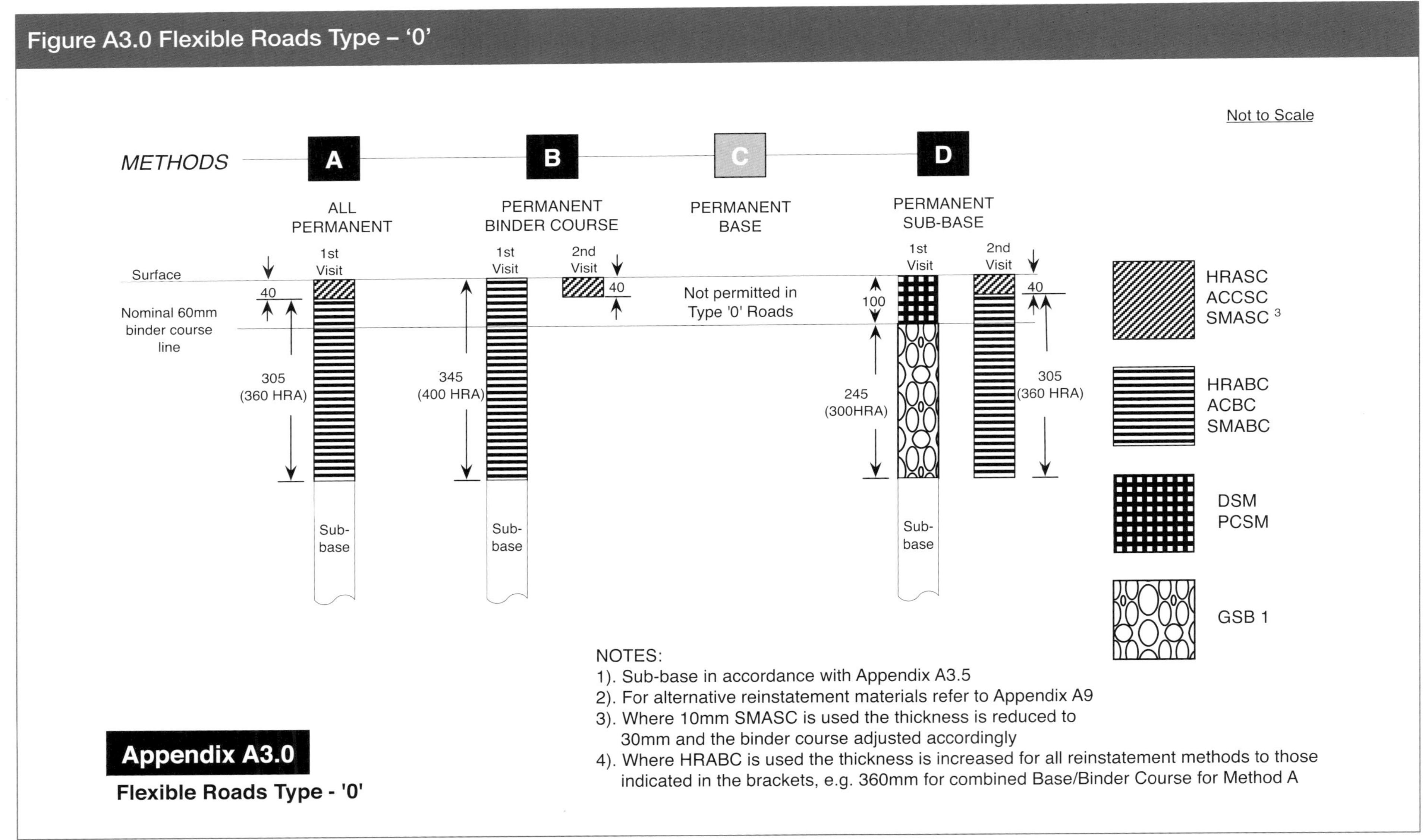

NOTES:
1). Sub-base in accordance with Appendix A3.5
2). For alternative reinstatement materials refer to Appendix A9
3). Where 10mm SMASC is used the thickness is reduced to 30mm and the binder course adjusted accordingly
4). Where HRABC is used the thickness is increased for all reinstatement methods to those indicated in the brackets, e.g. 360mm for combined Base/Binder Course for Method A

Appendix A3.0

Flexible Roads Type - '0'

Appendix A3.1

Flexible Roads Type - '1'

Figure A3.1 Flexible Roads Type – '1'

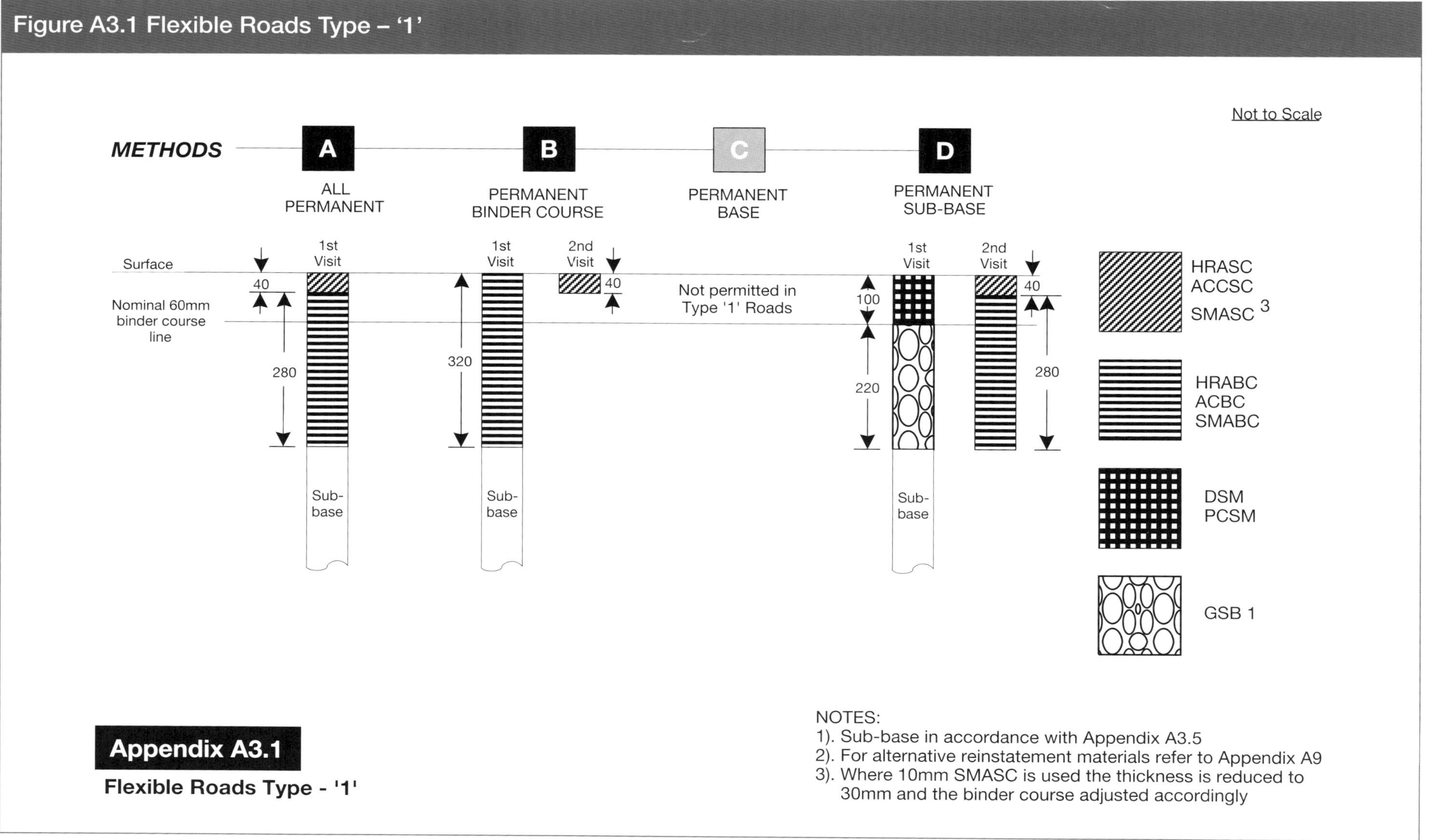

NOTES:
1). Sub-base in accordance with Appendix A3.5
2). For alternative reinstatement materials refer to Appendix A9
3). Where 10mm SMASC is used the thickness is reduced to 30mm and the binder course adjusted accordingly

Figure A3.2 Flexible Roads Type – '2'

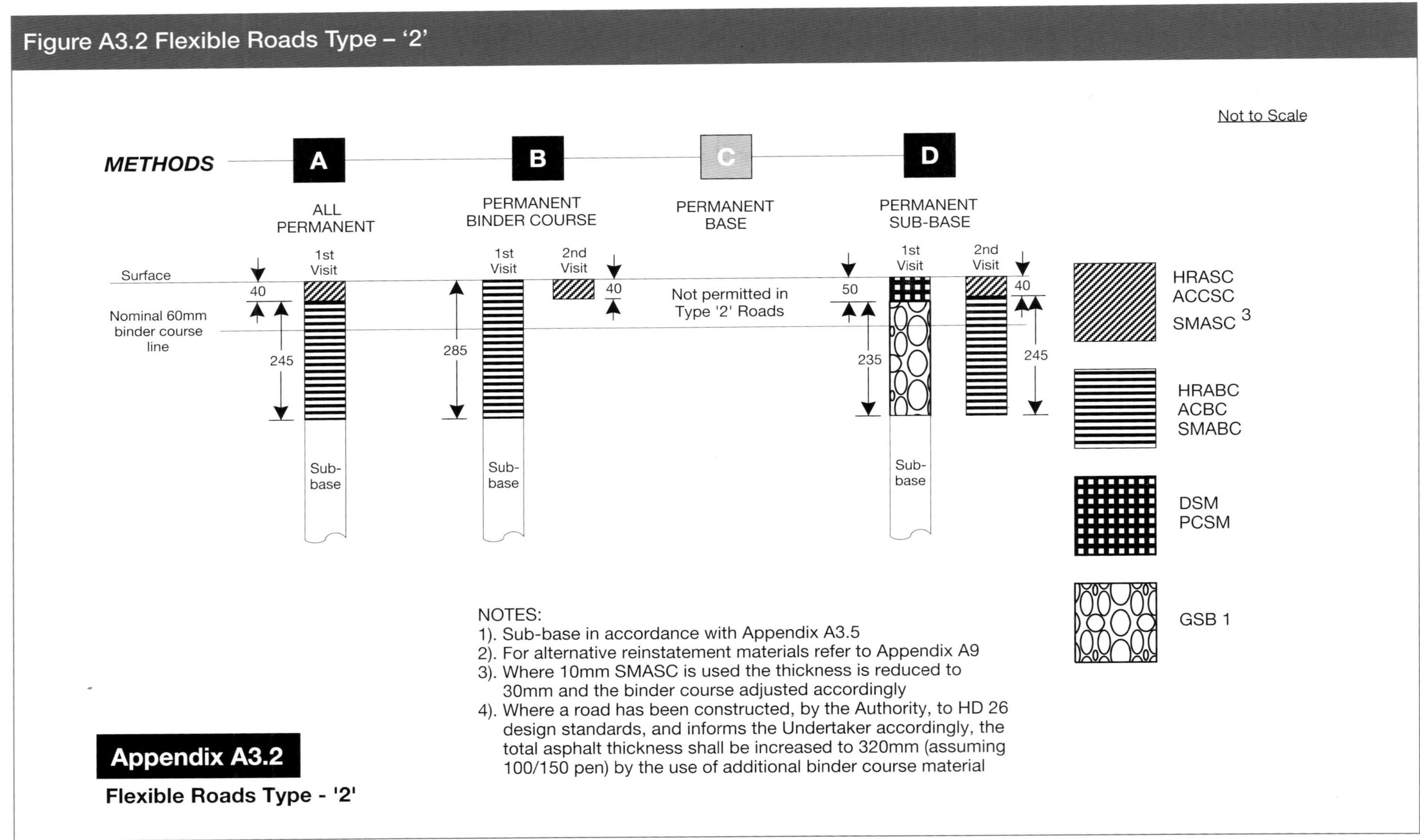

NOTES:
1). Sub-base in accordance with Appendix A3.5
2). For alternative reinstatement materials refer to Appendix A9
3). Where 10mm SMASC is used the thickness is reduced to 30mm and the binder course adjusted accordingly
4). Where a road has been constructed, by the Authority, to HD 26 design standards, and informs the Undertaker accordingly, the total asphalt thickness shall be increased to 320mm (assuming 100/150 pen) by the use of additional binder course material

Appendix A3.2

Flexible Roads Type - '2'

Figure A3.3 Flexible Roads Type – '3'

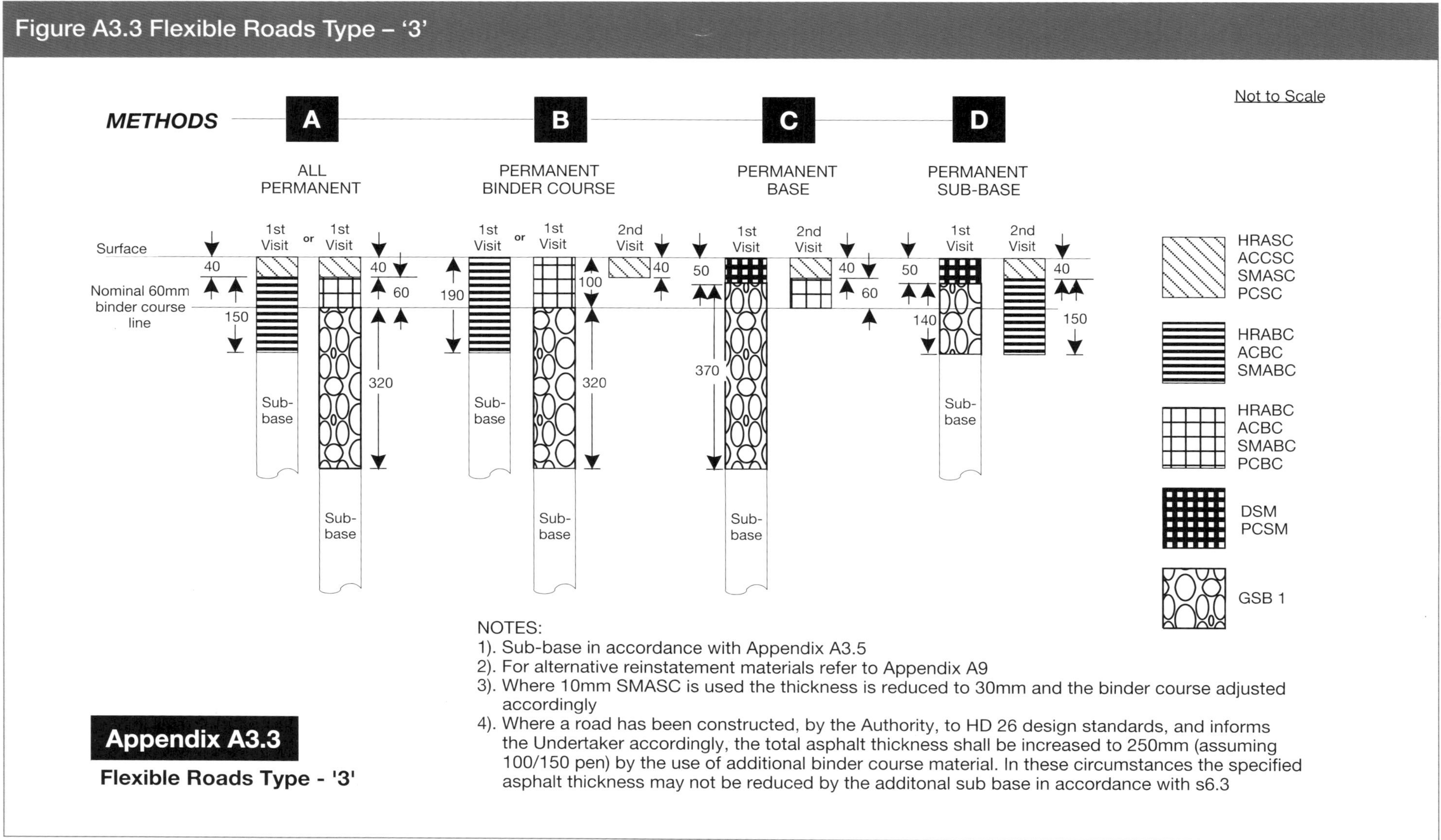

NOTES:

1). Sub-base in accordance with Appendix A3.5
2). For alternative reinstatement materials refer to Appendix A9
3). Where 10mm SMASC is used the thickness is reduced to 30mm and the binder course adjusted accordingly
4). Where a road has been constructed, by the Authority, to HD 26 design standards, and informs the Undertaker accordingly, the total asphalt thickness shall be increased to 250mm (assuming 100/150 pen) by the use of additional binder course material. In these circumstances the specified asphalt thickness may not be reduced by the additonal sub base in accordance with s6.3

Appendix A3.3

Flexible Roads Type - '3'

Figure A3.4 Flexible Roads Type – '4'

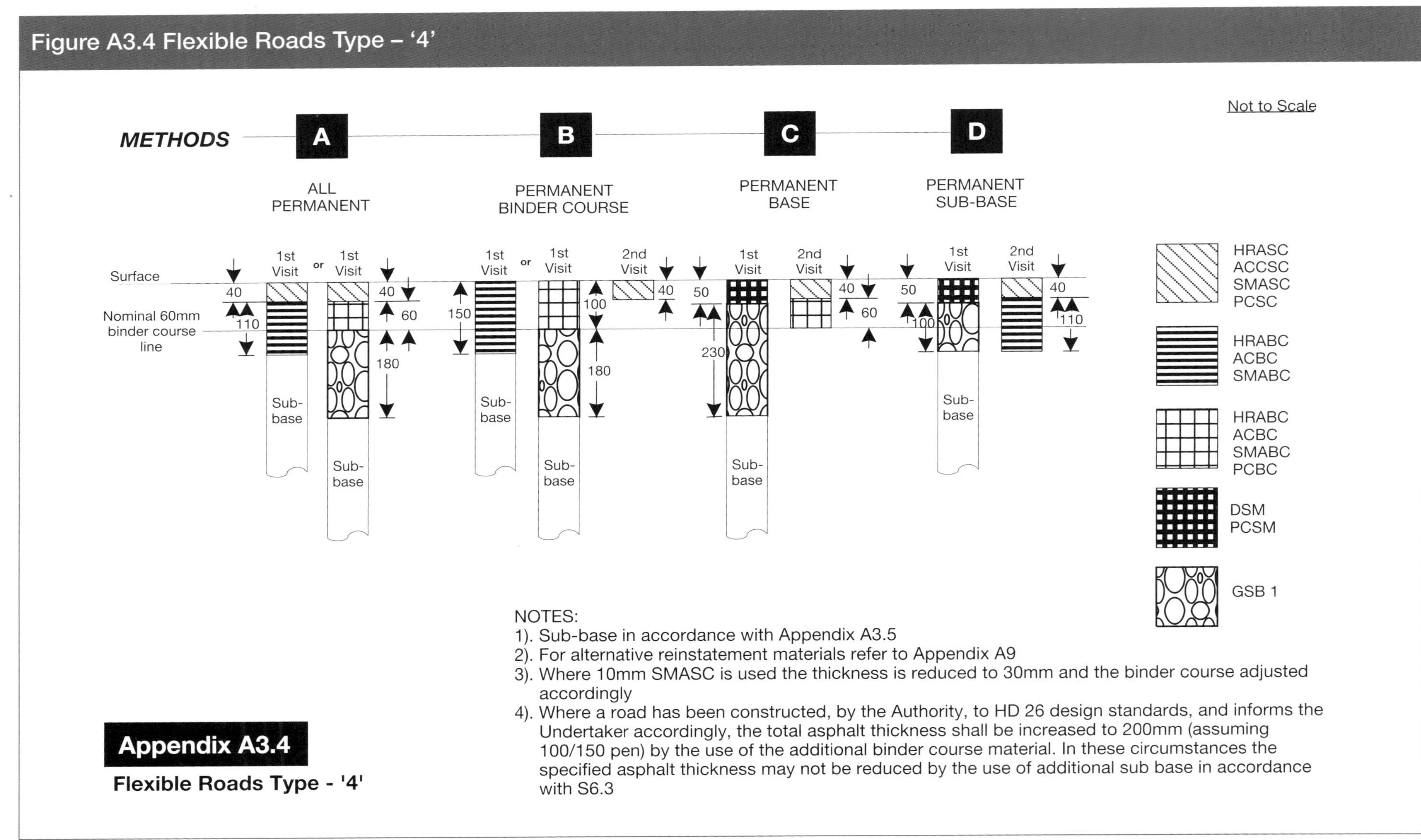

NOTES:

1). Sub-base in accordance with Appendix A3.5

2). For alternative reinstatement materials refer to Appendix A9

3). Where 10mm SMASC is used the thickness is reduced to 30mm and the binder course adjusted accordingly

4). Where a road has been constructed, by the Authority, to HD 26 design standards, and informs the Undertaker accordingly, the total asphalt thickness shall be increased to 200mm (assuming 100/150 pen) by the use of the additional binder course material. In these circumstances the specified asphalt thickness may not be reduced by the use of additional sub base in accordance with S6.3

Appendix A3.4

Flexible Roads Type - '4'

Figure A3.5 Sub-base Construction – Flexible Roads

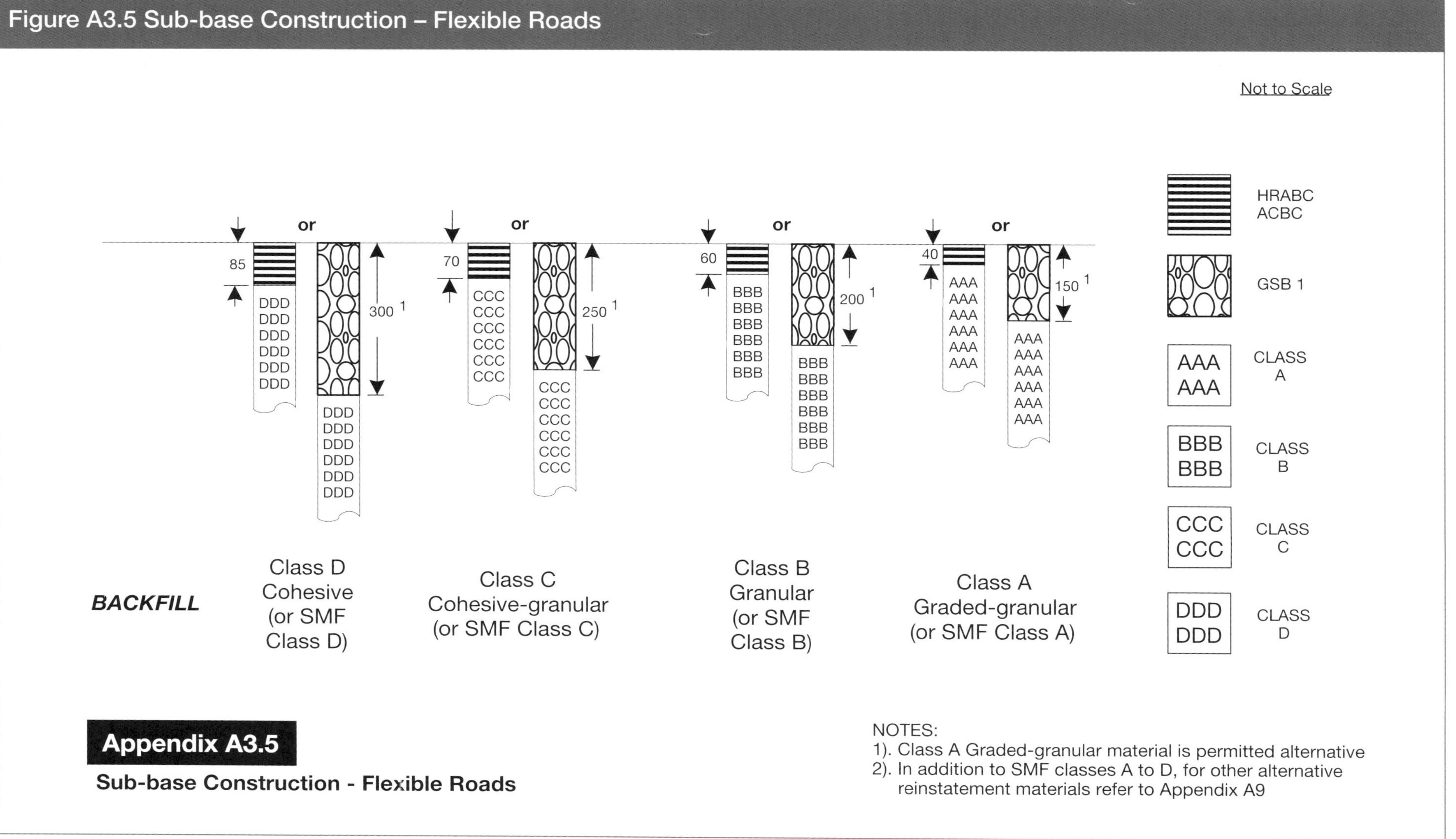

Appendix A3.5

Sub-base Construction - Flexible Roads

NOTES:

1). Class A Graded-granular material is permitted alternative

2). In addition to SMF classes A to D, for other alternative reinstatement materials refer to Appendix A9

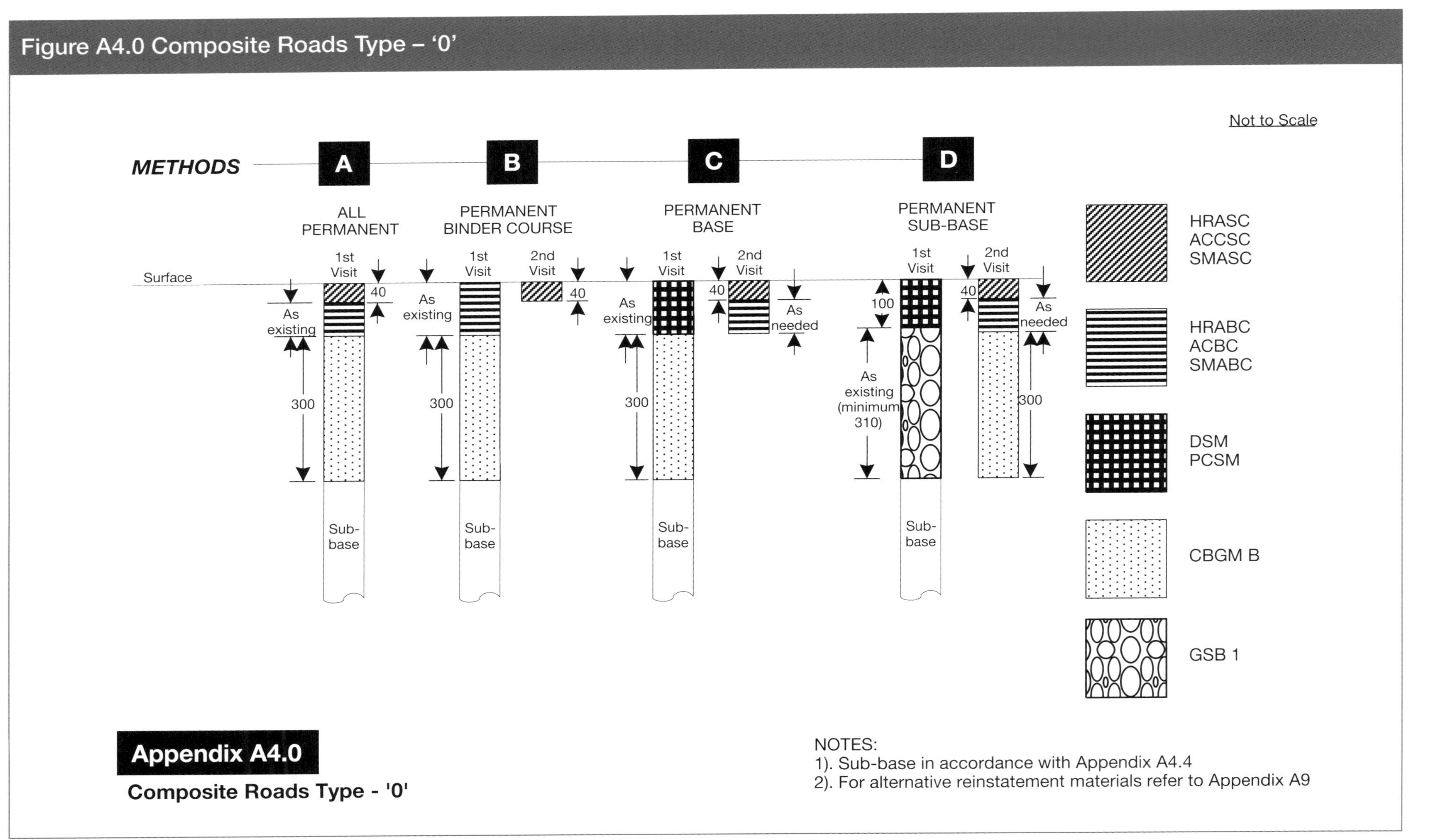

Appendix A4.0

Composite Roads Type - '0'

Figure A4.1 Composite Roads Type – '1'

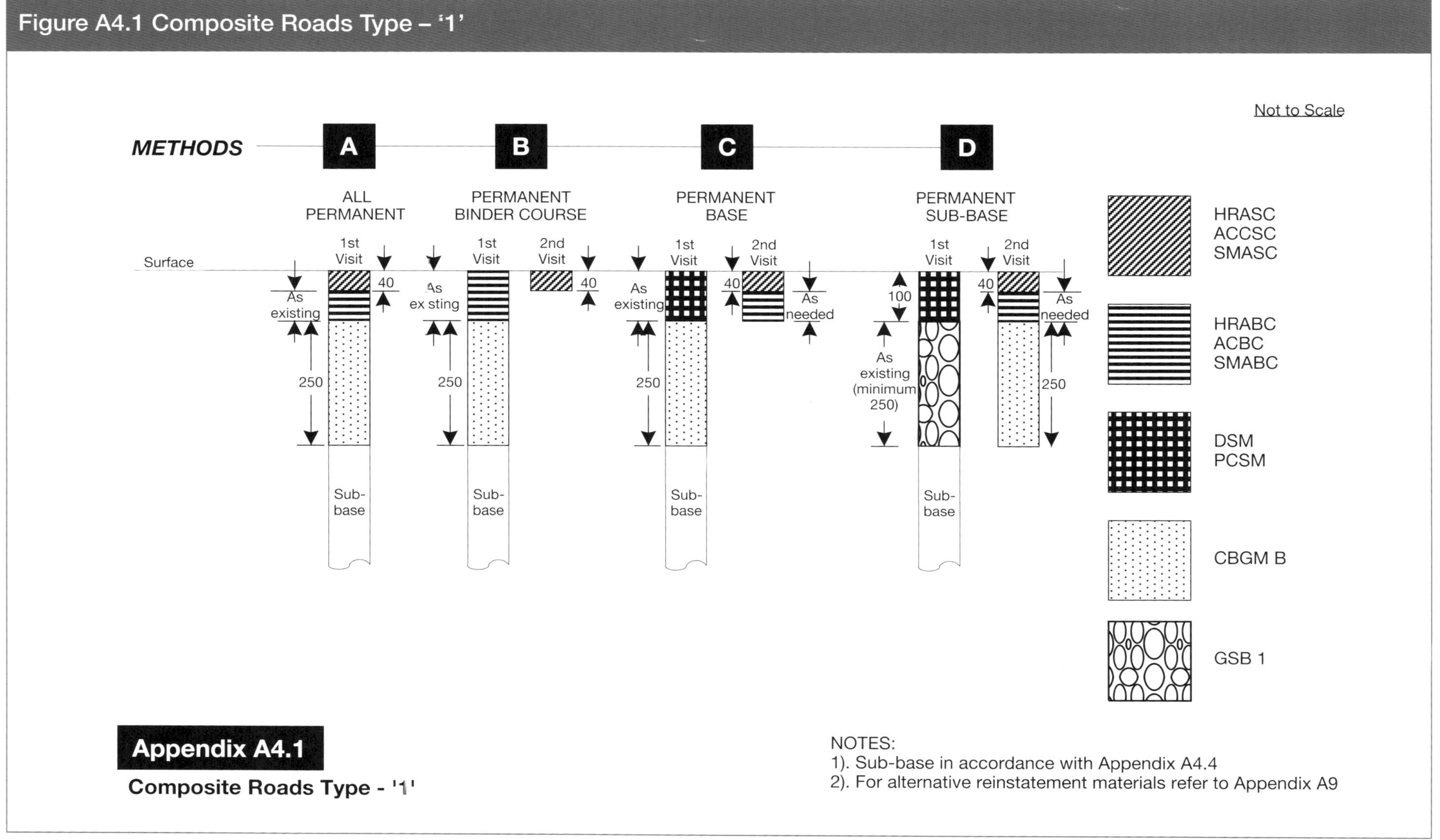

Figure A4.2 Composite Roads Type – ‘2’

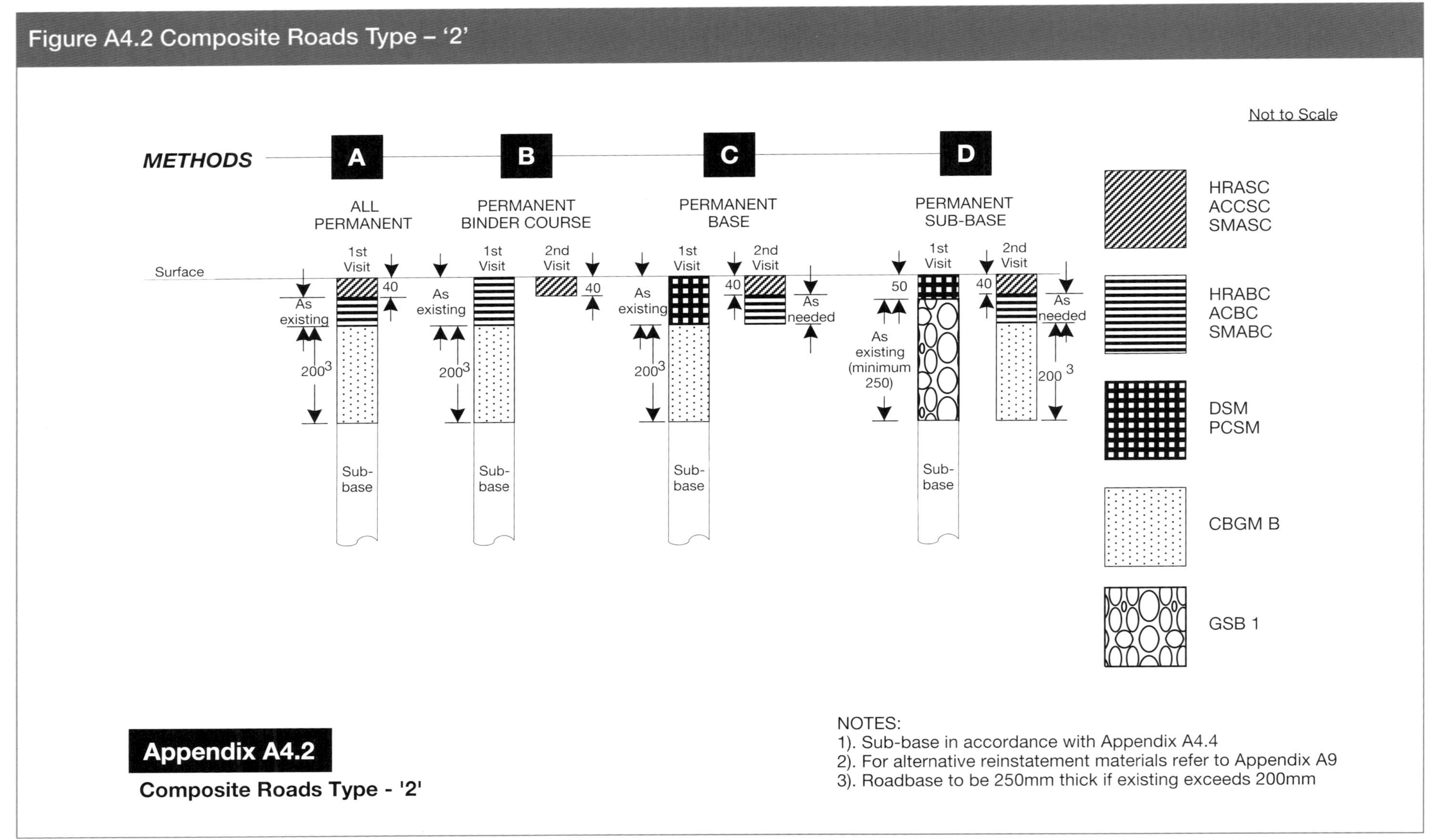

NOTES:
1). Sub-base in accordance with Appendix A4.4
2). For alternative reinstatement materials refer to Appendix A9
3). Roadbase to be 250mm thick if existing exceeds 200mm

Appendix A4.2

Composite Roads Type - '2'

Figure A4.3 Composite Roads Type – '3 & 4'

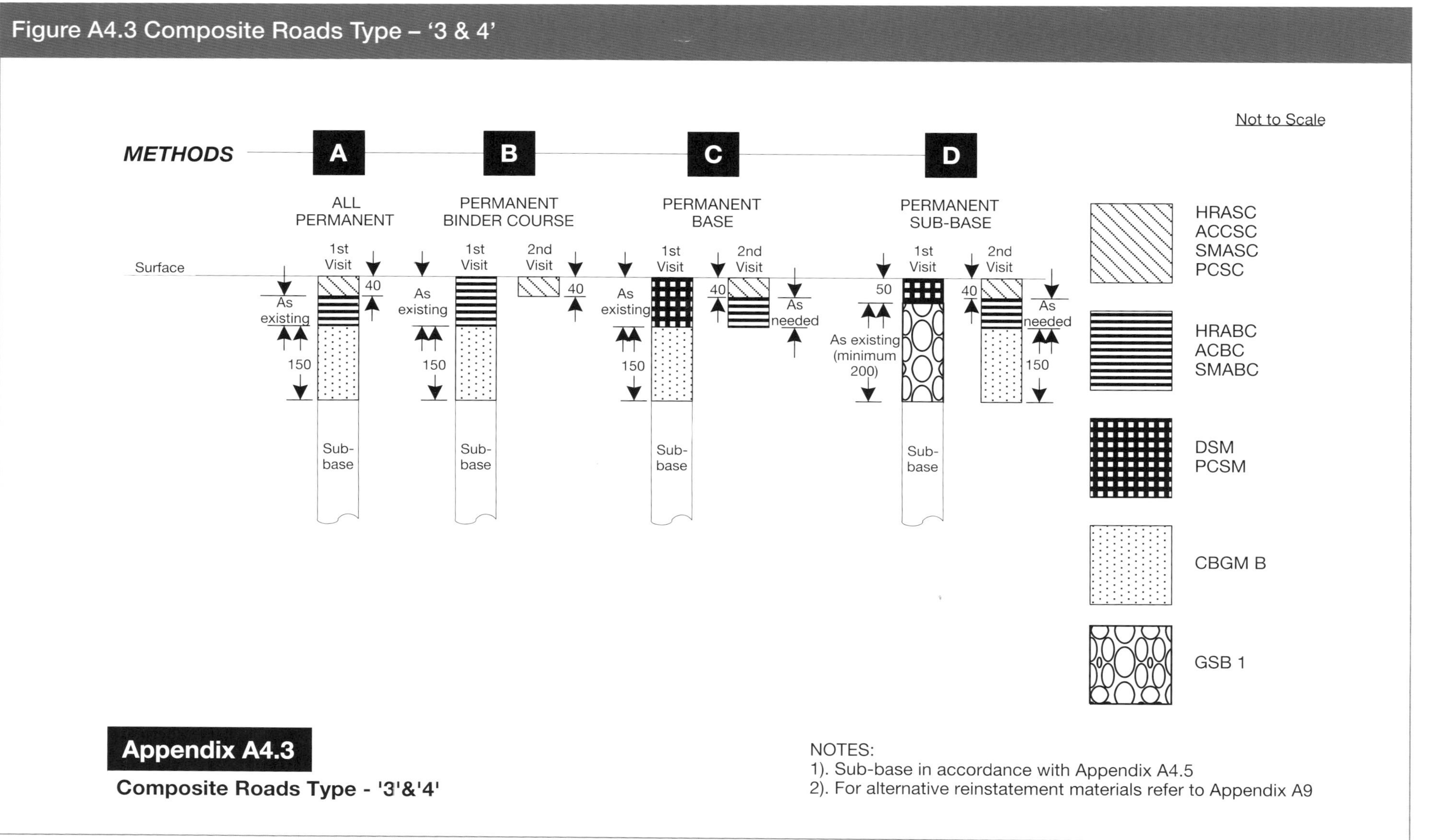

Appendix A4.3

Composite Roads Type - '3'&'4'

NOTES:
1). Sub-base in accordance with Appendix A4.5
2). For alternative reinstatement materials refer to Appendix A9

Figure A4.4 Sub-base Construction – Composite Roads – Types ‘0’, ‘1’ & ‘2’

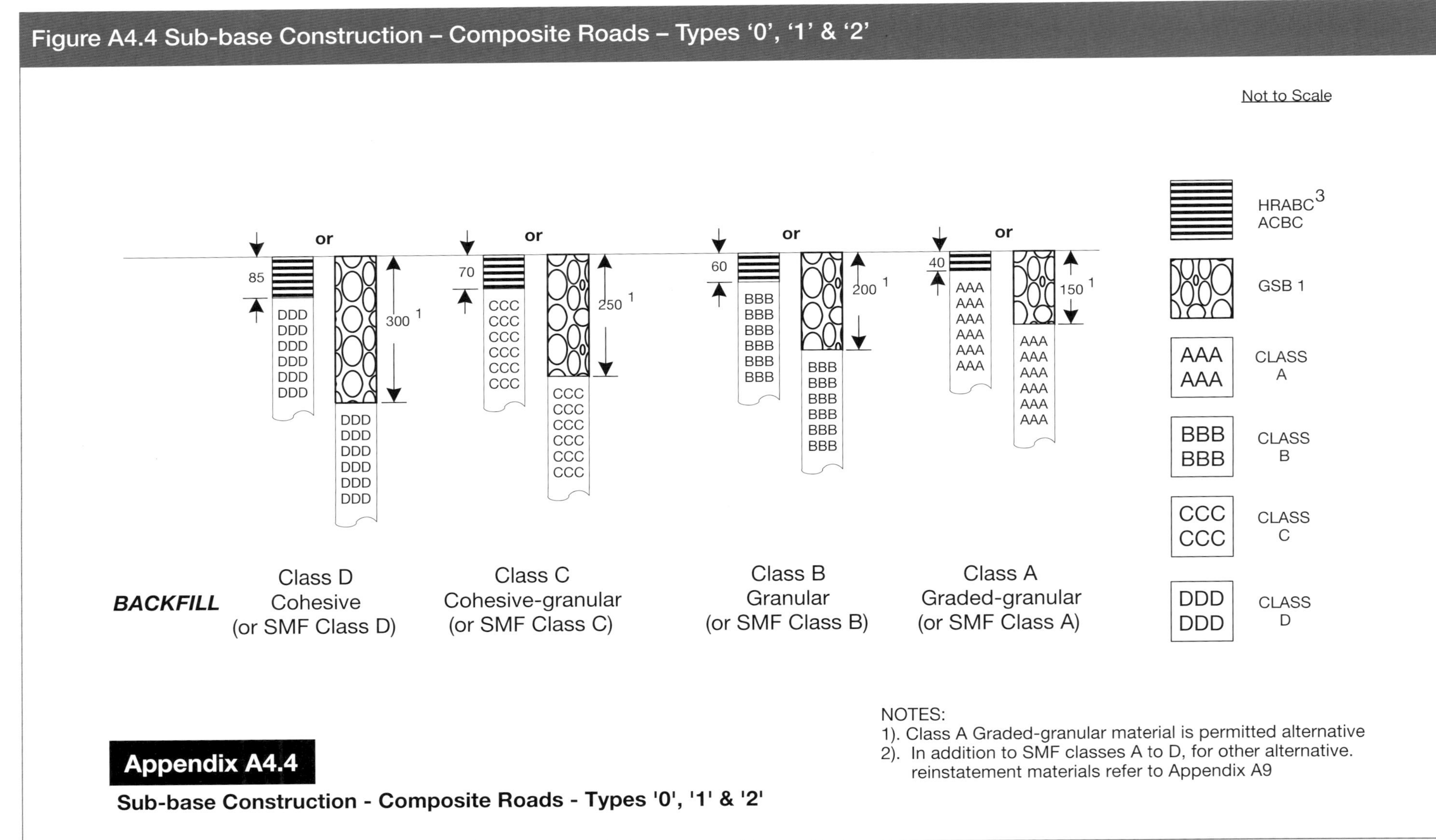

NOTES:
1). Class A Graded-granular material is permitted alternative
2). In addition to SMF classes A to D, for other alternative. reinstatement materials refer to Appendix A9

Appendix A4.4

Sub-base Construction - Composite Roads - Types '0', '1' & '2'

Figure A4.5 Sub-base Construction – Composite Roads – Types '3 & 4'

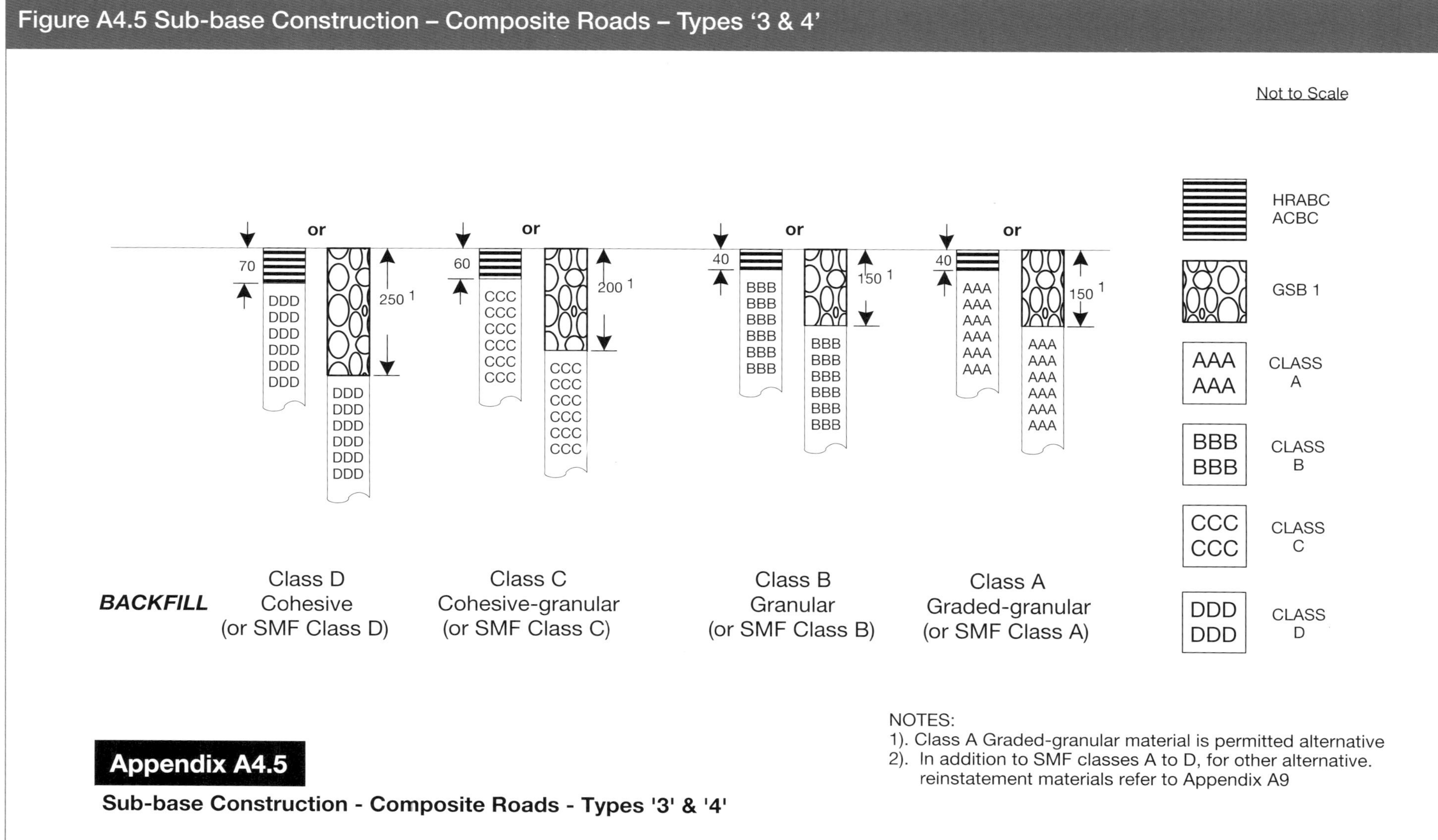

NOTES:
1). Class A Graded-granular material is permitted alternative
2). In addition to SMF classes A to D, for other alternative. reinstatement materials refer to Appendix A9

Appendix A4.5

Sub-base Construction - Composite Roads - Types '3' & '4'

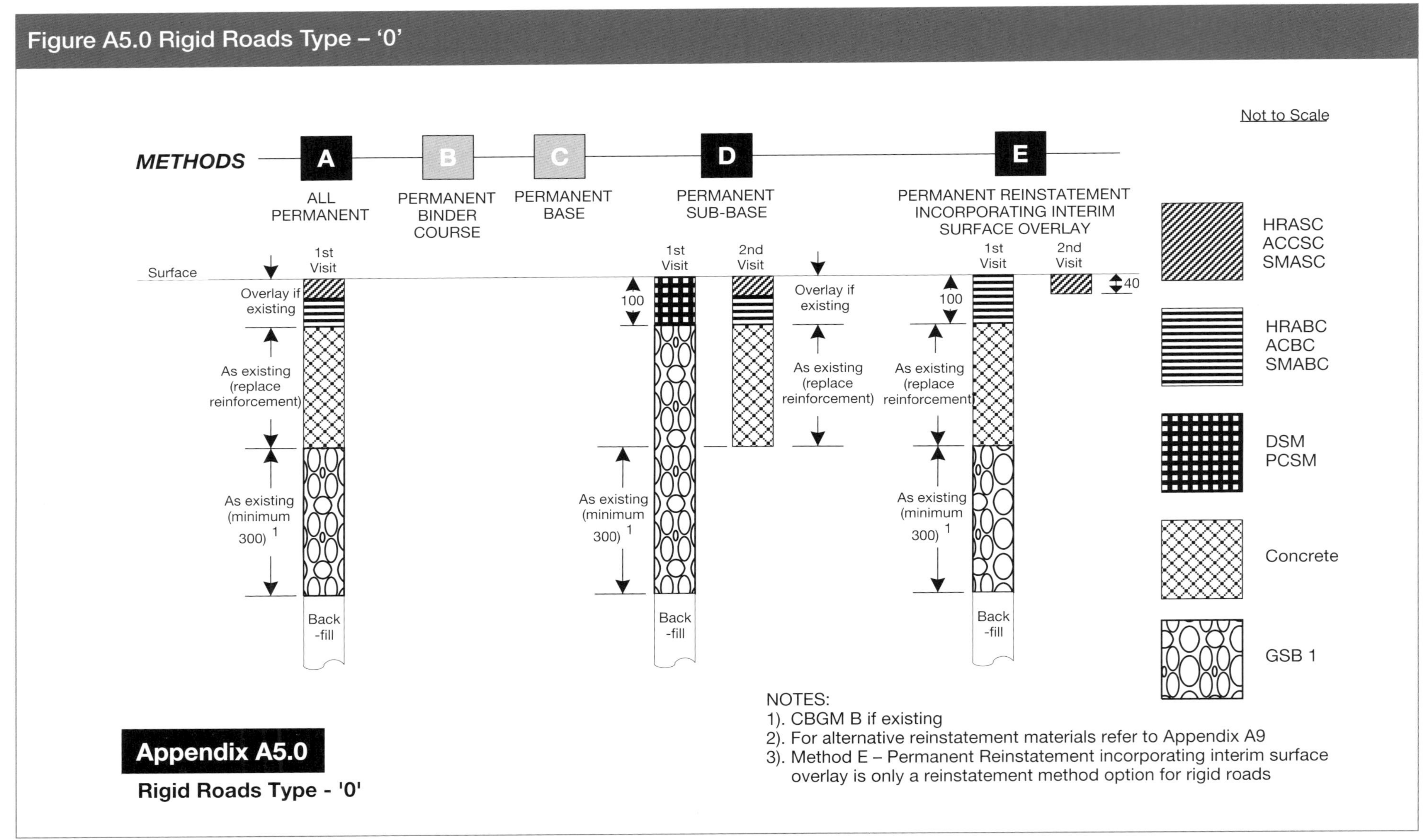
Figure A5.0 Rigid Roads Type – '0'
Not to Scale
METHODS
A
ALL PERMANENT
B
PERMANENT BINDER COURSE
C
PERMANENT BASE
D
PERMANENT SUB-BASE
E
PERMANENT REINSTATEMENT INCORPORATING INTERIM SURFACE OVERLAY
Surface
1st Visit
2nd Visit
Overlay if existing
As existing (replace reinforcement)
As existing (minimum 300) 1
100
40
Back -fill
HRASC
ACCSC
SMASC
HRABC
ACBC
SMABC
DSM
PCSM
Concrete
GSB 1
NOTES:
1). CBGM B if existing
2). For alternative reinstatement materials refer to Appendix A9
3). Method E – Permanent Reinstatement incorporating interim surface overlay is only a reinstatement method option for rigid roads
Appendix A5.0
Rigid Roads Type - '0'

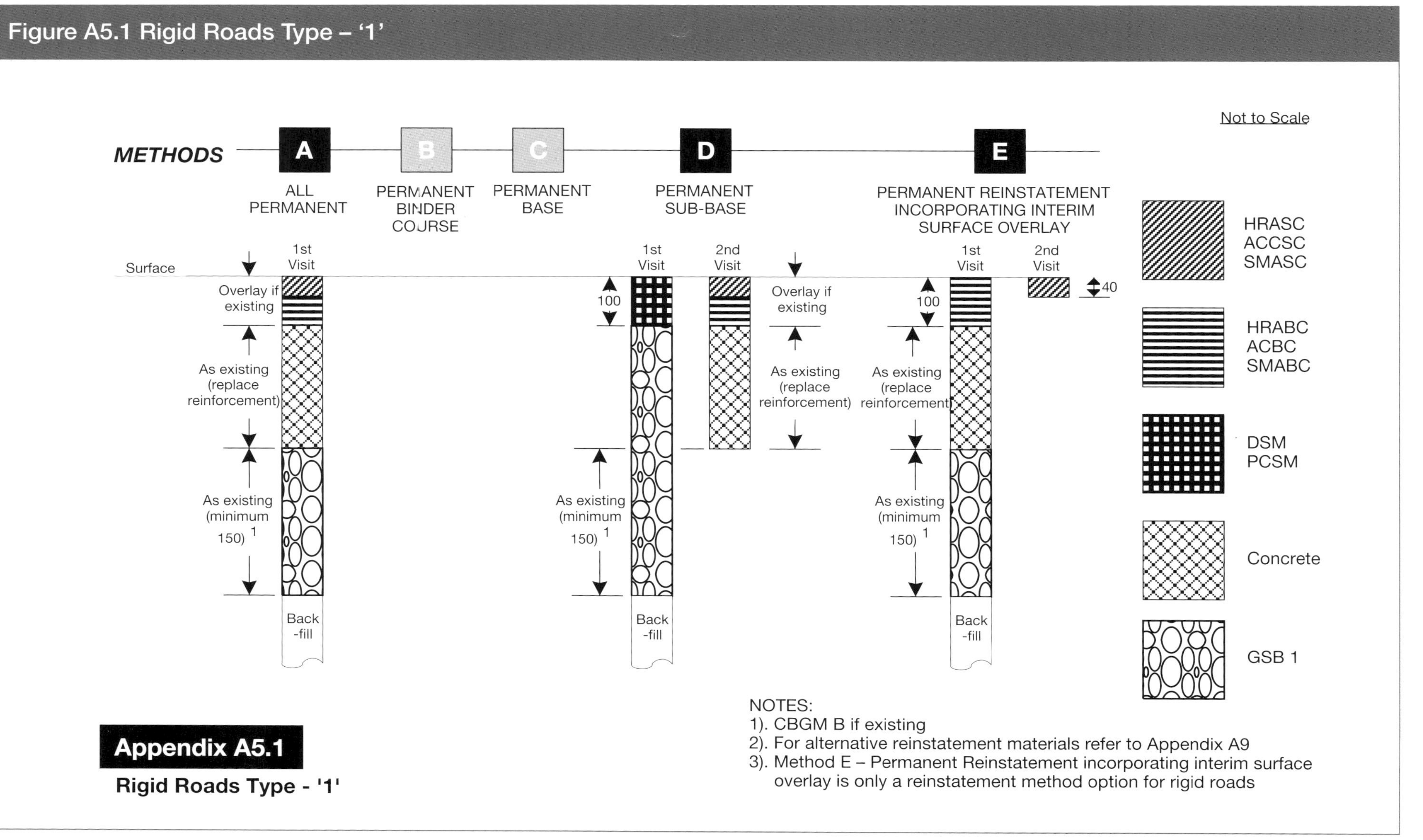

Figure A5.1 Rigid Roads Type – '1'
Not to Scale
METHODS
A
ALL PERMANENT
B
PERMANENT BINDER COURSE
C
PERMANENT BASE
D
PERMANENT SUB-BASE
E
PERMANENT REINSTATEMENT INCORPORATING INTERIM SURFACE OVERLAY
Surface
1st Visit
2nd Visit
Overlay if existing
As existing (replace reinforcement)
As existing (minimum 150) 1
100
40
Back -fill
HRASC ACCSC SMASC
HRABC ACBC SMABC
DSM PCSM
Concrete
GSB 1
NOTES:
1). CBGM B if existing
2). For alternative reinstatement materials refer to Appendix A9
3). Method E – Permanent Reinstatement incorporating interim surface overlay is only a reinstatement method option for rigid roads
Appendix A5.1
Rigid Roads Type - '1'

Figure A5.2 Rigid Roads Type – ‘2’, ‘3’ & ‘4’

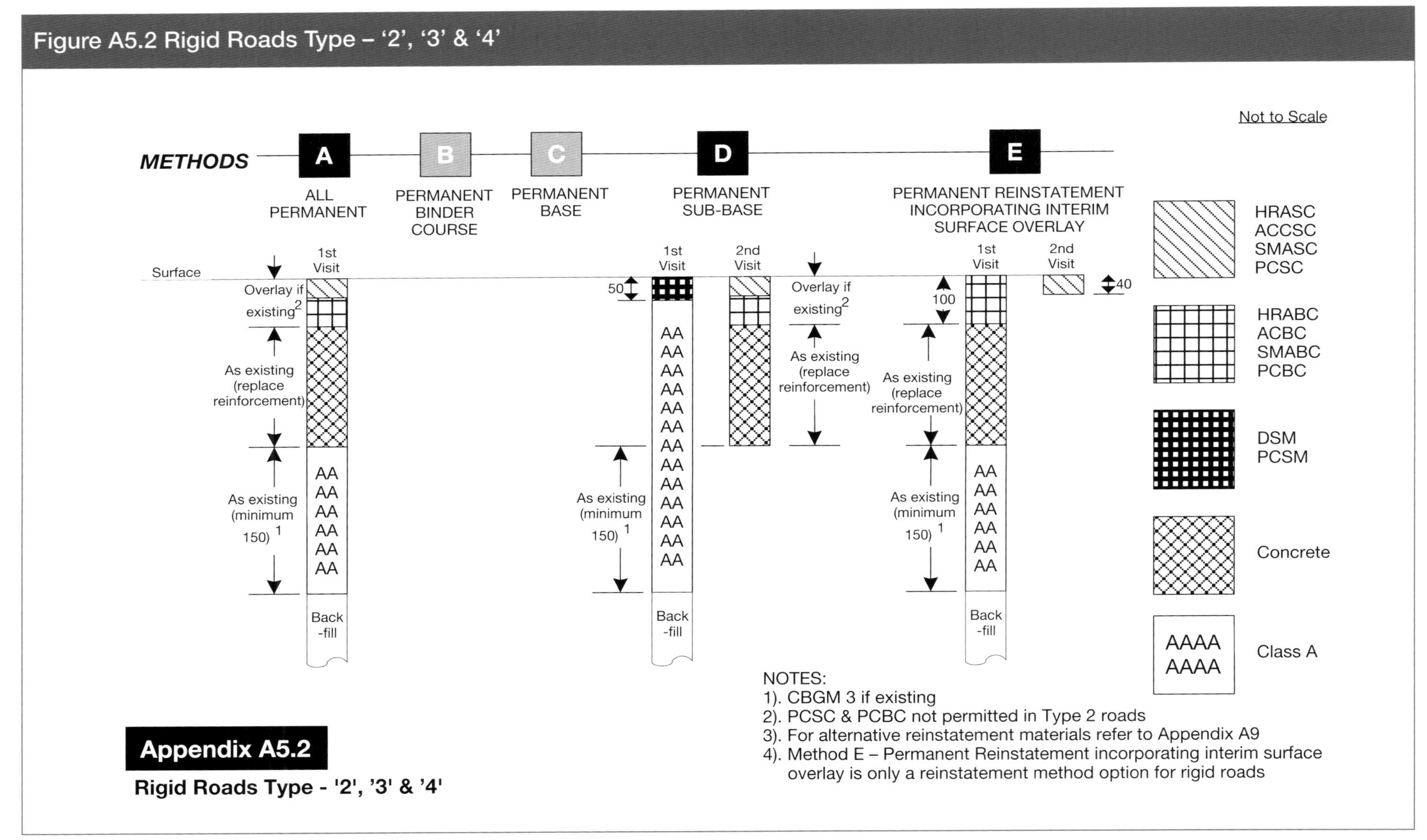

NOTES:
1). CBGM 3 if existing
2). PCSC & PCBC not permitted in Type 2 roads
3). For alternative reinstatement materials refer to Appendix A9
4). Method E – Permanent Reinstatement incorporating interim surface overlay is only a reinstatement method option for rigid roads

Appendix A5.2

Rigid Roads Type - '2', '3' & '4'

Figure A6.1 Modular Roads (Bituminous Base) Types – '3 & 4'

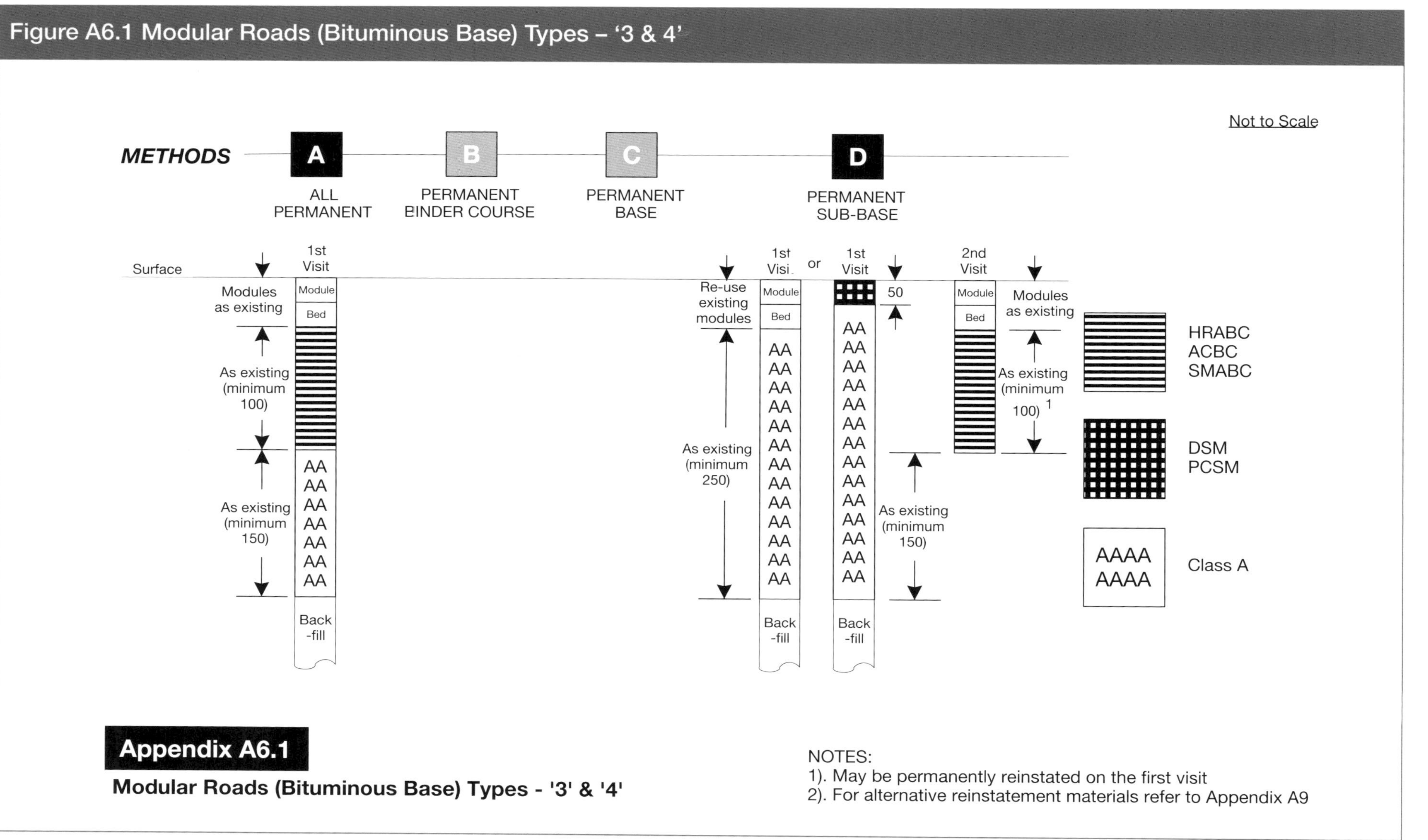

Appendix A6.1

Modular Roads (Bituminous Base) Types - '3' & '4'

NOTES:
1). May be permanently reinstated on the first visit
2). For alternative reinstatement materials refer to Appendix A9

Figure A6.2 Modular Roads (Composite Base) Types – '3 & 4'

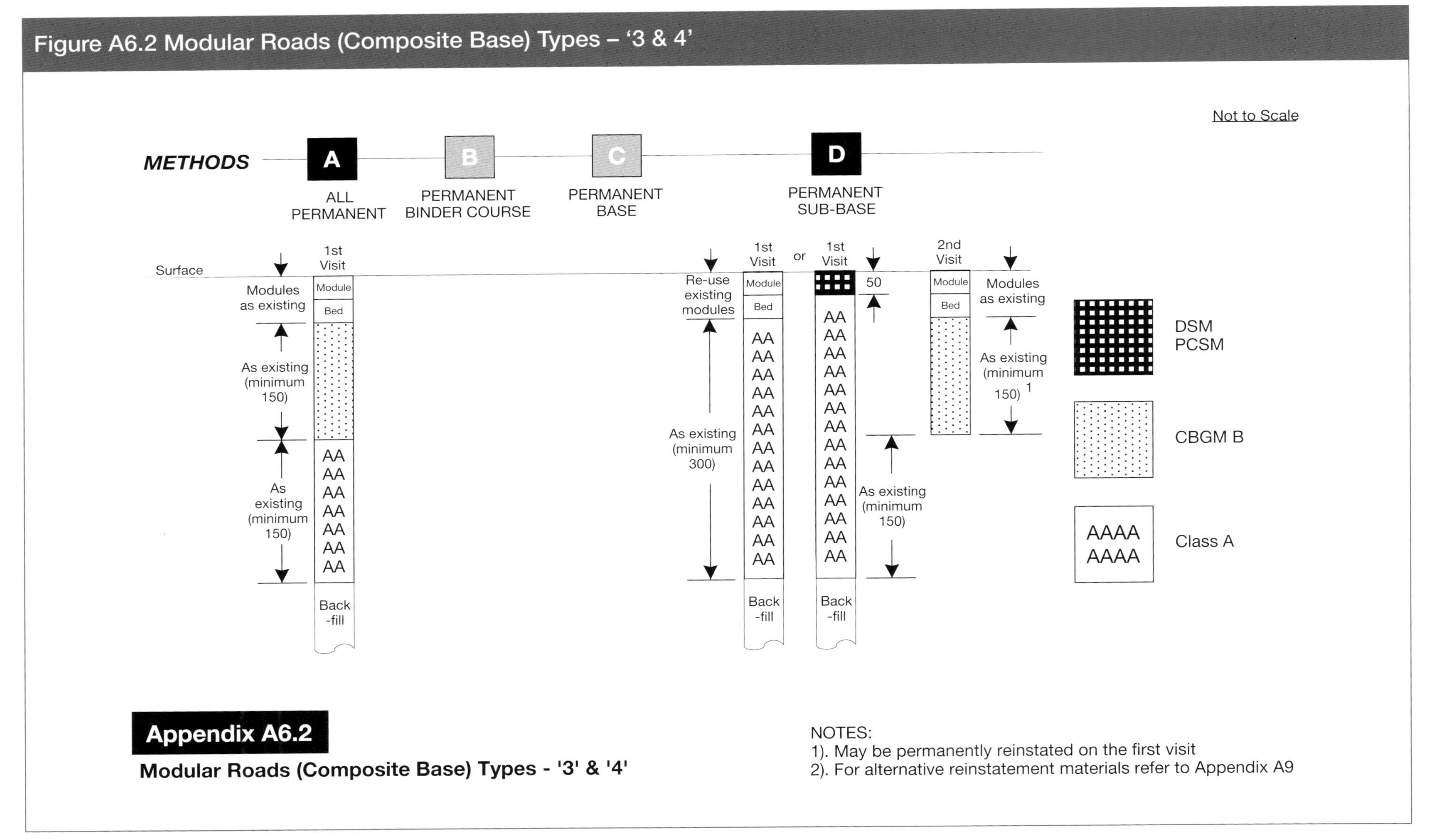

Appendix A6.2

Modular Roads (Composite Base) Types - '3' & '4'

NOTES:
1). May be permanently reinstated on the first visit
2). For alternative reinstatement materials refer to Appendix A9

Figure A6.3 Modular Roads (Granular Base) Types – '3 & 4'

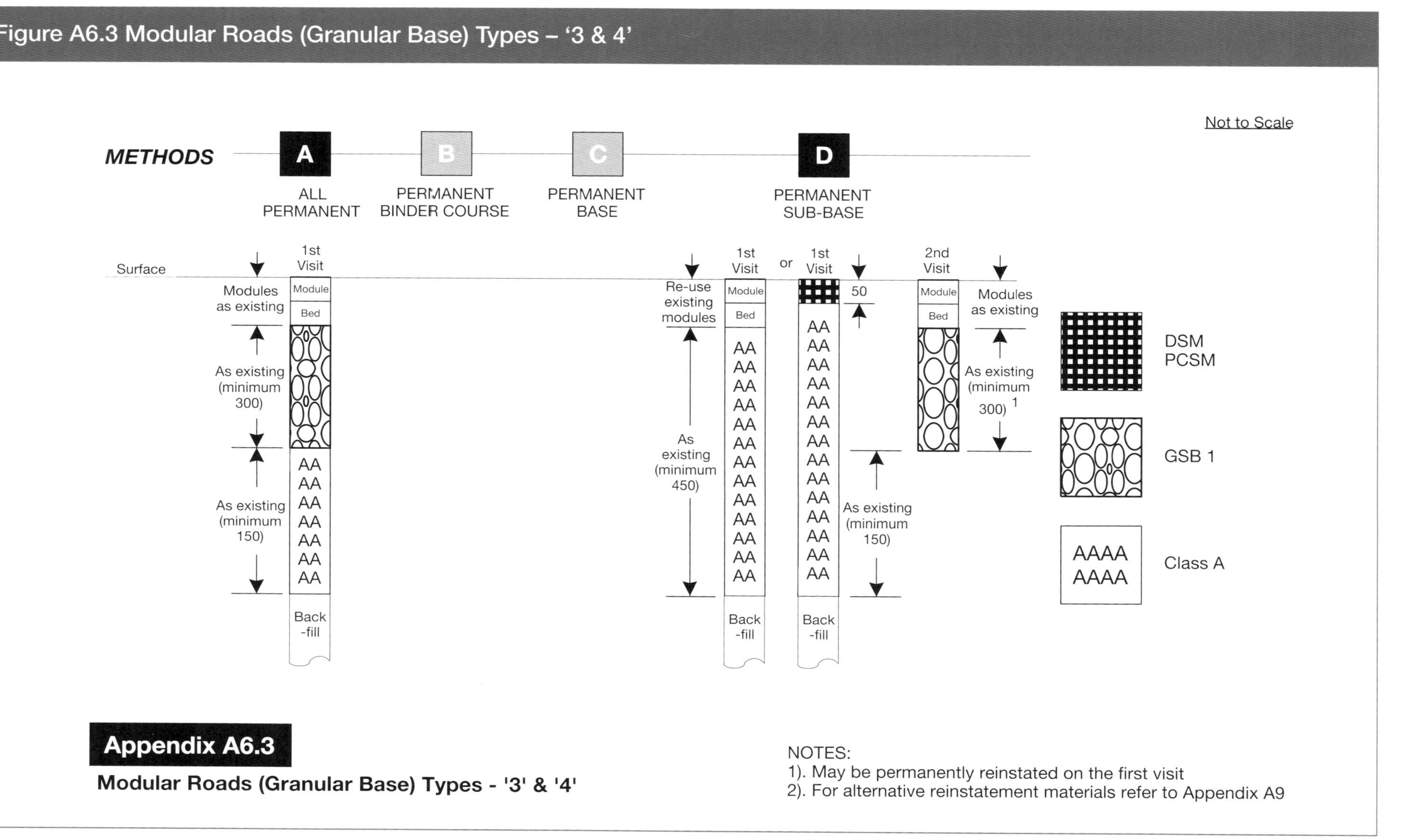

Appendix A6.3

Modular Roads (Granular Base) Types - '3' & '4'

NOTES:
1). May be permanently reinstated on the first visit
2). For alternative reinstatement materials refer to Appendix A9

Figure A7.1 Flexible Footways, Footpaths and Cycle Tracks

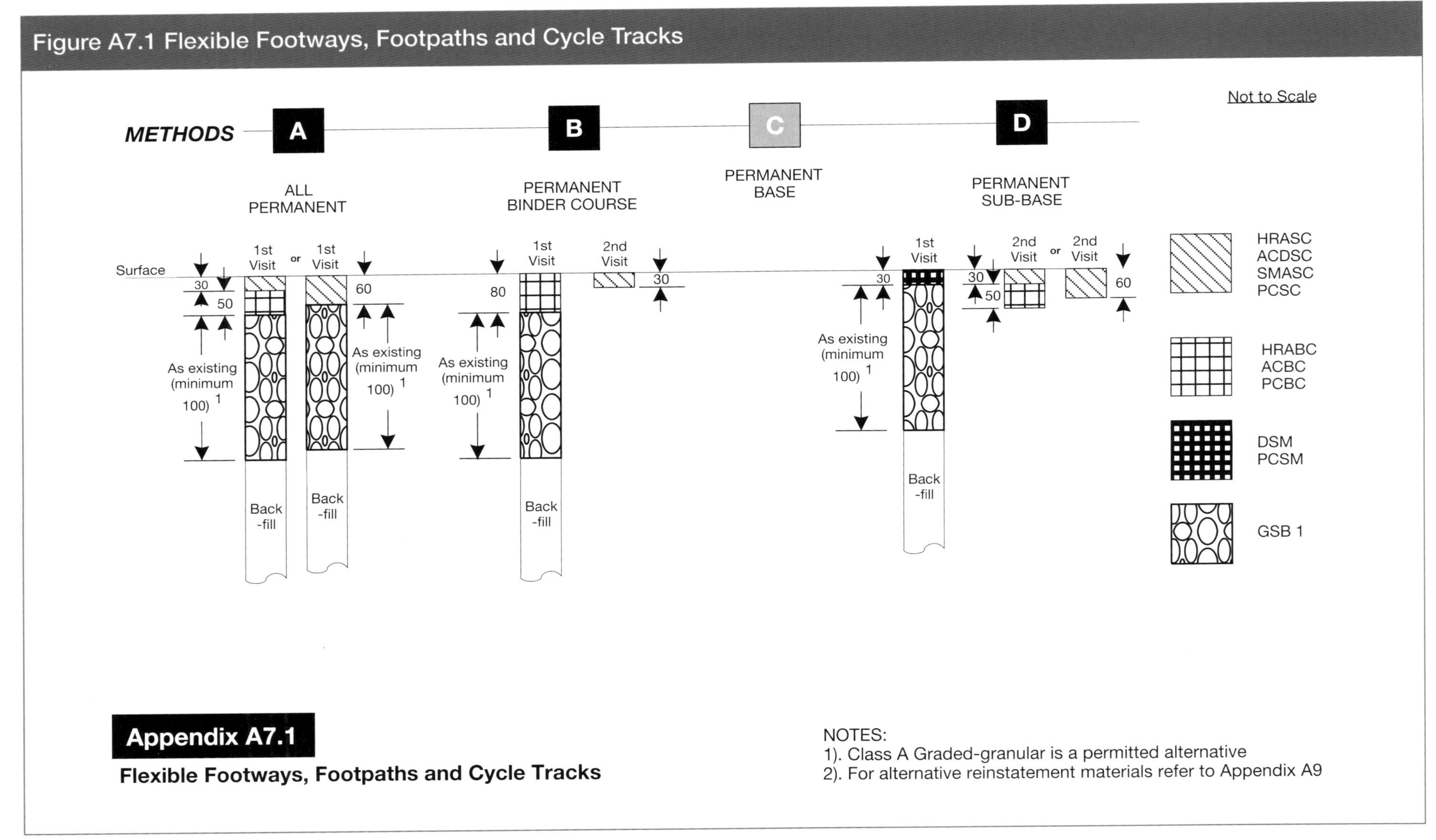

Appendix A7.1

Flexible Footways, Footpaths and Cycle Tracks

NOTES:
1). Class A Graded-granular is a permitted alternative
2). For alternative reinstatement materials refer to Appendix A9

Figure A7.2 Rigid Footways, Footpaths and Cycle Tracks

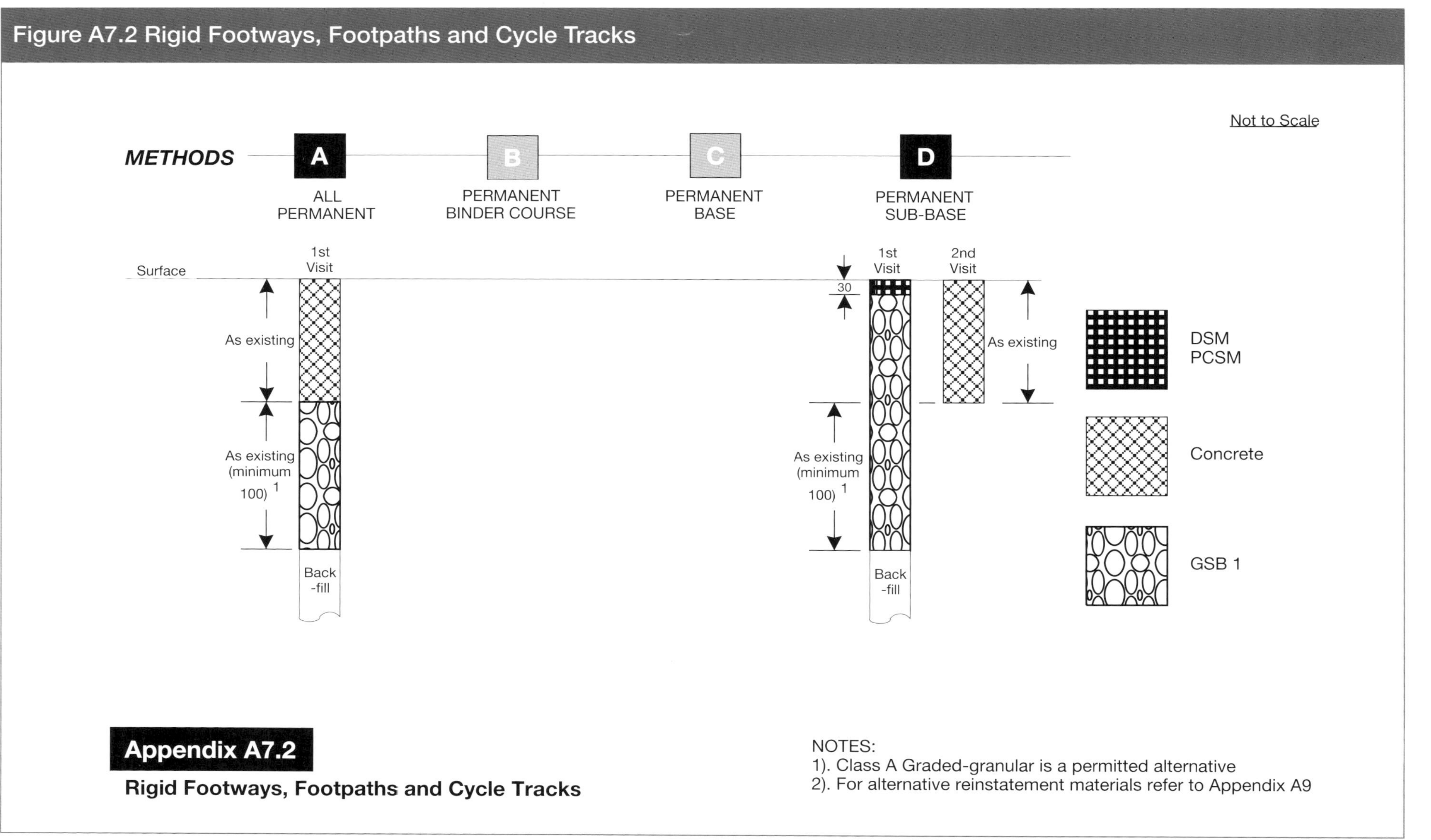

Appendix A7.2

Rigid Footways, Footpaths and Cycle Tracks

NOTES:
1). Class A Graded-granular is a permitted alternative
2). For alternative reinstatement materials refer to Appendix A9

Figure A7.3 Modular Footways, Footpaths and Cycle Tracks

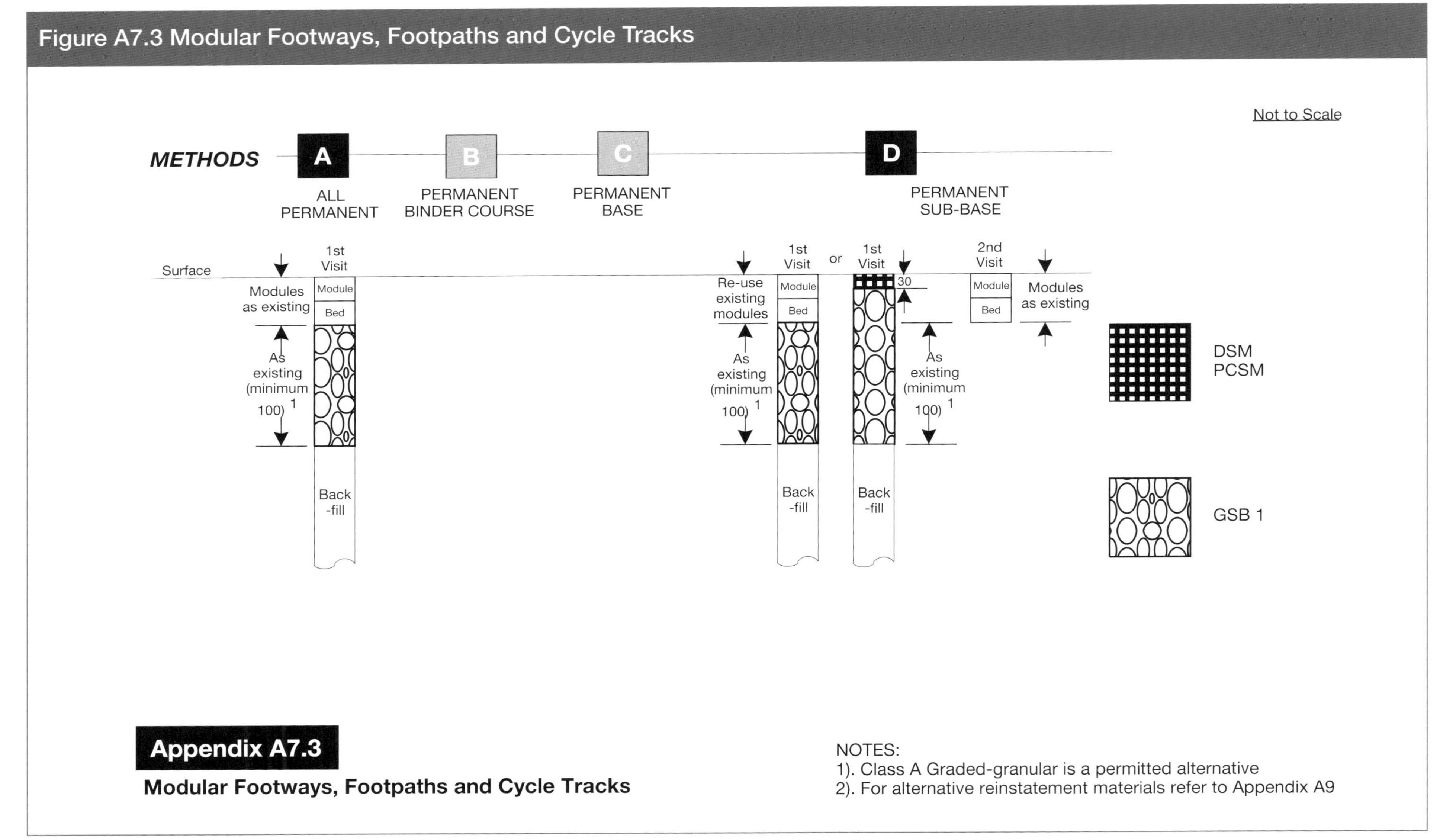

NOTES:
1). Class A Graded-granular is a permitted alternative
2). For alternative reinstatement materials refer to Appendix A9

Appendix A7.3

Modular Footways, Footpaths and Cycle Tracks

Appendix A8

Compaction Requirements

A8.1 Granular, Cohesive and Cement Bound Materials

All graded granular, granular, cohesive/granular, cohesive and cement bound materials laid above the surround to apparatus shall be compacted in accordance with Table A8.1.

Table A8.1 – Compaction Requirements for Granular, Cohesive and Cement Bound Materials

Compaction Plant and Weight Category	**Cohesive Material (less than 20% granular content)**			**Granular Material (20% or more granular content including cement bound material)**		
	Minimum Passes/Lift for compacted lift thickness up to			**Minimum Passes/Lift for compacted lift thickness up to**		
	100 mm	**150 mm**	**200 mm**	**100 mm**	**150 mm**	**200 mm**
Vibrotamper 50 kg minimum	4	8 **#**	NP	4	8	NP
Vibrating Roller **Single Drum**						
600-1000 kg/m	**NP**	**NP**	**NP**	12	**NP**	**NP**
1000-2000 kg/m	8	**NP**	**NP**	6	**NP**	**NP**
2000-3500 kg/m	3	6	**NP**	3	5	7
Over 3500 kg/m	3	4	6 **#**	3	4	6

Table A8.1 – Compaction Requirements for Granular, Cohesive and Cement Bound Materials						
Twin Drum 600-1000 kg/m 1000-2000 kg/m Over 2000 kg/m	**NP** 4 2	**NP** 8 3	**NP** **NP** 5 **#**	6 3 2	**NP** 6 3	**NP** **NP** 4
Vibrating Plate 1400-1800 kg/m^2 Over 1800 kg/m^2	**NP** 3	**NP** 6	**NP** **NP**	5 3	**NP** 5	**NP** 7
All Above Plant	For Maximum and Minimum compacted lift thickness See Appendix A2.6, Table A2.2					
Alternative Compaction Plant for Areas of Restricted Access (including small excavations and trenches less than 200 mm width)						
Vibrotamper 25 kg minimum	Minimum of 6 compaction passes Maximum of 100 mm compacted lift thickness					
Percussive Rammer 10 kg minimum						
Notes for Table A8.1: 1) **NP** = Not Permitted 2) **#** = Not permitted on wholly cohesive material i.e. clay and/or silt with no particles > 75 micron (μm) 3) Single drum vibrating rollers are vibrating rollers providing vibration on only one drum 4) Twin drum vibrating rollers are vibrating rollers providing vibration on two separate drums						

A8.2 Chalk Materials

All chalk materials, including medium and high-density chalks shall be compacted in accordance with Table A8.2. However, if the chalk is unstable after compaction, the unstable material shall be removed and replaced with fresh material. The fresh chalk shall be compacted in accordance with Table A8.2, except that the specified number of compaction passes shall be reduced by one pass. If the chalk is still unstable after compaction, it shall be deemed to be unsuitable for use as backfill and replaced with suitable material.

Table A8.2 – Compaction requirements for Chalk Materials			
Compaction Plant and Weight Category	**Chalk Material**		
	Minimum Passes/Lift For compacted lift thickness up to		
	100 mm	**150 mm**	**200 mm**
Vibrotamper 50 kg minimum	3	6	NP
Vibrating Roller **Single Drum**			
600-1000 kg/m	12	**NP**	**NP**
1000-2000 kg/m	6	8	**NP**
2000-3500 kg/m	**NP**	4	6
Over 3500 kg/m	**NP**	**NP**	4
Twin Drum			
600-1000 kg/m	6	8	**NP**
1000-2000 kg/m	2	4	6
Over 2000 kg/m	**NP**	3	4
Vibrating Plate			
1400-1800 kg/m^2	6	8	NP
Over 1800 kg/m^2	**NP**	6	8
Alternative Compaction Plant for Areas of Restricted Access (including small excavations and trenches less than 200 mm width)			
Vibrotamper 25 kg minimum	Minimum of 6 compaction passes Maximum of 100 mm compacted lift thickness		
Percussive Rammer 10 kg minimum			

Notes for Table A8.2:

1) **NP** = Not Permitted

2) Single drum vibrating rollers are vibrating rollers providing vibration on only one drum

3) Twin drum vibrating rollers are vibrating rollers providing vibration on two separate drums

A8.3 Bituminous Mixtures

All bituminous mixtures for permanent reinstatements permitted in Appendix A2 shall be compacted to the in-situ air void requirements of Section S10.2.3. Guidance on compaction procedures that may be capable of achieving the specified air voids values is given in NG A8

Compaction should be discontinued if the mixture shows any signs of distress, regardless of whether the minimum number of passes suggested in NG A8 have been applied; see Section NG10.2.3.

Compacted materials shall be capable of being wet flush cored as follows:

i) hot materials – upon reaching ambient temperature;

ii) PCSMs – at 6 months from the date of the permanent reinstatement.

Appendix A9

Alternative Reinstatement Materials (ARMs)

A9.1 Introduction

1) New or alternative materials have been, or may be, developed for use in highway construction and maintenance. These materials may allow more rapid, reliable and cost-effective reinstatements, with less dependence on the skill and physical effort of the operators. These materials may also offer significant environmental or practical advantages, and/or cost benefits, compared with conventional materials, including various combinations of the following:

   a) Reduced usage of virgin materials, by including recycled or secondary materials

   b) Lower energy requirements during manufacture and/or laying

   c) Reduced landfill requirements during construction or reconstruction

   d) Self-cementing properties to improve performance, reliability of laying and compaction

   e) Self-levelling or flowable, to avoid or reduce the need for compaction and to provide health and safety benefits

   f) May be placed in fewer lifts

2) These materials are termed Alternative Reinstatement Materials (ARMs), and are categorised by this Specification into two generic groups:

   a) Structural Materials for Reinstatements (SMRs)

   This generic group is intended to include proprietary or alternative bound reinstatement materials that include a cementitious, chemical or hydraulic binder or are inherently self-cementing. SMRs are categorised as follows:

   i) Foamed Concretes for Reinstatements (FCRs)

   These are cement-bound materials that have been prepared off-site, generally as "prescribed" mixes, at an approved mixing plant and under appropriate quality control procedures. They are flowable in nature and should not require compaction when placed. Such materials manufactured under these conditions, and any foamed concretes conforming to Clause 1043 and with aggregates of the Specification for Highway Works are deemed to be approved for use as ARMs. FCRs do not necessarily incorporate a coarse aggregate. Layer thickness and compressive strength requirements shall be in accordance with Table A9.1.

In accordance with the SHW the composition of all Recycled aggregate and Recycled concrete aggregate shall be tested as specified in Clause 710 of the MCHW1. The content of other materials (Class X) shall not exceed 1% by mass or by volume, which ever is the greater.

FCR permissible constituents shall exclude potash and bottom furnace ash.

ii) Flowable SMRs (FSMRs)

These materials comprise any type and/or combination of aggregates and binders. They are flowable mixes that should not normally require compaction, and are capable of achieving strengths equivalent to FCRs. These materials may only be used on a trial basis by prior agreement with the highway authority and following the approval trial procedure detailed in A9.5. Layer thickness and compressive strength requirements shall be in accordance with Table A9.1.

iii) Non-flowable SMRs (NFSMRs)

These materials comprise any type and/or combination of aggregates and binders. They are non-flowable mixes that will normally require compaction on site, and will be capable of achieving strengths equivalent to FCRs in their compacted state. These materials may be used on a trial basis by prior agreement with the highway authority and following the approval trial procedure detailed in Appendix A9.5.

iv) Hydraulically bound mixtures (HBM)

Hydraulically bound mixtures (HBMs) are mixtures that set and harden by hydraulic reaction. They include:

- cement bound materials (i.e. mixtures based on the fast setting and hardening characteristics of cement), and
- slow setting and hardening mixtures made from industrial by-products such as fly ash (FA) and ground granulated blast furnace slag (GGBS).

These materials comprise any HBM specified in BSEN 14227-1, -2, -3, -5, -10, -11, -12, -13 & -14, and shall be produced, handled, transported, used and tested in accordance with the SHW 800 series. Although not called up in the SHW, the HBM types, SBM B4, FABM 4 and HRBBM 4 from BSEN14227-2, -3, & -5 respectively are also included since they are purposely suited for trench reinstatement work. HBMs therefore should be produced, constructed and tested in accordance with the SHW 800 series as if they were SBM B3, FABM 3 and HRBBM 4 respectively. Layer thickness and compressive strength requirements shall be in accordance with Table A9.1 except that the specified compressive strength requirement shall be deemed to apply at 28 days as detailed in Appendix A9.3.4. All of the SHW or BSEN14227 HBM types are deemed approved for use as ARMs without a trial.

b) Stabilised Materials for Fills (SMFs)

This generic group is intended to include materials derived from excavated spoil, virgin, secondary or recycled materials, or any combination thereof, that have been stabilised or modified by re-processing, re-grading and/or by the inclusion of a cementitious, chemical or hydraulic binder. SMFs are generally non-flowable and shall therefore normally require compaction.

These materials may be used on a trial basis by prior agreement with the Authority and following the approval trial procedure detailed in Appendix A9.5 or may be deemed to be approved for use without trial if manufactured and used in accordance with SHW clause 840 or BS EN 14227-11.

3) ARMs complying with the SHW or BS EN14227 (specific for HBM types) are deemed approved for use as ARMs without a trial.

A9.2 General Requirements for ARMs

1) With the exception of FCRs and HBMs as described in Appendix A9.1.2 (a) (i) and (iv), (which are deemed to be approved for use), ARMs shall only be used with the prior agreement of the Undertaker and the Authority on an approved trial basis and following the trial procedure described in Appendix A9.5.

2) The producer shall establish and maintain a Quailty System which includes policy and procedures for production control. Details that should be included in the manual may be found in the annexe of the appropriate part of BSEN 14227. ARMs shall be produced, handled, transported and used in accordance with the approved mix formulations and procedures proven by prior development and testing.

3) Alterations to the proven mix formulations, mix proportions, aggregate type, admixtures, etc. shall not be undertaken without confirmation of their suitability, obtained by further development and testing. The approval of the Authority is required prior to the use of any ARM, subject to the trial procedure, whose formulation has been altered.

4) ARMs used within 450 mm of the road surface shall be non-frost susceptible subject to the exceptions referred to in Section S5.3.1.

5) Where the Authority is aware of areas with drainage or groundwater problems, it should notify the Undertaker. Following such notification the Undertaker shall provide, at backfill and sub-base levels within trench reinstatements, ARMs that are permeable to a degree not less than the surrounding ground. A backfill layer of pea gravel, of 100 mm minimum thickness and surrounded by a geotextile filter fabric where appropriate, may by considered to offer equivalent drainage potential.

6) Where the Authority is aware of any site where high sulphate levels are known to occur, it should notify the Undertaker. Following such notification, any Ordinary Portland Cement based binders in the ARMs shall be replaced with cement having a high sulphate resistance.

7) Surfacing materials shall not be reinstated until the ARM has attained sufficient strength to allow adequate compaction of asphalt materials and to sustain adequate traffic loading. A simple penetration or indentation or bearing capacity test appropriate to the ARM is recommended to allow confirmation of adequate strength prior to surfacing. Any appropriate standardised test procedure may be used and, with prior experience, will indicate the earliest time at which surfacing should be carried out.

8) Fluid ARMs may flow into damaged drainage or ducting within, or adjacent to, the excavation. Where required, plastic sheeting etc. may provide adequate protection during pouring and curing.

A9.3 Structural Materials for Reinstatements (SMRs)

A9.3.1 Permitted Uses of SMRs

1) SMRs may be used in any combination of the following, regardless of the nature of reinstatement materials used above and below:

   a) At any position within the surround to apparatus and/or backfill as the entire layer or combined with any other permitted backfill materials, in any proportion, within any reinstatement.

   b) As a sub-base within any reinstatement.

   c) As a combined sub-base and base within any reinstatement in Road Types 1, 2, 3 & 4 and as base within any reinstatement in Road Types 3 & 4.

   d) As a combined sub-base and binder course, within any reinstatement in footways, footpaths and cycle tracks.

2) SMRs shall not be used in place of surface course materials.

A9.3.2 General Requirements for SMRs

1) SMRs shall comply with the minimum layer thickness and compressive strength (R_c Class) requirements shown in Table A9.1.

Table A9.1 – SMR Minimum Layer Thickness and Compressive Strength Requirements						
Layer	**Road Type**					**Footway Footpath or Cycle Track**
	0	**1**	**2**	**3**	**4**	
Combined Binder Course & Sub-base	NP	NP	NP	NP	NP	150mm C 1.5/2
Base	NP	NP	NP	300 mm C 1.5/2	200 mm C 1.5/2	---
Base & Sub-base	NP	450 mm C3/4	450 mm C3/4	450 mm C 1.5/2	350 mm C 1.5/2	---
Sub-base &/or below	150 mm C 1.5/2	150 mm C 1.5/2	150 mm C 1.5/2	150 mm C 1.5/2	150 mm C 1.5/2	100 mm C 1.5/2
Crushing Strength at 28 days	C3/4 Minimum to C 9/12 Maximum C 1.5/2 Minimum to C9/12 Maximum					
Note to Table A9.1: NP = Not Permitted (see A9.3.1)						

2) Where the total thickness of SMR laid exceeds 1000 mm, the minimum crushing strength requirement of C3/4 shall apply to the top 1000 mm only and a minimum of C1.5/2 below this depth.

A9.3.3 Particular Requirements for FCRs and FSMRs

1) The compressive strength shall be determined in accordance with the principles of BS EN 12390 part 3, with the following exceptions or options:

   a) Test specimens may be prepared at the time of placement by casting within a test mould, or recovered from site after placement by the extraction of cores from the reinstatement.

   b) Specimen shape and dimensions shall be in accordance with BS EN 12390 part 1 with the addition that specimens may also be manufactured with an aspect ratio of 1. Flowable SMR moulds may be manufactured from cellular foam (preferably polystyrene) and include a cellular foam lid. The samples shall not be compacted, except for minimal tamping to allow the mould to be filled without leaving excessive areas of voids.

   c) Core test specimen top and bottom surfaces may be grouted to ensure flat, parallel loading surfaces.

d) Following preparation or recovery, the test samples shall be stored upright at either 20°C or 40°C, depending on the nature of the material, and tested in compression at 28 days after placement of the material on site.

2) Experience suggests that results obtained from 150 mm test cubes in moulds with cellular foam lids, stored at ambient temperature, are most representative of in-ground conditions.

3) FCRs and FSMRs shall not normally be tamped or compacted.

4) FCRs and FSMRs of density less than 1000 kg/m³ may not displace standing water. In excavations containing water, the minimum recommended density for foam concretes is 1050 kg/m³. FCRs may flow into, and block, damaged drainage or ducting within, or adjacent to, the excavation. Where required, plastic sheeting etc. may provide adequate protection during pouring and curing.

5) FCRs and FSMRs are unlikely to provide significant load bearing capacity for several hours after placement, depending on the ambient temperature. During this time, unguarded reinstatements may be a hazard to children and animals etc and should be protected.

A9.3.4 Particular Requirements for NFSMRs and HBMs to BS EN 14227

1a) NFSMRs

The compressive strength of NFSMRs shall be determined in accordance with the principles of BS 1924 Part 2 Section 4.2, with the following exceptions or options:

a) Test specimens may be prepared at the time of placement by compaction of a sample of material within a test mould or, preferably, recovered from site after placement by the extraction of cores from the reinstatement.

b) Specimens prepared on site may be placed in conventional steel test cubes or in cylindrical moulds. Compaction shall be applied in order to achieve a specimen density between 100% +/- 5% of that achieved on site.

c) Core test specimen top and bottom surfaces may be grouted to ensure flat, parallel loading surfaces.

d) Following preparation or recovery, the test samples shall be stored upright at either 20°C or 40°C, depending on the nature of the material, and tested in compression at 28 days after placement of the material on site.

1b) HBM

Following preparation using mixture recovered from the point of use, the test specimens shall be stored at either 20°C or 40°C in accordance with the procedures specified in the SHW 800 series and the relevant part of EN 14227, and tested in compression at 28 days.

2) NFSMRs and HBM shall normally require compaction to ensure adequate strength. The compaction regime (i.e. details of plant type, weight category, lift/layer thickness and number of passes) shall be specified before the NFSMR or HBM is used, and should be obtained by prior development and testing.

A9.3.5 SMR Material Production

A9.3.5.1 *FCR Material Production*

1) FCRs shall be produced to prescribed mix formulations by an approved mixing plant, in accordance with approved manufacturing processes under quality control procedures.

2) The wet density of the FCRs should be checked prior to placement. Depending on the method of manufacture, the quality of the foaming agent added at site should be checked prior to being incorporated in the mix. Any on-site addition of a foaming agent must be in accordance with the approved mix design.

A9.3.5.2 *FSMR and NFSMR Material Production*

1) FSMRs and NFSMRs shall be prepared in accordance with the procedures set out in the Approval Trial Agreement (see Appendix A9.5), to the approved mix formulation(s) (obtained by prior development and testing), in order to achieve the required compressive strength. Binders, additives and admixtures may be included based on prior development and testing.

2) FSMRs and NFSMRs may be delivered to site as ready-made materials or be prepared partly or wholly on site.

3) Mixing may be carried out using any equipment, adapted as necessary for the manufacture of FSMRs and NFSMRs in quantities appropriate to the intended use, provided the approved mixing procedure is used throughout. Mixing equipment should be maintained in accordance with the manufacturer's recommendations and checked regularly. All metering or weighing apparatus should be calibrated regularly according to a Quality Assurance Scheme.

4) All binders, additives and admixtures, including diluted solutions thereof, should be stored according to the manufacturer's recommendations and used within the recommended shelf life.

5) NFSMRs shall be compacted in accordance with the manufacturer's recommendations or an agreed compaction regime obtained from prior development and testing.

A9.3.5.3 *HBM production*

1) HBM may be delivered to site ready-made or be prepared partly or wholly on site.

2) Production shall be in accordance with the established Production Control System and the selected method from the SHW 800 series.

A9.4 Stabilised Materials for Fill (SMFs)

A9.4.1 Permitted Use of SMF Materials

1) SMFs may be used in place of other materials on a trial basis by prior agreement with the Authority, in the layers appropriate to their classification as defined by Table A9.2, and regardless of the nature of reinstatement materials used above and below, in any combination of the following:

   a) At any position within the surround to apparatus and/or backfill, as the entire layer or combined with any other permitted backfill materials, in any proportion, within any reinstatement.

   b) As a combined surround to apparatus and/or backfill within any reinstatement.

   c) If classified as a SMF Class A material as per Table A9.2, it may also be used in the sub-base layer within any road, footway, footpath or cycle track.

2) Soil stabilised with lime to BS EN 14227 – 11 Table 9 CBR_{15} shall be deemed equivalent to SMF Class A and shall not require an Appendix A9 trial.

A9.4.2 Overall Requirements for SMFs

1) Each stabilisation or modification method and formulation shall be classified as yielding SMF materials equivalent to one of the four defined classes of backfill material permitted in Appendix A1, as follows:

   a) Class A SMF Material – equivalent to Class A Graded Granular Backfill Material

   or

   b) Class B SMF Material – equivalent to Class B Granular Backfill Material

   or

   c) Class C SMF Material – equivalent to Class C Cohesive/Granular Backfill Material

   or

   d) Class D SMF Material – equivalent to Class D Cohesive Backfill Material.

2) The SMF material classification shall be based on the "soaked" %CBR or equivalent value proven during the development and laboratory testing, in accordance with Table A9.2.

Table A9.2 – SMF CBR Requirements	
SMF Class	**% CBR**
A	>15
B	7 to 15
C	4 to 7
D	2 to 4

3) The CBR value shall be determined by laboratory testing in accordance with the principles of BS1377, with the following requirements:

   i) Conventional steel test moulds may be unsuitable for some SMF materials (due to the requirement to remove any coarse aggregate >20 mm in size) and in-situ testing may need to be considered. The preparation of SMF test samples is not restricted and may include test cores extracted from site.

   ii) Following preparation, the test samples shall be stored at ambient temperature until a period of 90 days has elapsed from the placement of the material on site.

   iii) The laboratory CBR test shall be performed on samples in a soaked condition (soaked for 4 days prior to testing).

   iv) The test results shall be verified by a UKAS accredited laboratory unless mutually agreed otherwise.

   v) On site, a recognised appropriate direct or indirect equivalent test method may be used.

A9.4.3 SMF Material Production

1) SMFs shall be prepared in accordance with the procedures set out in the Approval Trial Agreement (see Appendix A9.5), to the approved mix formulation(s) and in accordance with the Quality System, obtained by development and testing, to achieve the required strength classification. Binders, additives and admixtures may be included as agreed and based on prior development and testing.

2) SMFs shall normally be prepared on site from basic constituents or delivered to site as a ready-mixed fill material. However, subject to experience gained by prior development testing, the SMF mix may, by prior agreement with the Authority, be transported. SMF mixes may be prepared, wholly or partially, away from the site.

3) Mixing may be carried out using any equipment, adapted as necessary for the manufacture of SMFs in quantities appropriate to the intended usage, providing the approved mixing procedure is used throughout. Mixing equipment should be maintained in accordance with the manufacturer's recommendations and checked regularly. All metering or weighing apparatus should be calibrated regularly according to a Quality Assurance Scheme.

4) All binders, additives and admixtures, including diluted solutions should be stored according to the manufacturer's recommendations and used within the recommended shelf life.

5) SMFs shall be compacted in accordance with the manufacturer's recommendations or an agreed compaction regime obtained by prior development and testing.

A9.5 Outline Scheme for Approval Trials

A9.5.1 Introduction

1) It is anticipated that an Undertaker or Authority's may wish to undertake or permit approval trials of ARMs for the purposes of development and/or performance assessment.

2) Trials may be carried out by formal agreement between an Undertaker and Authority, under an Approval Trial Agreement. This section outlines a scheme under which trials of ARMs should be carried out.

   Section A9.5.2.1 gives general guidance relating to the organisation of an Approval Trial.

   Section A9.5.2.2 describes special conditions relating to the scale of an Approval Trial and its effect on organisational and reporting matters.

   Section A9.5.2.3 outlines the intended duties of each party within the Approval Trial.

   Section A9.5.3 comprises a list of headings that describe the key requirements and stages of an Approval Trial. The headings are considered to represent the minimum essential information required to ensure that the Approval Trials are carried out in a controlled and agreed manner. The additional information under each heading given in parentheses is for guidance only. The parties to an Approval Trial (normally an Undertaker (who would generally initiate or request the trial) and an Authority) may, by agreement with the other party, add, amend or omit any details that do not affect the legal standing of the Agreement.

A9.5.2 General Requirements, Special Considerations and Duties of Parties to Approval Trials

A9.5.2.1 *General Requirements for Approval Trials*

1) Approval Trials may be undertaken in any Road Category, with the prior approval of the Authority. No Approval Trials shall be undertaken in a high amenity or high duty footway, footpath or cycle track, or a Site of Special Scientific Interest.

2) Approval trials in carriageways should be conducted on a minimum of three separate sites, representing a range of traffic conditions. A range of positions within the carriageway (i.e. within and outside of a wheel track, longitudinal and transverse orientation (for trench reinstatements)) should also be considered.

3) The duration of all Approval Trials shall be two years – the final inspection shall be completed within one month following the end of the two-year test period. The Undertaker shall notify the Authority of the inspection date at least seven working days in advance. The Authority shall confirm their intention to attend, or otherwise, within seven working days of receipt of such notification. The inspection measures should be carried out on the notified date at an agreed time or an agreed alternative date. Where the Authority does not attend the final inspection, the Undertaker shall provide the Authority with a summary of the investigation within 28 days of the inspection. The Undertaker should keep a photographic record of the Approval Trial reinstatements at the time of inspection and send copies to the Authority.

4) Core sampling and interim inspections of any type may be carried out on Approval Trial reinstatements at any time. Where required, as part of the Approval Trial agreement, the Undertaker shall notify the Authority at least five working days in advance of such works. Any holes created during these activities shall be reinstated in accordance with the relevant requirements of this Specification.

5) Approval Trial reinstatements may be accidentally damaged during the trial and rendered unsuitable for accurate assessment. It is therefore recommended that trials should include duplicate sites for each road type, category, position, orientation, etc.

6) Where an Approval Trial reinstatement requires remedial action, regardless of the reason, the Undertaker shall provide the Authority with details of the remedial measures within one month of completion. Where practicable, records of surface measurements, photographs etc taken before and after the remedial work should be kept by the Undertaker and copies provided to the Authority.

7) With the written approval of the Authority further use of the ARM's under trial may be permitted before completion of the trial. Such approval shall only apply to works carried out within the boundary of the Authority. Further use of ARMs shall be only in Road Categories up to and including the highest category used for the Approved Trial.

8) On successful completion of the Approval Trial the results, audit trail and Factory Production Control or Quality System documentation should be shared with other Street Authorities from whom permission for further use is to be sought. By agreement between the parties involved, some or all of the details of the trials shall be forwarded to Regional HAUC or National HAUC to allow such details to be made available nationally. Further use of ARMs shall be only in Road Categories up to and including the highest category used for the Approved Trial.

9) After the successful completion of an Approval Trial permission for further use of the ARM shall not be unreasonably withheld by any other Authority and shall only be denied for engineering reasons. Where reasonable engineering concerns are expressed, the nature of which shall be stated, then additional assessment may be required by the Authority.

10) It is recognised that the scope, extent and duration of ARM approval trials may vary widely.

A9.5.2.2 *Special Considerations for Approval Trials*

1) For small-scale Approval Trials intended to take place on a small number of sites and over a fixed time period (e.g. for specially prepared Approval Trial excavations), the Undertaker shall notify the Authority at least one month in advance of the start of an Approval Trial.

   Specially prepared excavations should be of similar depth and plan dimensions to the Undertaker's routine excavations, and generally not less than 500 mm by 500 mm in plan, or not less than 200 mm wide for trench excavations. The total combined surface area of all Approval Trial sites should not be less than 2 square metres.

   The location and position of the Approval Trial reinstatements should represent as wide a range as possible (see Appendix A9.5.2.1(2)). If specially prepared sites are to be used, the site locations may be jointly selected.

2) Approval Trials of a larger extent, (e.g. trials that use an Undertaker's routine excavation sites as Approval Trial sites) may take place over a longer time period and the Undertaker shall notify the Authority at least one month in advance of the start of the Approval Trial period. Arrangements for notification and attendance at these Approval Trials should be included in the Trial Agreement.

3) Any restrictions as to the size, location and position, total number of Approval Trial sites and/or the period during which the Approval Trial reinstatements may be carried out, should also be included in the Approval Trial agreement.

4) A two-year Approval Trial period shall apply to each Approval Trial site, commencing on its date of installation. An interim report on the Approval Trial should be provided within six months of the start date of the Trial. The final review or reporting need not be carried out until the final Approval Trial site has reached an age of two years.

A9.5.2.3 *Duties of Parties to Approval Trials*

1) The initiator (usually the Undertaker) would be expected to have carried out documented development work to ensure a high level of confidence in the proposed process before the commencement of the Approval Trial. The results of such development work should not be unreasonably withheld from the Authority.

2) The Undertaker shall provide as much notice of the Approval Trial reinstatement operation(s) (e.g. location, date/time, excavation, mixing, reinstatement, sampling, post-construction activities etc) as practically possible, in accordance with the requirements of Appendix A9.5.3.1 of the Approval Trial agreement.

3) The Undertaker shall not unreasonably withhold information relating to any aspect of the Approval Trial from the Authority.

4) The Authority shall not unreasonably obstruct the commencement, progress, or cause the termination of the Approval Trials provided they are carried out in accordance with the terms of the Approval Trial agreement.

5) Either party shall have the right to request confidentiality on any matter relating to the Approval Trial.

A9.5.3 **Suggested Information for Inclusion in Approval Trial Agreement**

Prior to the commencement of an Approval Trial, the following information should be considered by both parties for inclusion in the Approval Trial Agreement.

A9.5.3.1 *General Information*

1) **Parties to trial** – names of Undertaker and Authority agreeing to Approval Trial

2) **Confidentiality** – parties (if any) to whom trial information may be divulged

3) **Geographical extent of trial** – county or district border, utility region or area boundary

4) **Scope of trial** – total number of trial reinstatements or maximum number of sites

5) **Time limit for trial** – start/end dates

6) **Termination** criteria – conditions under which agreement may be ended and notice of termination

7) **Signatories/witnesses** – approved officers of appropriate seniority who are permitted to commit their organisation to the execution of the Approval Trial and who can approve the terms and conditions of the trial.

A9.5.3.2 *Procedural*

1) **Contemporary records** – details of records required, responsibility for record-keeping

2) **Notification details** – notice periods, arrangements for contacting relevant parties to an Approval Trial

3) **Attendance at trials** – parties who may attend an Approval Trial

4) **Review periods/meetings** – dates, attendees, procedures for calling ad hoc meetings

5) **Post-construction assessment** – test methods to be employed and arrangements for periodic surveying, sampling, etc

A9.5.3.3 *Technical*

1) **Type of trial site** – routine utility excavations or specially excavated Approval Trial
2) **Location of trial site** – non high-amenity or non high-duty footway, cycle track, (including road classification Type 2 to 4) etc
3) **Positioning of trial site** – "as excavated" , within wheeltrack, etc
4) **ARMs to be trialled** – generic SMR or SMF materials
5) **ARM details** – Mix design, binder details, additives, dependencies on site conditions or excavated/base material type and condition, details of prior development work
6) **ARMs preparation** – batching, mixing and placement procedures.
7) **Quality control on site** – any tests to be applied in order to ensure that an ARM has been prepared to the required design
8) **Compaction regime** – NFSMRs and SMRs only
9) **Sampling requirements** – types of samples and sampling frequency
10) **Testing laboratories** – contact details of accredited laboratories or otherwise
11) **Remedial measures for "failed" sites** – replacement with an alternative SMR or SMF material or other approved material or remove from the Approval trial Agreement
12) **Future of trial sites** – remove after trial completion or leave in place, future monitoring and/or testing

Appendix A10

Not used

Appendix A11

Bitumen Binder Equivalence

A11.1 Introduction

In some road types, particular binder grades are not permitted or are not permitted for machine-lay. In general, hand laying is not recommended where the material is likely to be difficult to compact adequately, especially in cold conditions.

A11.2 Base and Binder Course Materials

Binder grades permitted for Base and Binder Course materials are shown in Table A11.1, provided that the layer thickness is amended to that shown in the table.

Table A11.1 – Permitted Base/Binder Course Binder Grades and Layer Thickness

Material	Bitumen Pen Grade	Combined Base/Binder Course (mm)					Binder Course Only (mm)	
		Road Type					Road Type	
		0	1	2	3	4	3	4
SMA BC	40/60	305	260	200	120	100	60	60
	70/100	NP	285 **H**	225	135	105	60	60
	100/150	NP	NP	245	150	110	60	60
20 mm ACBC	40/60	305	260	200	120	100	60	60
	70/100	340 **H**	285 **H**	225	135	105	60	60
	100/150	375 **H**	310 H	245	150	110	60	60
	160/220	NP	NP	NP	NP	155 **H**	NP	85 **H**
50/20 or 60/20 HRABC	40/60	350	295	230	150	110	60	60
	70/100	340 **H**	285 **H**	255	185	135	75	75
	100/150	NP	NP	275 **H**	215 **H**	155 **H**	85 **H**	85 **H**

Notes to Table A11.1:

1) **NP** = Not Permitted
2) **H** = Hand-lay only – not recommended for hot weather & not permitted for machine-lay
3) Shaded cells denote the thicknesses for the preferred binder grades noted in Appendix A2 against the binder courses for SMA, AC and HRA.
4) Thicknesses for combined binder and base course for Flexible Roads noted in Appendix A3 generally reflect ACBC material, being the more commonly used material.

Appendix A12

Reinstatement of Modular Surface Layer

A12.1 Interim Reinstatement

1) Where an interim reinstatement is required, the existing modules should be reused, including the use of broken modules. Where damage has resulted in fragmentation or widespread breakage of modules [subject to the special case of natural material modules (as set out in Appendix A12.2.2)], then bituminous mixtures may be used for interim reinstatement, provided they meet the performance requirements of Section S2 and that compaction of such mixtures does not result in further damage to adjacent modules.

A12.2 Permanent Reinstatement

A12.2.1 General

1) Permanent reinstatement of modular surface layers should be generally carried out in accordance with BS 7533.

2) Permanent reinstatement of modules shall include all modules, which are situated within or extend beyond the effective width of the reinstatement (W) described in Section S2.1.4 and shall also include any other modules which are disturbed in the course of carrying out the excavation or reinstatement.

3) Clean undamaged modules shall be re-used for permanent reinstatement; broken modules shall not be used for permanent reinstatement and shall be replaced.

4) Laying course material shall be sand or mortar, to match the characteristics of the existing type and thickness. Unless otherwise notified by the Authority, where sand is present, laying course and jointing materials shall be in accordance with BS7533:Part 3. For all roads and footways, the grading of the laying course material shall be in accordance with Table D.3 Category II. Jointing materials to Section D1.2, shall be applied to gaps between individual modules at the time of permanent reinstatement. Where mortar has been used for laying course material the Undertaker shall seek guidance from the Authority as to the specification to be used. This information shall not be unreasonably withheld.

A12.2.2 Requirements for Natural Material Modules

A12.2.2.1 *General for whole Natural Material Modules*

1) The reinstatement of whole natural material modules shall be in accordance with the general requirements of Appendix A12.2.1.

A12.2.2.2 *Damaged Natural Material Modules*

1) Where damaged modules are to be re-used in the reinstatement, a joint inspection shall be arranged prior to the commencement of excavation, to agree the extent of usage of damage modules and the minimum size acceptable for re-use.
2) The Undertaker should take photographic records at the joint inspection which should be agreed between the Undertaker and the Authority.
3) The Undertaker shall use its best endeavours to match existing profiles and meet the tolerances specified in Section S2. However, where the pre-existing profile of damaged modules is near or in excess of current intervention and construction tolerances specified in Section S2, it will be difficult for the Undertaker to construct a complying reinstatement. The Undertaker shall use its best endeavours to ensure that the interface between its reinstatement and the adjoining surfaces avoid creating hazardous trips.

A12.2.3 Infills in Modular Reinstatements

A12.2.3.1 *General*

1) Gaps greater than 5mm between the nearest module and the immediately adjacent fixed feature (such as edgings, channel blocks, drainage features, surface boxes, ironware) or boundary feature (such as walls, fences and the like), which are caused as a direct result of any works by the Undertaker, should be filled to the full depth of the adjacent paving module, as follows:
   (a) for smaller gaps, or infills - a 1:4 cement:sand mortar should be used;
   (b) for larger gaps or infills, where aggregate can be used – a 1:5:3 cement:sand:aggregate concrete infill should be used, with a maximum aggregate size of 10 mm.
2) Infills should be generally as small as possible, subject to the proviso that where the physical characteristics of the bond, fixed feature, or proximity of other fixed features do not allow for a small infill, then best endeavours should be used to achieve the smallest infill possible.
3) Infills should match existing work by the Authority.

A12.2.3.2 *Infill Widths and Limitations*

1) Where possible, infills should be limited to a maximum width of 50mm in all modular areas, irrespective of whether the existing footway area was originally constructed in accordance with BS7533.

2) In the case of modules where one side of the module is greater than 300mm, there are instances where it shall be permissible to increase the width of the infill to a maximum of 150mm, in order to achieve a better engineering and aesthetically pleasing reinstatement. These include instances where the intervening distance is less than 150mm:

   (a) between the Undertaker's newly laid apparatus and the nearest module (on any side), or

   (b) between two or more pieces of Undertaker's newly laid apparatus, or

   (c) to an existing fixed or boundary feature.

   Where it can be shown to be acceptable custom and practice, in exceptional cases, the maximum permissible infill width may be increased to 200mm, for irregularly shaped apparatus. Typical examples are in Notes for Guidance Section NGA12.

3) In the case of modules where all sides are 300mm or less, there are similarly instances where it is permissible to increase the width of the infill to the same as the full width of module (measured on the shortest side), again in order to achieve a better engineering and aesthetically pleasing reinstatement. These include instances where the intervening distance is less than the full width of a module plus 25mm (measured on the shortest side):

   (a) between the Undertaker's newly laid apparatus and the nearest module (on any side), or

   (b) between two or more pieces of Undertaker's newly laid apparatus, or

   (c) to an existing fixed or boundary feature.

   Typical examples are in Notes for Guidance Section NGA12.

A12.2.3.3 *Acceptable localised loss of Modular Pattern*

1) Physical characteristics may prevent or limit the possibility of completing a uniform and closely matching modular reinstatement immediately adjacent to features. The physical characteristics of the module itself, the existing as-laid bond, as well as the physical characteristics of the fixed or boundary feature, may individually or collectively contribute to such a situation.

2) In all instances, the Undertaker should attempt to minimise the width of the infill. However, the following exceptions are permissible:

   (a) Where the above physical characteristics are present, permanently reinstated modules immediately adjacent to the feature may be laid with a degree of localised loss of bond pattern. The introduction of a stringer (or in some cases, soldier) course immediately adjacent to the feature should not be considered as a loss of bond pattern. The loss of bond pattern should be limited, where practicable, to the first two rows beyond any stringer course, being laid in such a manner as to aesthetically integrate with the surrounded bond pattern. Typical examples are indicated in Notes for Guidance Section NGA12.

(b) If adjacent modules abut an existing, contiguous infill, such as at a property boundary, then the infill shall match the existing.

(c) In the case of fixed features that are not rectangular, there is no requirement to cut modules to match the edge profile of the fixed feature to otherwise reduce the infill at irregular edges.

(d) Where localised custom and practice adopted by the Authority for its own works differs to the above, infills may be laid to a standard consistent with that of the Authority.

A12.3 Provision of Replacement Modules

1) Where insufficient modules remain for reinstatement use and identical replacement modules are no longer available, then a reasonably similar colour, shape and size shall be the preferred order of criteria in the choice of acceptable replacements.

2) Where replacement modules are required due to breakage at some time prior to the Undertaker's works, the Authority may provide suitable replacements to the Undertaker, free of charge.

3) Where replacements modules are required due to breakages caused during the course of the Undertaker's works, the Undertaker shall reinstate using modules purchased at the Undertaker's expense or purchased from the Authority at reasonable cost.

4) Authorities are recommended to retain stocks of modules used within their areas to enable them to provide replacements when required. Where no stocks of suitable replacements are available, Authorities should assist Undertakers in locating a source of suitable replacement modules. This is becoming especially prevalent with the proliferation of modules sourced from around the world.

A12.4 Pre-existing Surface Damage outside limits of Undertaker's Works

1) Some modular surfaces outside the limits of the Undertaker's works may be broken or have settled or deformed. Where the existing profiles are near or exceed the current intervention and construction tolerances specified in Section S2, it will be difficult for the Undertaker to construct a complying reinstatement. Subject to the Authority agreeing to meet the costs of the works necessary to reinstate the surfaces outside the limits of its works, the Undertaker shall extend its reinstatement works to include such surfaces. In the absence of agreement, the Undertaker shall be under no obligation whatsoever to extend its reinstatement works but shall use its best endeavours to ensure that the interface between its reinstatement and the adjoining surfaces avoid creating hazardous trips. In such situations, it must be recognised that it may be necessary to install different sized modules or fillets to minimise surface irregularities at the interfaces. The Undertaker shall use its best endeavours to match existing materials and profiles and meet the tolerances specified in Section S2.

2) Where the area of permanent reinstatement needs to be substantially extended, to include an existing area of broken or settled modular surfacing, the Undertaker shall notify the Authority prior to the commencement of works.

A12.5 Joint Inspections and Recovery of Costs

1) Within Limits of Undertaker's Works – Following notification from the Undertaker, a joint inspection shall be arranged prior to the commencement of all standard or major works to agree the extent of damaged, settled or deformed surfacing within the limits of the works. Where the Authority does not provide suitable replacements to the Undertaker in accordance with paragraph A12.3 (2) above, it may contribute to the Undertaker the sum notified by the Undertaker as the cost of replacing the same.

2) Outside Limits of Undertaker's Works – Following notification from the Undertaker, a joint inspection shall be arranged to agree the need and extent of any remedial measures outside of the limits of the Undertaker's works. An apportionment of the additional costs, based on the relative areas of permanent reinstatement, shall be agreed. In the event of an Authority failing to agree to meet a proportion of the costs of reinstating modules, the Undertaker shall proceed in accordance with paragraph A12.4 (1).

3) Prior joint inspections will usually be impractical for minor and immediate works. However, such works are usually small individual excavations and a proportion of such works will be inspected by the Authority, within the sample inspection regime. On completion of all minor and immediate works, the Undertaker shall be free, at its discretion subject to paragraphs A12.3 (2) and A12.4 (1), to recover all reasonable costs from the Authority, according to the procedure illustrated in Figure A12.1.

Figure A12.1 Procedure for Pre-Existing Damage to Modular Surfaces

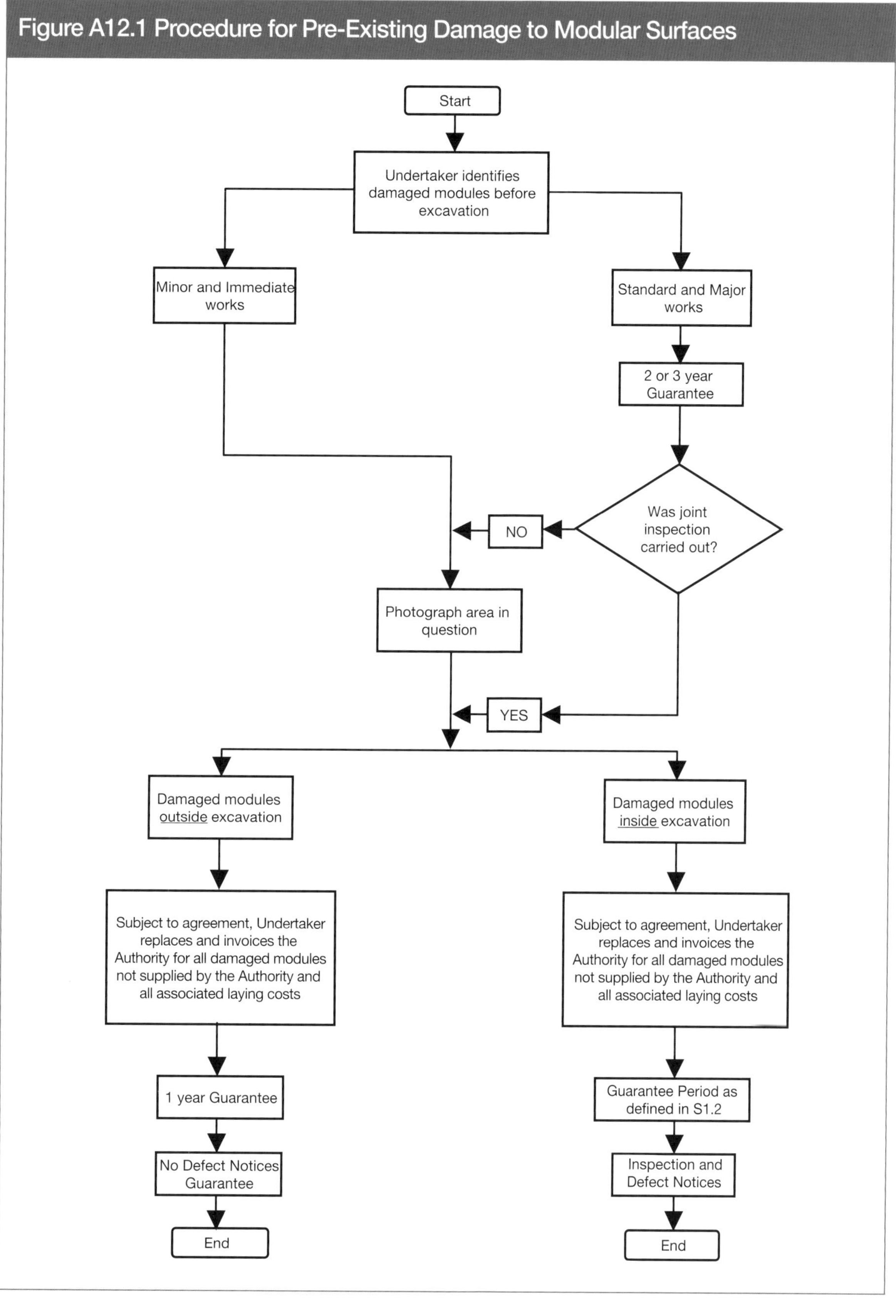

Notes For Guidance

NG0 Preamble to the Specification

There are no Notes for Guidance

NG1 Introduction

NG1.1 General

1) The primary objectives of this Specification are to ensure that all Undertakers' reinstatements, within highways, are completed to a permanent standard, as soon as is practicable and to a consistent high quality. Undertakers and Authority personnel should work together, in close co-operation, in order to achieve these objectives.

2) This Specification may require a joint inspection of any reinstatement site, depending on the existing site conditions, before the commencement of works. Such joint pre-inspections may be of an informal nature, by agreement, and should be carried out at the earliest convenience of both parties. Where either party fails to attend any agreed pre-inspection, or where existing site conditions warrant concern, it is recommended that the Undertaker retains a photographic record of the existing surfaces, prior to the commencement of works.

3) This Specification may require a formal notification of circumstances or other requirements, depending on the existing conditions of any reinstatement site, prior to the commencement of works. Such pre-notifications should be issued at the earliest possible opportunity. Undertakers shall comply with such notification issued at the street works notice stage, and should make reasonable efforts to comply with any notification issued thereafter.

4) Where this Specification allows several options, it is recommended, wherever practicable, to agree a preferred option from the alternatives available. This principle should be applied to all sections where alternatives are provided.

NG1.2 Guarantee Period

1) Where an Authority intends to resurface or reconstruct a section of road, the Undertaker may complete any reinstatement to an alternative interim standard, by agreement. The guarantee period shall thereafter be waived, unless the Undertaker's reinstatement can be shown to be grossly substandard. It is expected that agreement to this procedure will be conditional upon all savings in costs made by not carrying out a permanent reinstatement being shared, equally, between the Undertaker and the Authority.

2) Where site circumstances are considered to militate against a successful permanent reinstatement, an additional interim period of up to a further 6 months may be adopted, before it is necessary to complete the permanent reinstatement.

3) In designated high amenity locations and areas with high quality surfaces there is benefit in completing the permanent reinstatement immediately or as expeditiously as possible. To facilitate a permanent reinstatement, materials need to be identified and ordered early in the works planning process. Advance notification through the normal co-ordination process is necessary to achieve this and the Authority should assist the Undertaker to locate sources of suitable similar or equivalent modules, especially if no stocks are available from the Authority itself.

NG1.3 Road Categories

1) Road categories 0 to 4 are based on the number of millions of standard axles (msa) carried by the road over a 20-year period. Reinstatements are designed on this basis. The traffic loading is calculated in accordance with the following:.

   a) Road Type 0 & 1 – HD 26/06

   b) Road Type 2 – Intermediate between HD 26/06, HD 24/96 & LR1132

   c) Road Type 3 & 4 – TRL reports LR1132, RR 87 & Road Note 29

   Some roads that have been constructed in recent years (particularly new housing estate roads constructed under the auspices of Section 38 of the Highways Act 1980) may have been designed and constructed to *HD* 24/96 or HD 26/06 standards. In these cases the Authority shall notify the Undertaker, in advance of the works, and the Undertaker shall reinstate the excavation to match the existing construction thickness. It is not possible to match the engineering integrity of existing well-consolidated unbound layers with unbound reinstatement materials. Therefore there may be significant differences between the existing carriageway construction and the requirements of the Specification. The increased thickness of reinstatement materials compensate for this.

2) For any road, its msa rating gives the number of standard axle loads which it is expected to carry over a defined period of time. This msa rating is calculated using the following input data:

   a) 24 hour annual average daily flow (AADF) of commercial vehicles in one direction. The use of AADF data in one direction, averaged from data in each direction, is recommended.

   b) Average vehicle axle factor over a 20-year service life.

   c) Actual sustained annual growth rate of commercial vehicles, averaged over several years, from valid census data.

   These data, processed in accordance with HD 26/06 procedures, provide the maximum number of commercial vehicles per day, in each direction, for all road types. Table NG1.1 has been prepared in accordance with HD 26/06, showing the maximum annual average daily flow (AADF) in one direction, in commercial vehicles per day (cvd), for a single carriageway road, or for both lanes of a dual carriageway, for all road types, from 2002 onwards, for all likely traffic growth rates. Appropriate AADF rates for all Intermediate years within each five-year period can be calculated by interpolation, pro rata.

Table NG1.1 – Maximum Commercial Vehicle Traffic per Road Type

Year of Traffic Count	Daily Traffic Flow – Commercial Vehicles/Day One Direction – Single or Dual Carriageway					Average Growth Rate %
	Type 4	Type 3	Type 2	Type 1	Type 0	
2002	66	240	638	1383	4499	**0**
2006	66	240	638	1383	4499	
2011	66	240	638	1383	4499	
2016	66	240	638	1383	4499	
2021	66	240	638	1383	4499	
2002	60	217	578	1253	4079	**1**
2006	62	226	601	1304	4245	
2011	65	237	632	1370	4461	
2016	68	249	664	1440	4689	
2021	72	262	698	1514	4928	
2002	54	196	521	1132	3690	**2**
2006	58	212	564	1225	3994	
2011	64	234	623	1353	4410	
2016	71	259	687	1494	4869	
2021	78	286	759	1649	5376	
2002	49	176	469	1020	3333	**3**
2006	55	198	528	1148	3751	
2011	64	230	612	1331	4349	
2016	74	266	709	1543	5041	
2021	86	309	822	1789	5844	
2002	43	157	420	916	3005	**4**
2006	50	184	491	1072	3515	
2011	61	223	598	1304	4277	
2016	74	272	727	1586	5204	
2021	91	331	885	1930	6331	
2002	39	140	375	821	2704	**5**
2006	47	170	456	998	3287	
2011	61	217	582	1274	4195	
2016	77	277	742	1626	5354	
2021	99	354	948	2075	6833	

Table NG1.1 – Maximum Commercial Vehicle Traffic per Road Type

2002	35	125	334	734	2430	
2006	44	158	422	927	3068	
2011	59	211	564	1240	4105	**6**
2016	79	283	755	1660	5494	
2021	106	378	1011	2221	7352	
2002	31	111	297	655	2180	
2006	41	145	389	859	2858	
2011	57	204	546	1204	4008	**7**
2016	80	286	766	1689	5621	
2021	112	401	1074	2369	7884	
2002	27	98	263	584	1953	
2006	37	133	358	795	2657	
2011	54	196	526	1167	3904	**8**
2016	79	288	772	1715	5736	
2021	117	423	1135	2520	8429	

3) Where the actual AADF rates for any road are significantly different for each direction and Table NG1.1 indicates different road types in each direction, the highest traffic category shall be applied in each direction.

4) Where one-way traffic systems and/or other traffic management schemes result in multi-lane traffic, standard growth rate predictions and lane correction procedures may result in an inaccurate road classification overall. In such cases, whenever reasonably practical, the flow of commercial vehicles should be monitored separately, and traffic calculations completed for each traffic lane.

5) Where an existing road is near, or beyond, its service life, and is expected to be re-constructed within the foreseeable future, a temporary re-classification of the road will usually be appropriate, pending its re-construction. Such temporary re-classifications should be undertaken by agreement between the parties involved. Similarly, where roads are expected to be re-constructed within the guarantee period of the reinstatement, it will usually be appropriate to amend methods, materials or performance requirements for those reinstatements, by agreement.

6) The national network of roads carrying, up to 125 msa within a 20-year period, and classified as Types 0 to 4 roads according to the requirements of this Specification, will yield a distribution similar to that shown in Table NG1.2.

Table NG1.2 Estimated Highway Classification

Road Type	% of Total
0	< 1
1	< 1
2	< 5
3	< 9
4	> 84

7) It is expected that the roads in any Authority area will show a distribution similar to that shown in Table NG1.2, although there will be some local variations. In future years, there may be cases where traffic flows change, to such a degree, that re-classification will be necessary.

NG1.4 – NG1.5 *There are no Notes for Guidance*

NG1.6 Alternative Options

1) New Materials

Research into new or improved reinstatement materials is often undertaken by various organisations and such work may produce materials that perform as well as, or better, than those given in this Specification. In order to allow such materials to be proven by development testing, the materials and relevant layer thickness quoted in this Specification may be amended or supplemented, subject to prior agreement.

2) Local Materials

Materials may be available locally that have not been defined in any national Specification, but which, by experience, are known to give acceptable performance in service. In order to allow the use of such local materials, the materials and relevant layer thickness quoted in this Specification may be amended or supplemented, subject to prior agreement.

3) Alternative compaction equipment

Alternative compaction equipment, including any compaction device, not specifically permitted within Section S10 and Appendix A8, may be permitted, provided it has been proven to be capable of achieving the performance requirements permitted in Section S10, Appendix A2 and/or Appendix A8.

a) For all compaction plant not shown in Appendix A8, an approved operating procedure should be established, by development testing, in an appropriate trench environment with the relevant material options to meet the performance requirements permitted in Section S10, Appendix A2 and/or Appendix A8. The development testing may be verified by an independent, accredited laboratory.

b) Where alternative compaction plant is intended to be used on more than one type of material, as defined in Appendix A8, an approved compaction procedure shall be established, as defined in section NG1.6 (3) (a) above, for each intended category of material.

NG1.7 Immediate Works

The minimum thickness of bituminous surfacing material, required by Section S1.7.1 for the reinstatement of all immediate works, is 40 mm. A greater thickness may be required, in areas subject to frequent or heavy traffic, if further remedial works, during the 10 days permitted duration of immediate works, are to be avoided.

NG1.8 Apparatus within the Road Structure

1) Some apparatus may already be present at shallow depth, within many existing road structures and special requirements may apply to their reinstatement. Both the Undertaker and the Authority are likely to have particular criteria and this Specification may be altered, or supplemented, subject to prior agreement, to accommodate any such requirements.

2) Not all new apparatus will need to be installed to the full depth or width expected by this Specification; an example is small diameter cabling and/or ducting for telecommunications, traffic controls, etc. This Specification may be altered, or supplemented, subject to prior agreement, to accommodate these applications.

NG1.9 Geosynthetic Materials, Geotextiles and Reinforcement Grids

Where these materials are used, the manufacturer's instructions shall be followed, particularly in relation to appropriate overlaps, fixing and the like.

NG1.10 Trees

NG1.10.1 Prohibited, Precautionary and Permitted Zones

PROHIBITED ZONE – 1m from trunk. Excavations of any kind must not be undertaken within this zone unless full consultation with Local Authority Tree Officer is undertaken. Materials, plant and spoil must not be stored within this zone.

PRECAUTIONARY ZONE – beneath canopy or branch spread. Where excavations must be undertaken within this zone the use of mechanical excavation plant should be prohibited. Precautions should be undertaken to protect any exposed roots. Materials, plant and spoil should not be stored within this zone. Consult with Local Authority Tree Officer if in any doubt.

PERMITTED ZONE – outside of precautionary zone. Excavation works may be undertaken within this zone however caution must be applied and the use of mechanical plant limited. Any exposed roots should be protected.

NG1.10.2 Precautions during Excavation and Reinstatement

1) THE PROHIBITED ZONE

Don't excavate within this zone.

Don't use any form of mechanical plant within this zone.

Don't store materials, plant or equipment within this zone.

Don't move plant or vehicles within this zone.

Don't lean materials against, or chain plant to, the trunk.

Do contact the local authority tree officer or owner of the tree if excavation within this zone is unavoidable.

Do protect any exposed roots uncovered within this zone with dry sacking.

Do backfill with a suitable inert granular and top soil material mix as soon as possible on completion of works.

Do notify the local authority tree officer or the tree's owner of any damage.

2) THE PRECAUTIONARY ZONE

Don't excavate with machinery. Where excavation is unavoidable within this zone excavate only by hand or use trenchless techniques.

Don't cut roots over 25mm in diameter, unless advice has been sought from the local authority tree officer.

Don't repeatedly move / use heavy mechanical plant except on hard standing.

Don't store spoil or building material, including chemicals and fuels, within this zone.

Do prune roots which have to be removed using a sharp tool (e.g. secateurs or handsaw). Make a clean cut and leave as small a wound as possible.

Do backfill the trench with an inert granular material and top soil mix. Compact the backfill with care around the retained roots. On non highway sites backfill only with excavated soil.

Do protect any exposed roots with dry sacking ensuring this is removed before backfilling.

Do notify the local authority tree officer or the tree's owner of any damage.

3) THE PERMITTED ZONE

Don't cut roots over 25mm in diameter, unless advice has been sought from the local authority tree officer.

Do use caution if it is absolutely necessary to operate mechanical plant within this zone.

Do prune roots which have to be removed using a sharp tool (e.g. secateurs or handsaw). Make a clean cut and leave as small a wound as possible.

Do protect any exposed roots with dry sacking ensuring this is removed before backfilling.

Do notify the local authority tree officer or the tree's owner of any damage.

NG1.11 *There are no Notes for Guidance*

NG2 Performance Requirements

NG2.1 *There are no Notes for Guidance*

NG2.2 Surface Profile

NG2.2.1 *There are no Notes for Guidance*

NG2.2.2 Edge Depression – Intervention

Freedom from excessive edge depressions, or 'trips', for all pedestrians and two wheeled vehicles, is considered to be one of the most important performance requirements. Given that pedestrians and various two wheeled vehicles are likely to use or cross any roads, footways and cycle tracks, it is considered necessary to set a single limit for all edge depressions.

NG2.2.3 Surface Depression – Intervention

Excessive surface depressions will reduce ride quality and give rise to noise and vibration. The maximum depth of surface depression within the area of a reinstatement is limited to approximately 2.5% of the width of reinstatement, which represents a mean slope of 1 in 20 (5% gradient). In order to prevent excessive areas of standing water, it is considered necessary to limit the maximum depth of a surface depression to 25 mm, regardless of the reinstatement width.

NG2.2.4 Surface Crowning – Intervention

Excessive surface crowning will reduce ride quality and give rise to noise and vibration. The maximum height of crowning within the area of a reinstatement is limited to approximately 2.5% of the width of the reinstatement, which represents a mean slope of 1 in 20 (5% gradient). In order to prevent excessive surface irregularity, it is considered necessary to limit the maximum height of crowning to 25 mm, regardless of the reinstatement width.

NG2.2.5 Combined Defect – Intervention

The intervention limits specified for surface depressions and surface crowning include a reduction in the intervention limit, to 80% of the tabulated value, subject to a minimum of 10 mm, where surface depressions and/or crowning and/or edge depressions abut. The individual features shall be measured, and the reduction applied, as follows:

1) Combination Depressions

   Where an edge depression abuts an area of surface depression, then the area of abutting depression should be measured as shown in Figure NG2.2. Any surface crowning also abutting the area of combined depressions should be measured separately, as shown in Figure NG2.3. The permitted depth of a combination depression is further limited if the depression results in standing water.

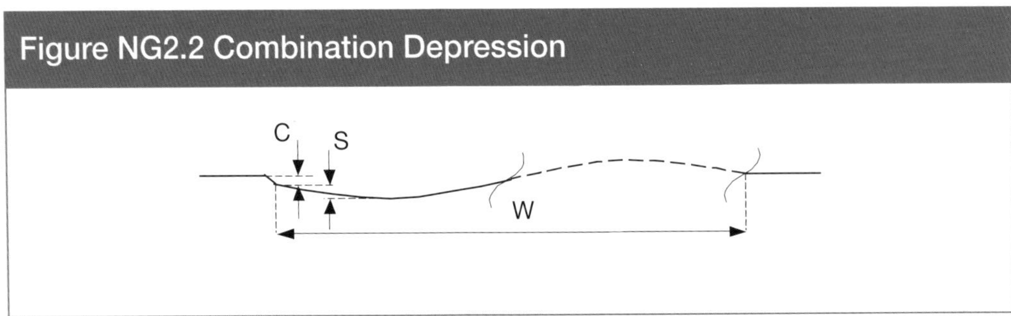

Figure NG2.2 Combination Depression

E = Edge Depression Contribution	=	10 mm	whichever is the greater
S = Surface Depression Contribution	=	10 mm or 80% of tabulated value	

2) Combination Crowning

   Where an area of surface crowning abuts an edge depression, or a surface depression, or any combination thereof, then the area of abutting crowning should be measured as shown in Figure NG2.3. The area of abutting depression should be measured separately, as shown in Figure NG2.2. The maximum height of combination crowning is further limited if the crowning results in standing water.

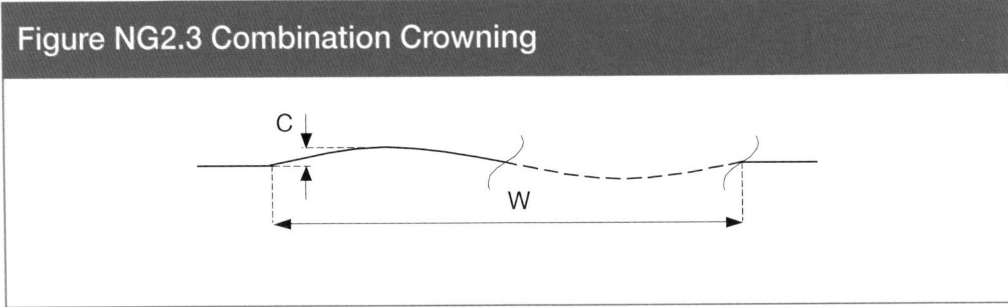

Figure NG2.3 Combination Crowning

C = Surface crowning contribution = 10 mm or 80% of tabulated value } whichever is the greater

NG2.2.6 *There are no Notes for Guidance*

NG2.3 Fixed Features

Fixed features, e.g. kerbstones and related precast concrete products, channel blocks and drainage

fixtures, surface boxes and ironware, should be bedded on a sound foundation, in accordance with the owner's requirements. In order to prevent excessive areas of standing water, it is considered necessary to set separate intervention limits for channel blocks, drainage fixtures, surface boxes and ironware.

NG2.4 Surface Regularity

Where the use of a rolling straightedge is not permitted, the surface regularity shall be assessed on an agreed basis. One method could be the use of a two metre or three metre straightedge.

NG2.5 Structural Integrity

1) Reinstatement materials and compaction requirements have been specified in order to safeguard the pavement structure, both within and adjacent to the reinstatement. Any substantial or rapid settlement within a reinstatement may therefore indicate a potential reduction in the stability of the adjacent pavement structure, as well as potential defects within the reinstatement.
2) There will be cases, in adverse circumstances, where the correct application of this Specification, in all respects, will still result in levels of settlement within the reinstatement that do not meet the requirements of Section S2.5, Structural Integrity. For example, the type and condition of the adjacent ground and/or pavement structure may limit the degree of compaction that can be achieved, so influencing the amount of settlement that could occur.
3) Any engineering investigation is intended only to determine the likelihood and extent of any further settlement, and the most cost-effective and convenient method of restoring the structural stability and surface performance of failed sections of a reinstatement, to a satisfactory condition.
4) In the case of large or deep excavations, it may be appropriate for an Authority and an Undertaker to agree an extended interim guarantee period, with additional interim surfacing materials laid to restore the running surface. When no further consolidation or settlement is considered likely, a permanent binder course and surface course may be laid, and the permanent guarantee period initiated. In any event, the location and extent of any re-excavation should be mutually agreed, taking full advantage of any bound materials already in place.

NG2.6 Skid Resistance

1) An adequate skid resistance of the reinstated running surface must be maintained, by selection of the polished stone value (PSV), aggregate abrasion value (AAV) and texture depth of the aggregate exposed at the road surface. The exposed aggregate may be precoated chippings rolled into the surface (HRA), coarse aggregate within the surface course, coated material to BS 594987 or any chippings or other aggregate applied in any form of surface dressing or slurry sealing treatment.

2) Smaller reinstatements constitute a much lower degree of skidding risk, but the measurement of skid resistance, texture depth and surface regularity become progressively more difficult as the reinstatement width reduces. However, material requirements and laying conditions remain unchanged and it is expected that the skid resistance of smaller reinstatements will not be significantly different.

3) For the purposes of identifying reinstatement sites where the risk of skidding is potentially high (Site A), sections of carriageway of greater than 10% gradient should be identified from existing steep hill warning signs or by notification from the Authority. Similarly, bends of less than 100 metres radius in roads where the speed limit is greater than 40 mph (65 kph) should be identified from existing bend, double bend or chevron warning signs or by notification from the Authority.

4) Given good site conditions, it is possible to obtain reasonably representative measurements of skid resistance and surface regularity on narrower reinstatements but amended test procedures and/or extra care are required. The TRL Mini Texture Meter and TRL Rolling Straightedge should always be fully contained within the limits of the reinstatement. The actual minimum practicable width for these instruments will depend on the trench alignment and radius of curvature. Measurements can be particularly difficult when testing on tight radius bends.

5) The Undertaker should require the suppliers of bituminous materials to regularly supply details of the constituent materials within their bituminous mixtures and in particular PSV/AAV test results for the coarse aggregate in Surface Course mixtures and the aggregate used for precoated chippings in HRA.

6) The past use of Table S2.7 has indicated that the minimum values noted are appropriate in most cases.

NG2.7 *There are no Notes for Guidance*

NG3 Excavation

NG3.1 Breaking the Surface

NG3.1.1 High Amenity and Natural Materials Surfaces

1) When excavating in modular construction within high amenity areas, or in natural materials within any footway area (as defined in Section S1.4), the Undertaker shall lift the existing modules carefully and store for re-use.
2) More recent construction tolerances of existing modules in NG3.1(1) often make it unlikely that the first module in an individual excavation can be lifted without the module itself being damaged. In such circumstances, this damage may be inevitable, but it is expected that the damage is limited to only one module in an individual excavation.

NG3.1.2 Aesthetics

1) The shape and line of larger trenches and their reinstatement should have regard wherever possible to the aesthetic appearance of the reinstatement and its impact on the street scene.

NG3.2 Excavation

1) HSG 185 "Health and Safety in Excavations" gives guidance to those carrying out excavations.
2) Where possible, all excavations should be planned before commencement of works on site.
3) Work must be undertaken and supervised by properly qualified personnel.

NG3.3 *There are no Notes for Guidance*

NG3.4 Side Support

1) Where required, there must be sufficient quantities of appropriate materials available to provide safe trench support.

NG3.5 – NG3.7 *There are no Notes for Guidance*

NG4 Surround to Apparatus

NG4.1 General

1) It is often necessary for an Undertaker to require a specific type or quality of material, and/or special protective components, to be laid within the immediate vicinity of certain types of underground apparatus. This material is usually referred to as the surround to the apparatus, and may include fine unbound granular materials (usually termed 'finefill'), bound materials, tiles, covers, tubular shields, etc., or any combination thereof. The resulting surround may be required for a variety of reasons, including structural support, low corrosion potential, protection for non-metallic materials or special coatings, etc.

2) The nature of the Undertakers apparatus, and/or the protective features of the surround, especially any fine unbound granular materials used within the surround, may impose additional restrictions on the type of compaction equipment that can be used and the necessary operating procedures. However, the entire surround will effectively form a foundation structure for the remainder of the reinstatement and must be capable of providing adequate support for all loading imposed on the reinstatement surface, as well as the weight of the reinstatement structure.

3) In selecting a material for the surround to apparatus, Undertakers should be mindful of the potential for the migration of fines from the adjacent ground, and/or the overlying backfill, into any surround material that is open-textured. Such migration will normally result in settlement of the adjacent ground, and/or the backfill. Migration of fines can be prevented by using a close textured surround or, if this is undesirable, by enclosing the surround within a suitable filter membrane.

NG5 Backfill

NG5.1 Backfill Material Classification

The assumed limiting performance of the five classes of backfill material defined in Appendix A1 is shown in Table NG5.1.

Table NG 5.1 – Backfill Material Performance	
Backfill Material Class	**Material Performance % CBR**
A	Over 15
B	7 to 15
C	4 to 7
D	2 to 4
E	Less than 2

NG5.2 *There are no Notes for Guidance*

NG5.3 Additional Requirements

1) Frost Heave Susceptibility

The frost heave test described in BS 812: Part 124 (as amended by SHW Clause 801.8) is costly and time consuming and is not suitable for routine on-site control checks. The test is primarily intended as a method to establish whether an aggregate from a particular source is likely to be frost susceptible when used in road pavement construction. Material for the frost heave test must be representative of the source or sub-grade encountered. Authorities usually maintain a list of "Approved Suppliers of Non-frost Susceptible Materials" and should have knowledge of frost susceptible sub-grades in their locality.

The following notes on identification of potentially frost heave susceptible material are for guidance but are not, in themselves, exhaustive:

a) Clay materials can be regarded as non-frost susceptible, particularly when the plasticity index is greater than 15%. Clay/silt mixtures are more difficult to assess and are likely to be of marginal frost susceptibility.

b) Silts, particularly those with more than 10% passing a 75 micron (μm) BS sieve size, are likely to be frost susceptible.

c) Cohesive/granular materials will often be frost susceptible; the quantity and type of granular aggregate and, to a lesser degree the silt fraction are the controlling factors. If the aggregate is a frost susceptible type, then it is very probable that the mixture will also be frost susceptible.

d) Granular materials with more than 10% passing a 75 micron (μm) BS sieve size have a high potential for frost susceptibility and granular materials with more than 12% passing 75 micron (μm) are likely to be frost susceptible.

e) All crushed chalks are frost susceptible and the magnitude of the frost heave will increase with the saturation moisture content of the chalk.

f) Oolitic and magnesium limestones are likely to be frost susceptible, particularly those where the aggregate saturation moisture content exceeds 3.5%.

g) Hard carboniferous limestones are unlikely to be frost susceptible unless they have been contaminated with clay or have more than 12% passing 75 micron (μm).

h) Crushed granites will only be frost susceptible if the percentage passing 75 micron (μm) exceeds 12% and is partially plastic.

i) 'As dug' sands and gravels are frequently frost susceptible especially if the percentage passing 75 micron (μm) BS sieve size is greater than 12% or if it is plastic. Sands and gravels won by "wet working" techniques are unlikely to be frost susceptible unless contaminated by a clay or a high silt fraction.

j) Burnt colliery shales, slags, PFAs, etc. are secondary materials, and it is not possible to give general guidance to their potential for frost heave resistance. Each source is different and will need to be assessed by the frost heave test. The exception to this is graded bottom furnace ash produced by modern power stations, which has been found to be non-frost susceptible.

k) Foamed concretes can generally be regarded as non-frost susceptible.

NG6 Flexible and Composite Roads

NG6.1 *There are no Notes for Guidance*

NG6.2 Sub-base Reinstatement

1) It may be reasonable to expect that an adequately compacted sub-base should achieve an in-situ CBR value in excess of 30%.
2) It is expected that a bituminous sub-base will only be selected where the Base is also bituminous.
3) When placing bituminous material directly on to the backfill it is important to ensure that the exposed surface of the backfill has been compacted. This operation is essential to minimise the risk of a build up of pore water pressure causing the subgrade to become spongy. It is also imperative that construction is phased such that excavated areas are covered, on the same day, with the first layer of bituminous material, to prevent the ingress of water. Care should be taken in the compaction of this first layer. If pore water pressure builds up in the backfill at this stage, then rolling should cease and the material left overnight, or longer if necessary, prior to the placement of any further layers.
4) The condition of sub-base material can be assessed using Field Identification Test No. 3 in Appendix A1.

NG6.3 Base Reinstatement

Overlaid Modular Layers

1) This Specification permits the re-use of cobbles and setts for the reinstatement of the relevant layer. However, it is often extremely difficult to achieve a performance from such reinstatements that is similar to that of the original, i.e. well interlocked and 'stress hardened' layer. Failure to achieve this structural stiffness could result in failure of the reinstatement and particularly any surfacing materials laid thereon.
2) The Specification does not permit the re-use of penning, in which the layer of modules is laid upright, in an interlocking manner, exhibiting a greater stiffness than an equivalent layer of cobbles/setts.

NG6.4 Surface Reinstatement

NG6.4.1 Hot Rolled Asphalt Surfaces

1) HRA design mixtures give better resistance to deformation where queuing of heavy traffic is likely to occur and may be more economical to lay.

2) Type C mixtures use fine aggregates of a coarser grading than Type F mixtures, usually associated with the use of crushed rock fines. Such mixtures tend to be stiffer and less well suited to the reinstatement of small excavations.

NG6.4.2 – NG6.4.5.1 *There are no Notes for Guidance*

NG6.4.5.2 *High Friction Surfacings*

1) High friction surfacings will usually have been laid for safety reasons and should be reinstated as soon as is practicable.

2) Performance on concrete may not be as good as on bituminous surfacings and the suitability of a system should be checked by reference to its HAPAS Certificate.

3) Suppliers of some high friction surfacing systems may have specific requirements relating to the condition of the surface to which it is to be applied. Guidance on this should be sought either from the supplier or the HAPAS Certificate.

4) It is recommended that High Friction surfacing systems are applied to a surface course that has been trafficked for some weeks. This is to help prevent cracking extending into the surface course induced by the application of a newly laid high friction surface.

NG6.4.5.3 *Porous Asphalt*

1) Edge sealing requirements specified in Section S6.5.2.2 may not be appropriate with porous asphalts because the free-flow characteristics of the material may be impeded.

2) Application rates in this specification are quoted in kg/m^2 of residual bitumen. This differs from the previous specification, which quoted rates in l/m^2 of total emulsion. For example, the rate of 0.50kg/m^2 residual bitumen equates approximately to 1.2 l/m^2 of K1-40 or 0.80 l/m^2 of K1-60 emulsion.

NG6.4.5.4 *Coloured Surfacings*

1) Coloured surfacings are sometimes used for marking bus lanes, accident prevention measures, traffic prioritisation schemes, etc. The use of warning signs, e.g. “Temporary Road Surface”, should be considered until the special surface can be restored.

2) It may not be possible to obtain coloured surfacings in a wide selection of colours and Authorities may have to accept limitations in colour matching. In addition, coloured surfacings can fade or undergo other changes in colour as the materials age.

NG6.4.5.5 *Other Specialist Surfacing Materials*

Texture depth requirements specified in Section S2.6.2 may not be appropriate for the increasing number of specialist surfacing materials currently being used by some Authorities.

NG6.4.6 Surface Treatments

In all roads, where the overall quality of existing surface dressings or surface treatments are to a high standard, it may be difficult to produce small excavations or narrow trenches with surface dressings or other surface treatments that closely and uniformly match the existing adjacent surfaces. Under such circumstances, some localised variation in surface quality may be acceptable to the Authority.

NG6.4.7 – NG6.4.10 *There are no Notes for Guidance*

NG6.5 Base and Edge Preparation

NG6.5.1 Base Preparation

1) Tack coating materials are generally based on rapid curing anionic or cationic bitumen emulsions to BS 434, with approximately 40% bitumen content. New tack coating materials are becoming available, and the trial use of more modern variants is recommended.

2) Application rates in this specification are quoted in kg/m^2 of residual bitumen. This differs from the previous specification, which quoted rates in l/m^2 of total emulsion. For example, the rate of 0.15 kg/m^2 residual bitumen equates approximately to 0.35 l/m^2 of 1-40 or 0.25 l/m^2 of K1-60 emulsion.

3) Further guidance on application of tack coats and bond coats can be found in BS594987.

NG6.5.2 Edge Preparation

1) Edge sealant materials are generally based on rapid curing bitumen emulsions to BS EN 13808, typically in the range 40 to 100 pen and approximately 70% bitumen content, or hot bitumens to BS EN 12591 typically 50 or 70 pen. An increasing number of high build and rubberised edge sealants are becoming available and, in general, are preferred. Alternatives to these materials exist and, if there are any doubts as to their effectiveness, they may be used on a trial basis.

2) When using edge sealant materials, strict adherence to manufacturer's instructions is essential. Dependant on weather conditions brushed

sealant drying times may vary between 5 minutes and 2 hours, whilst spray sealant times may vary between 1 and 15 minutes before reinstatement can take place.

Additionally prior to application:

- All excess water and loose material should be removed from the cut faces of the reinstatement;
- All bound vertical edges must be clean and free from slurry and dust etc. with the stone in the existing layers clearly visible.

3) The following case study data sheets illustrate the results of edge sealant application under different edge conditions:

- Example 1 – dry and clean;
- Example 2 – wet;
- Example 3 – dirty and damp.

Example 1

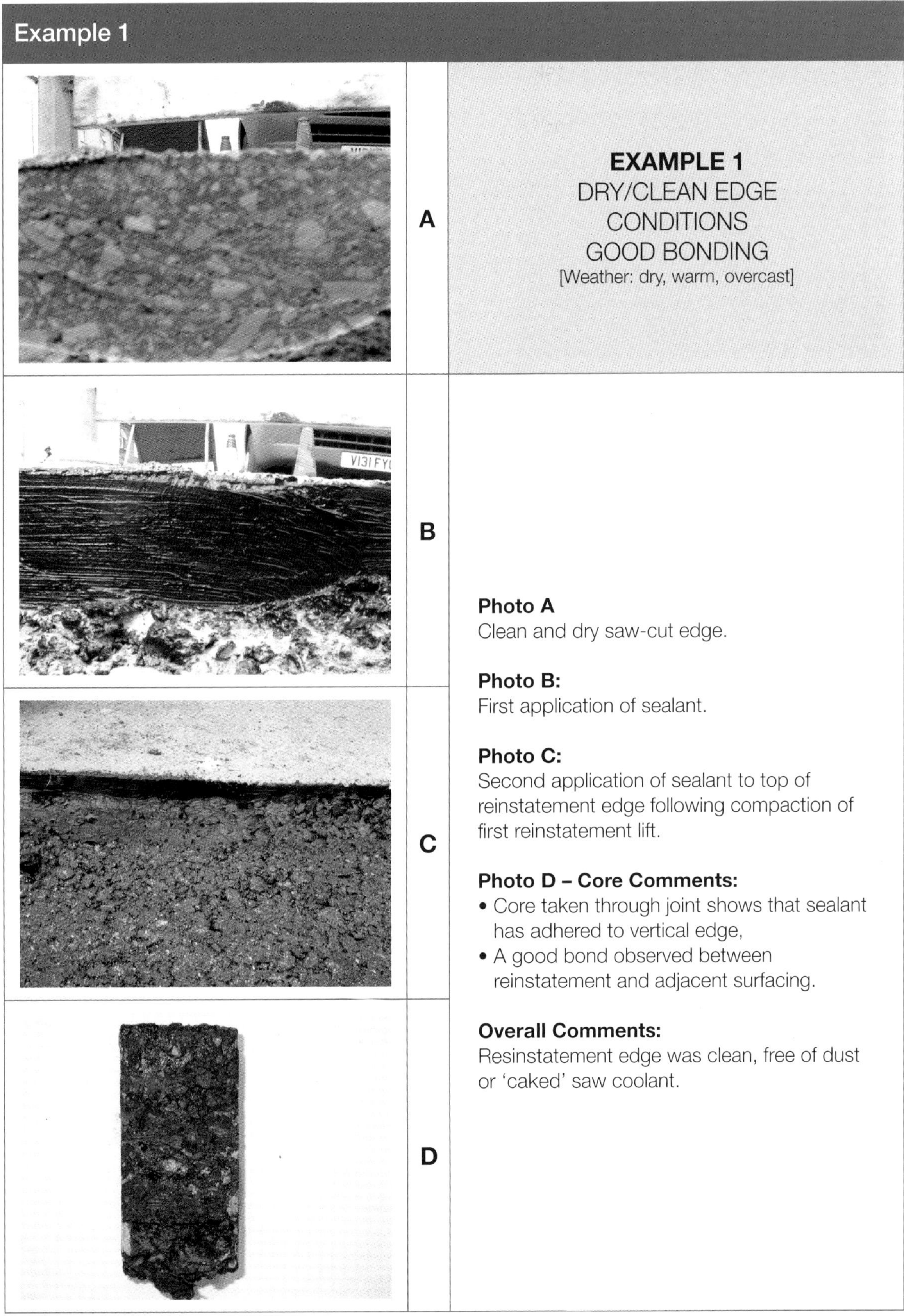

EXAMPLE 1
DRY/CLEAN EDGE
CONDITIONS
GOOD BONDING
[Weather: dry, warm, overcast]

Photo A
Clean and dry saw-cut edge.

Photo B:
First application of sealant.

Photo C:
Second application of sealant to top of reinstatement edge following compaction of first reinstatement lift.

Photo D – Core Comments:

- Core taken through joint shows that sealant has adhered to vertical edge,
- A good bond observed between reinstatement and adjacent surfacing.

Overall Comments:
Resinstatement edge was clean, free of dust or 'caked' saw coolant.

Example 2

A

EXAMPLE 2
WET EDGE
CONDITIONS
POOR BONDING
[Weather: dry, hot sunny]

B

C

D

Photo A
Coating of wet slurry on saw-cut edge.

Photo B:
First application of sealant. [Only 5 minutes of drying time allowed before reinstatement commenced].

Photo C:
Second application of sealant to top of reinstatement edge following compaction of first reinstatement lift.
[Only 2 minutes of drying time allowed before reinstatement commenced].

Photo D – Core Comments:
- Core taken through joint shows that sealant has not adhered to vertical edge,
- No bond observed between reinstatement and adjacent surfacing.

Overall Comments:
- Resinstatement edge should have been washed and substantially dried before application of spray sealant.
- Allowed drying time does not conform with Manufacturer's Instructions.
- Incorrect application of edge sealant could permit water penetration into joint, potentially leading to early life edge deterioration, settlement of trench and future (avoidable) defects.

Example 3

	A	**EXAMPLE 3** DIRTY/DAMP EDGE CONDITIONS POOR BONDING [Weather: light rain]
	B	**Photo A** Coating of wet slurry on saw-cut edge. **Photo B:** First application of sealant. [Only 5 minutes of drying time allowed before reinstatement commenced]. **Photo C:** Second application of sealant to top of reinstatement edge following compaction of first reinstatement lift. [Only 2 minutes of drying time allowed before reinstatement commenced]. **Photo D – Core Comments:** • Core taken through joint shows that sealant has not adhered to vertical edge, • No bond observed between reinstatement and adjacent surfacing. **Overall Comments:** • Resinstatement edge should have been washed and substantially dried before application of spray sealant. • Allowed drying time does not conform with Manufacturer's Instructions. • Incorrect application of edge sealant could permit water penetration into joint, potentially leading to early life edge deterioration, settlement of trench and future (avoidable) defects.
	C	
	D	

NG6.6 *There are no Notes for Guidance*

NG7 Rigid and Modular Roads

NG7.1 Reinstatement Methods

1) The requirements of this Specification shall apply to all rigid roads up to 125 msa traffic flow. All rigid roads with existing traffic flows exceeding 30 msa must be identified by the Authority, prior to the commencement of works, so that reinstatement requirements can be agreed.
2) Some modern concrete roads, constructed in accordance with current Government standards and specifications, may incorporate special design philosophies that are beyond the scope of this Specification. Similarly, there may be other existing rigid road designs that will also require the use of particular reinstatement methods. Such roads must also be identified by the Authority, prior to the commencement of works, so that reinstatement requirements can be agreed.

NG7.2 – NG7.3.1 *There are no Notes for Guidance*

NG7.3.2 For small excavations a proprietary C32/40 site-batched concrete may be used.

NG7.3.3 – NG7.6 *There are no Notes for Guidance*

NG7.7 Modular Roads

1) When excavating in modular roads, the existing modules shall be lifted carefully and stored for re-use.
2) It is particularly important to ensure that bedding and jointing sands should meet the performance demands in areas subject to heavy vehicular traffic.

NG7.8 *There are no Notes for Guidance*

NG8 Footways, Footpaths and Cycle Tracks

NG8.1 *There are no Notes for Guidance*

NG8.2 Sub-base and Binder Course Reinstatement

NG8.2.1 – NG8.2.3 *There are no Notes for Guidance*

NG8.2.4 Excavations Adjacent to Roads

The most heavily stressed area of a road is usually the inside wheel track adjacent to the road edge. Depending on ground conditions, it is often necessary to support the road edge by providing lateral restraint within the adjoining footway, footpath, cycle track or verge. The most common form of edge support is a section of unbound or cement bound granular materials. This construction will most commonly be encountered when the horizontal distance, between the edge of the Undertakers' excavation and the edge of the road surface, is less than the expected depth of cover of the Undertakers' apparatus.

NG8.3 Surface Reinstatement

NG8.3.1 *There are no Notes for Guidance*

NG8.3.2 High Duty and High Amenity Areas

1) In high duty footways, the durability of the wearing surface is of prime importance and simple cosmetic matching of materials may not be adequate. Specific grades of material such as York stone modules, or specific types of construction such as asphalt sand carpet/mastic, may have been laid in order to give an acceptable performance under extreme conditions. In these cases, similar or equivalent grades of materials will need to be reinstated.
2) In high amenity footways, the cosmetic matching of materials at the wearing surface may be of primary importance with durability of secondary importance.

NG8.3.3 **Areas Surfaced with Asphalt Concrete**

A wide range of surface treatments exist and commonly these are less than 6mm aggregate size. Where available, a similar surface finish will be reinstated. The surface course material may be reinstated using any of the allowed binder course or surface course materials, with a final surface treatment applied as soon as practicable following the laying of the permanent surface course.

NG8.3.4 **Other Asphalt Areas**

Mastic asphalt is sometimes used as a footway surfacing material for its appearance and durability. Where an Authority has a policy of using this material and reinstating with it then it is reasonable to expect the Undertaker to similarly comply with this. However, the cost of small quantities of mastic asphalt is disproportionate to the size of the reinstatement and can result in significant wastage. Consequently it is not unreasonable for an Undertaker to wish to compile a programme of such works to achieve an efficient utilisation of resources. Therefore an Authority should expect such work to be programmed so that sites requiring mastic asphalt are batched to produce a package of work.

NG8.3.5 **Concrete Material Areas**

1) In general, reinstatements in a concrete footway, footpath or cycle track should match the existing surfacing as closely as is practicable.
2) Generally, the use of all flexible permanent reinstatements in overlaid concrete, mastic asphalt, asphalt carpet, sand carpet or other derivative surfaces etc., has proven to be entirely adequate in practice.

NG8.3.6 – NG8.3.8 *There are no Notes for Guidance*

NG8.4 – NG8.5 *There are no Notes for Guidance*

NG9 Verges and Unmade Ground

NG9.1 – NG9.5 *There are no Notes for Guidance*

NG10 Compaction Requirements

NG10.1 Introduction

1) Research has shown that failure to operate and maintain compaction equipment in accordance with manufacturer's schedules and recommended practices is likely to result in inadequate compaction with serious implications for the short term performance of individual structural layers and the long term integrity of the entire reinstatement.

2) All compaction equipment covered by this Specification must be frequently checked, adjusted and maintained, as necessary, in accordance with the manufacturer's recommended practices, in order to ensure that the manufacturer's recommended operating frequency is maintained throughout each compaction operation.

3) All compaction equipment covered by this Specification must be used in accordance with the manufacturer's recommended operating procedures.

NG10.2 Reinstatement Materials

NG10.2.1 Unbound Granular and Cohesive Materials

For granular or cohesive materials, a vibrating roller may be unsuitable in small excavations because of the restricted manoeuvrability of large heavy rollers required to achieve adequate levels of compaction with an acceptable number of passes.

NG10.2.2 *There are no Notes for Guidance*

NG10.2.3 Bituminous Mixtures

1) With some combinations of compaction plant and certain types of bituminous mixtures if compaction is continued as the material approaches its maximum density the following may result:

   a) The migration of fines or binder to the surface.

   b) The development of shear surfaces and or crushing of aggregates.

2) Provided that the material has been laid and compacted within the appropriate temperature range, fewer passes will be required when any signs of distress become apparent.

3) Asphalt maximum density values, used in the calculation of air voids content, are specific to particular asphalt mixtures incorporating constituents from specific sources. Any variation in mix proportions or constituents requires the maximum density to be re-established.

4) Although consistent asphalt supply may allow an established maximum density for a particular mixture and source to be used for some time in routine situations, the definitive method to be used in the event of dispute will require the maximum density to be determined for the mixture actually used. The maximum density may be determined from bulk samples, if available, or from material obtained from additional core samples.

5) When taking cores near surface apparatus, Section S10.2.3(4) requires a minimum clearance of 100mm to avoid damaging the apparatus or structure it is bedded on. However it is possible that some surface apparatus may have wider than normal flanges and there may be instances where a greater clearance is required to avoid damage. If doubt exists, liaison with the owner of the apparatus should be undertaken in advance.

NG10.2.4 *There are no Notes for Guidance*

NG10.2.5 Modular Surfacing Materials

Depending on the size and type of paving module to be laid, and/or the extent of the area to be surfaced etc., the use of additional mechanical compaction may become necessary.

NG10.3 Equipment Operation and Restrictions

1) A single pass of any compaction plant is deemed to be completed when the foot, roll or plate of the compactor has impacted the entire surface area of the layer.

2) Where the excavation width is more than 50 mm greater than the foot, roll or plate width (i.e. side clearances between the compacting surface and the wall of the excavation exceed 25 mm per side), two or more traverses of the compaction device will be required to ensure coverage of the entire surface and all will be deemed to constitute a single pass.

3) Compaction plant should be steered along a line offset from that steered on the previous pass so that alternate passes are run close in to each side wall of the excavation.

4) Small items of compaction plant will frequently be required and additional provisions must be considered for use in trenches of less than 200 mm width, small excavations and other areas of restricted access. In general, lightweight vibrotampers and poletampers are capable of achieving the same degree of compaction as the heavier items of plant specified in Appendix A8. However, small plant is usually not self-advancing and therefore more difficult to operate effectively.

NG10.3.1 Hand Rammers

1) Hand rammers may be used for initial tamping of fine fill material or immediately adjacent to street furniture, reinstatement edges etc.

2) In all cases, full machine compaction complying with Appendix A8 will normally be applied immediately after the required thickness of material has been built-up. However, hand ramming alone may be necessary around standpipes and other isolated fixed features.

NG10.3.2 Percussive Rammer

1) A percussive rammer is deemed to be a hand-held and/or pedestrian guided machine in which an electric, pneumatic or hydraulically operated reciprocating mechanism acts on a plate or 'foot'.

2) Percussive rammers may only be used to provide full machine compaction in areas where restricted access prevents the effective use of conventional compaction equipment.

NG10.3.3 Vibrotamper

1) A vibrotamper is deemed to be a free-standing, pedestrian guided machine in which a reciprocating mechanism, driven by an integral engine or motor, acts on a spring system through which oscillations are set up in a base plate or 'foot'.

2) Vibrotampers may be operated at reduced speed, for the first pass only, with cohesive materials.

3) Vibrotampers are not preferred for any permanent surface course application or any other application involving a layer thickness of less than 50 mm.

NG10.3.4 Vibrating Roller

1) A vibrating roller is deemed to be a self-propelled, pedestrian steered machine with a means of applying mechanical vibration to one or more rolls.

2) Vibrating rollers should be operated in the lowest available gear, except for the first pass, which should be at maximum forward speed.

3) All compaction passes should be carried out with full vibration, except for the first pass, which should be carried out without vibration in order to nip in the material adjacent to the reinstatement edges and to prevent uneven displacement of material within the remainder of the reinstatement area.

4) Vibrating rollers are the preferred method of compaction for all permanent surface courses.

5) The use of twin drum rollers is preferred to single drum for the compaction of bituminous mixtures and will improve the quality of the permanent surface course. However, single drum vibrating rollers are permitted, as detailed in Appendix A8.

NG10.3.5 Vibrating Plate Compactor

1) A vibrating plate compactor is deemed to be a pedestrian guided plate equipped with a source of vibration consisting of one or more rotating, eccentrically weighted shafts.

2) Vibrating plate compactors should be operated in the lowest available gear, except for the first pass, which should be at maximum forward speed.

NG10.3.6 Other Compaction Equipment

Compaction plant not referenced in Appendix A8, including machine-mounted, modified and other alternative compaction equipment, may be permitted for the compaction of reinstatement materials, in accordance with the following relevant requirements:

1) Machine-Mounted Compactors

   A machine-mounted compactor is deemed to be any compaction equipment that is mounted, as an attachment or accessory, to the chassis or front or rear booms of an excavator, tractor, skid-steer vehicle or other proprietary vehicle, for the purposes of compaction.

   All machine-mounted compactors, whether integral to the vehicle design or special attachments for front or rear mounting to the chassis or booms of any excavator, tractor or skid-steer vehicle etc. should be operated in accordance with the recommendations of the compactor or attachment manufacturer, to the relevant compaction procedure required by Appendix A 8. However, other operational variables should also be considered prior to the operation of such plant as follows:

   a) Compactor Downforce

      The total downforce will vary depending upon the weight of the vehicle chassis or compactor frame, and any additional downforce applied by hydraulic rams etc. However, changes in the configuration of any vehicle, by the addition or removal of other accessories etc, changes in the width of the vibrating foot, roll or plate etc, movement of any boom resulting in a significant change of loading geometry or outreach etc, attaching of the compactor to other vehicles of differing types or weights etc, can all result in a significant reduction of compactive performance that is seldom apparent. All operators should be aware of the potential reduction in compactive performance resulting from such changes in configuration.

   b) Applied Downforce

      The mounting of compaction equipment to the front loader arms of an excavator, where the downforce is sensibly limited by the lifting of the front wheels, is preferred. All compactors mounted to the backhoe of an excavator should be fitted with a downforce-limiting device, correctly set, or with a simple indicating device allowing the amplitude to be estimated.

c) Compactor Set-up

Where vibration frequency or amplitude, or any other parameter affecting the dynamic output of a compactor, is expected to be adjusted on a routine basis, all parameters should be set in accordance with the manufacturer's recommendations unless specific testing, meeting the requirements of Section NG1.6.3, has shown other settings to be at least as effective.

2) Modified Compaction Equipment

Modified compaction equipment shall include any proprietary vibrotamper, vibrating roller, vibrating plate compactor, percussive rammer or other compaction plant which has been adapted, converted, revised or otherwise changed from the original manufacturer's Specification, resulting in a significant change to the original configuration, dimensions, operational weight or power output.

Modified compaction equipment shall be permitted, provided it is operated in accordance with compaction procedures meeting the following requirements:

a) The original manufacturer shall provide written confirmation that the modified compaction equipment, operated in accordance with the original compaction procedure, is capable of achieving the same degree of compaction as any other option permitted in Appendix A8, or

b) A revised compaction procedure is developed in accordance with the requirements of Section NG1.6.

3) Alternative Compaction Equipment

Alternative compaction equipment shall include all other compaction devices not specifically permitted within Section NG10.3. Alternative compaction equipment may be permitted, provided it is operated in accordance with compaction procedures developed in accordance with the requirements of Section NG1.6 (3).

NG11 Ancillary Activities

NG11.1 Traffic Signs, Road Markings, Studs and Verge Markers

NG11.1.1 General

In the interests of safety generally and particularly in the interests of people with disabilities, all traffic signs, road markings, studs and verge markers removed during the course of the works should be replaced immediately following completion of works.

NG11.1.2 *There are no Notes for Guidance*

NG11.1.3 Road Markings – General

Cold applied road markings (e.g. Methylmethacrylate) are often laid thinner than thermoplastic materials and may require longer setting or curing times. Different glass beads and other surface treatments, e.g. for skid resistance, may need to be applied to these materials. Guidance on this shall be sought from the manufacturer of the material and this guidance must be followed.

NG11.1.4 *There are no Notes for Guidance*

NG11.2 Street Furniture and Special Features

In the interests of safety generally, and particularly in the interests of the disabled, all street furniture, tactile paving and any other special features removed during the course of works should be replaced immediately following the completion of works.

NG11.3 Traffic Sensors etc.

1) Examples of sensors include ice warning sensors, buried queue and traffic detectors, other electronic detectors and various data collection devices.
2) The replacement of some traffic sensors may require the use of specialist contractors.

NG11.4 Water-related Matters

NG11.4.1 and NG11.4.2 *There are no Notes for Guidance*

NG11.4.3 Water Egress (Street Surface and Utility Apparatus)

1) If water issues from the street surface or an Undertaker's apparatus, the Authority shall initiate an investigatory works procedure to determine the cause and source of the water egress. Prior to commencement of the investigatory work, the Authority should contact any Undertaker or Undertakers which it believes may be responsible for the egress of water. Undertakers shall cooperate with the Authority in its investigation and may take trial holes and check apparatus for water leakage or surcharge through the apparatus, ducts and surround to the apparatus.
2) If following the investigation, the Authority has reasonable cause to believe that water egress is caused or associated with the Undertaker's apparatus, remedial measures shall be agreed between the Authority and the Undertaker and shall be at the Undertaker's cost. In the absence of agreement between the Authority and the Undertaker, liability for any damage shall be determined in accordance with section 82 of the Act (Liability for any damage or loss caused).

NG11.5 Ironwork and Apparatus

NG11.5.1 Access Covers, Frames and Surround

1) The access surround is a critical feature because of the load transfer and point loads impacting on the fixed feature and as a potential point of weakness. It is therefore important that the surround is constructed to adequately withstand and transfer the applied loads.
2) The access surround should be of sufficient width to enable adequate compaction if constructed in an asphaltic material or a flowable material.

NG11.5.1.1-NG11.5.1.4 *There are no Notes for Guidance*

NG11.5.1.5 *Reinstatement Materials*

1) Apparatus bedding materials should be compliant with the current version of HA104 and used in accordance with its requirements.
2) If the bedding material depth is greater than the manufacturers recommendations, an appropriate product should be used to infill this gap. e.g. C32/40 strength concrete.

NG11.6 *There are no Notes for Guidance*

NG11.7 Overbanding

Research by TRL has indicated overbanding may provide some benefits in terms of long-term performance of the reinstatement. However, poorly applied overbanding can pose a significant risk in terms of poor resistance to skidding especially for two wheeled vehicles and horses. It is therefore recommended that site-specific risk assessments should be documented by the Undertaker before any use of overbanding on potentially high risk sites as defined in Section S2.6.3.

NG12 Remedial Works

NG12.1 – NG12.5 *There are no Notes for Guidance*

NGA1 Backfill Materials

There are no Notes for Guidance for this Appendix

NGA2 Key to Materials

NGA2.0 Introduction

For guidance on the terminology for asphalt mixtures refer to PD6691

NGA2.1 Hot Rolled Asphalt (HRA) Mixtures

1) HRA design mixtures give better resistance to deformation where queuing of heavy traffic is likely to occur and may also be more economical to lay.

2) Type C mixtures use fine aggregate of a coarser grading than Type F mixtures – usually associated with the use of crushed rock fines. Such mixtures tend to be stiffer and are less well suited to the reinstatement of small excavations.

NGA2.2 Stone Mastic Asphalt (SMA) Mixtures

NGA2.2.1 General

1) SMA is a high stone content, gap graded material which has the voids between aggregate particles essentially filled with a bitumen-rich mortar.

2) SMAs are very rich in bitumen to the extent that measures have to be taken to prevent bitumen from 'draining' from the mix during transport. Most commonly bitumen drainage is prevented by addition of either polymer modifiers or cellulose fibre.

3) True SMA is intended to be virtually impermeable and has very good resistance to deformation by virtue of its 'stone to stone' skeleton. The level of texture depth achieved is largely a function of the material design, texture depth achieved is therefore likely to be more consistent than with HRA, where the application rate and the embedment of the surface applied coated chippings is critical.

NGA2.2.2 Specification

1) There is a European Standard for SMAs, BS EN 13108-5 and, in the UK, a Published Document PD6691 "Guidance on the use of BS EN 13108 Bituminous mixtures – Material specifications".

2) There are also a number of proprietary mixes that fit the generic description of an SMA.

3) HAPAS approved thin surface course systems may also comply with the HAUC requirements but there is no guarantee. Some HAPAS materials can have void contents in excess of that permitted in this specification. Purchasers should make it clear to suppliers that the work has to comply with the air void specification.

NGA2.2.3 Transport

1) As with all asphalt materials it is important that temperature loss is minimised during transport, handling and storage to allow effective placement and compaction. The high bitumen content of mixtures means that provided material temperatures remain elevated then compaction is relatively easy.

2) Transporting should comply with the requirements of this specification and BS 594987.

3) To minimise the risk of segregation and temperature loss it is preferable to use the material direct from the delivery vehicle or hot box. Material should never be tipped on to adjacent surfaces for use sometime later.

NGA2.2.4 Preparation

1) Preparation should comply with this specification and BS 594987. A polymer-modified bond coat is preferable when using SMA.

NGA2.2.5 Laying

1) Placement of the SMA should be done in such a way as to avoid segregation of the mix. Where possible this is to be accomplished by careful use of a shovel. The use of a rake is to be avoided. Care must be taken with the use of some "hot boxes" as these can also cause segregation of mixes through the discharge augers.

2) Areas showing segregation should be removed as these are not acceptable at any time.

3) Where initial skid resistance of >40 SRV is required (all carriageway applications) or in areas where equestrian usage is likely the material should be gritted using a clean, dry, crushed quartzite or similar very hard angular aggregate to a grading similar to that shown in Table NGA2.1 or 3mm steel slag shall be applied evenly to the surface during the initial rolling, i.e., whilst the material is still warm. The rate of application shall be to provide about 80% surface coverage (approximately 1000 grammes per square metre). Where the authority uses a lightly coated grit for the treatment of SMA this may also be suitable.

4) After the final rolling all surplus aggregate should be removed before the reinstatement is opened to traffic.

5) It is important to take care that the application of grit should not reduce compliance with any texture depth requirement.

Table NGA2.1 – Recommended Aggregate Grading for Gritting SMA Surfaces	
BS test sieve:	**% passing**
6.3 mm	100
5.0 mm	95-100
3.35 mm	66-90
1.18 mm	0-20
600 µm	0-8
75 µm	0-1.5

NGA2.2.6 Compaction

1) Compaction of the material is best carried out using a smooth wheeled roller. Vibration may be applied provided that this does not bring about excessive movement of the bitumen to the surface of the layer, i.e. "bleeding". On narrow reinstatements compaction equipment in accordance with Table A8.3 may be used but care must be taken to ensure that there is no excessive loss of surface texture or bleeding.

NGA2.3 and NGA2.4 *There are no Notes for Guidance*

NGA2.5 Structural Layer Thickness Tolerances

Excessive layer thicknesses of HRA surface course can lead to localised rutting likely to exceed the surface profile performance requirements set out in Section S2.2.

NGA2.6 – NGA2.10 *There are no Notes for Guidance*

NGA3-7

There are no Notes for Guidance

NGA8 Compaction Requirements

NGA8.1-
NGA8.2 *There are no Notes for Guidance*

NGA8.3 Bituminous Mixtures

Table NGA8.3 provides guidance for compaction procedures that may be capable of achieving the specified air voids values.

Table NG A8.3 Compaction requirements for Bituminous Mixtures

Compaction Plant and Weight Category	Bituminous Mixtures – Minimum Passes/Lift for compacted lift thickness up to			
	40 mm	**60 mm**	**80 mm**	**100 mm**
Vibrotamper 50 kg minimum	5 #	7 #	**NR**	**NR**
Vibrating Roller				
Single Drum				
600-1000 kg/m	10	12	**NR**	**NR**
1000-2000 kg/m	6	10	**NR**	**NR**
2000-3500 kg/m	5	7	8	**NR**
Over 3500 kg/m	4	6	7	**NR**
Twin Drum				
600-1000 kg/m	5	7	**NR**	**NR**
1000-2000 kg/m	4	5	6	8
Over 2000 kg/m	3	4	4	6
Vibrating Plate				
1400-1800 kg/m^2	6	**NR**	**NR**	**NR**
Over 1800 kg/m^2	3	5	6	8

Table NG A8.3 Compaction requirements for Bituminous Mixtures	
All Above Plant	For Maximum and Minimum compacted lift thickness See Appendix A2.6, Table A2.1
Alternative Compaction Plant for Areas of Restricted Access (including small excavations and trenches less than 200 mm width)	
Vibrotamper 25 kg minimum	Minimum of 6 compaction passes Maximum of 75 mm compacted lift thickness
Percussive Rammer 10 kg minimum	
Notes for Table NG A8.3: 1) **NR** = Not Recommended 2) **#** = Vibrotamper not recommended on permanent surface course of trenches > 500 mm width 3) Twin drum vibrating rollers are preferred for compaction of bituminous mixtures 4) Single drum vibrating rollers are vibrating rollers providing vibration on only one drum 5) Twin drum vibrating rollers are vibrating rollers providing vibration on two separate drums	

NGA9 Alternative Reinstatement Materials (ARMs)

Alternative Reinstatement Materials, particularly slow cure Hydraulically Bound Mixtures, may not achieve their full design strength for some time after placement. It is therefore recommended that Structural Materials for Reinstatement, used as sub base or base, should achieve a minimum Immediate Bearing Index (CBR without surcharge) of 30 prior to overlaying or trafficking.

For further information on the production of ARMs from recycled and secondary materials refer to the WRAP Quality protocol for the production of aggregates from inert waste (2005 and 2004). Available at http://www.wrap.org.uk/downloads/0083_quality_protocol_A4.67caadd5.87.pdf

NGA10-11

There are no Notes for Guidance

NGA12 Reinstatement of Modular Surface Layers

NGA12.1 General

1) For the purposes of this Specification, modules where one side of the module is generally greater than 300mm, are expected not to rely on infill sand between the vertical faces of the modules. Rather, the gaps between these modules are normally filled, or pointed, with a cement: sand mortar.

2) Modules with sides generally up to and including 300mm rely on jointing sand between the vertical faces of the modules, normally affected through vibration methods, with jointing sand subsequently brushed into joints upon completion. It is essential that the jointing sand is kiln dried and free flowing. Sharp sand or building sand are not normally deemed to meet these requirements, although in some situations the use of sharp sand has been found to provide increased durability.

3) It should be noted that there may be a need to revisit sites to top up jointing sand following subsequent trafficking.

4) It should also be noted that there may be a need for the application of a sealant on sites subject to mechanical/vacuum sweeping.

NGA12.2 Examples of Cement or Concrete Infills

1) Figures NGA12.1 to NGA12.3 provide guidance as to acceptable treatment of cement or concrete infills between the nearest practical module and the immediately adjacent fixed feature or boundary feature, as described in Appendix A12. Figures NGA12.1 and NGA12.2 show fillets in modules of one side greater than 300mm, whilst Figure NGA12.3 shows fillets in modules with sides up to and including 300mm.

NGA12.3 Examples of Reinstatement of Modular Patterns

1) Figures NGA12.4 to NGA12.6 provide guidance as to acceptable treatment of modular patterns in localised reinstatements immediately adjacent to fixed features or boundary features. The principle of an acceptable loss of local pattern is indicated, together with the use of larger cut and/or shaped pavers, both leading to an improved aesthetic and structural arrangement of the modules within the reinstatement.

Figure NGA12.1 Extension of Infill Concrete – Modules greater than 300mm [Picture 1]

Infill concrete extended to nearest module to accommodate irregular shape of ironwork and avoid 'cutting' or 'trimming' of modules [modules of side greater than 300mm in this example].

Maximum width of infill measured orthogonally from ironwork face increased to 200mm (maximum) to accommodate irregular shape.

Figure NGA12.2 Extension of Infill Concrete – Modules greater than 300mm [Picture 2]

Infill concrete extended to nearest module to accommodate irregular shape of ironwork and avoid 'cutting' or 'trimming' of modules [modules of side greater than 300mm in this example].

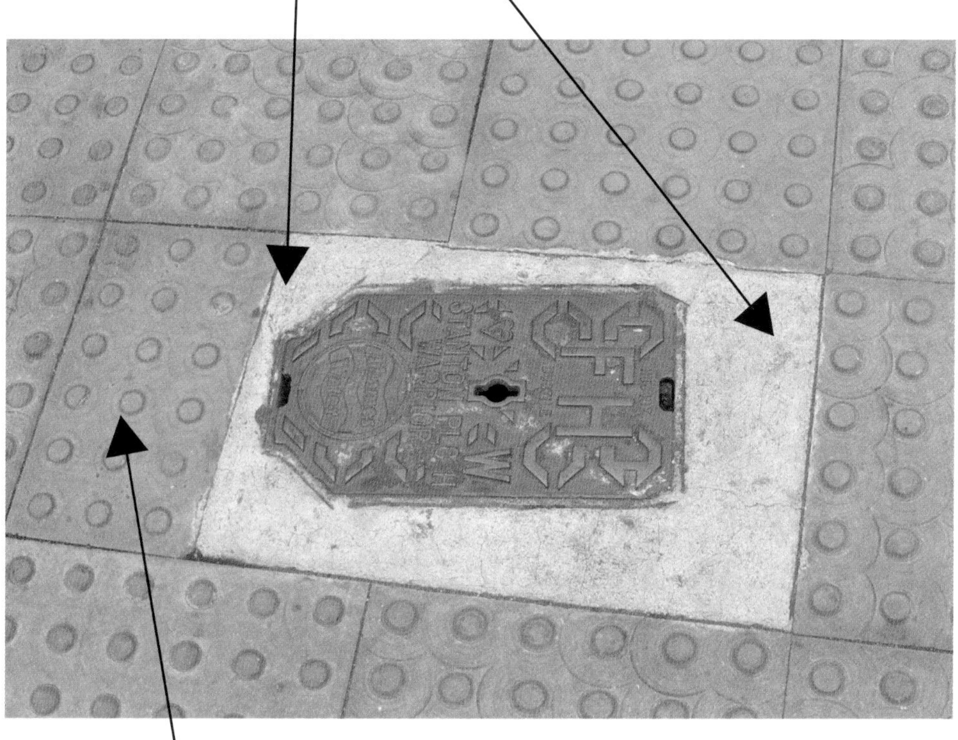

Use of varying width of infill limits 'cutting' or 'trimming' of existing surround modules (half-size in this example)

Figure NGA12.3 Extension of Infill Concrete – Modules up to 300mm

Use of varying width concrete to form an 'external' regular boundary shape (rectangular) with existing modules avoids 'cutting' or 'trimming' of existing surround modules

Infill concrete extended to nearest appropriate (full) module to accommodate orientation of ironwork and avoid 'cutting' or 'trimming' of modules to undesirably small sizes[modules of side up to 300mm in this example].

Maximum width of infill measured orthogonally from ironwork face up to module width + 25mm

Figure NGA12.4 Acceptable Loss of Module Pattern – Modules up to 300mm [Picture 1]

Use of cut 'half' blocks (100mm x 100mm) minimises apparent loss of local module/paver pattern (herringbone in this example)

Use of larger cut/shaped blocks leads to acceptable loss of local pattern (herringbone in this example). This is preferred to small and/or angular cut blocks otherwise necessary to maintain regularity of existing block paver pattern.

Figure NGA12.5 Acceptable Loss of Module Pattern – Modules up to 300mm [Picture 2]

Use of grouped larger cut/shaped blocks leads to acceptable loss of local pattern (herringbone in this example). This is preferred to small and/or angular cut blocks otherwise necessary to maintain regularity of existing block paver pattern

Use of larger cut and/or shaped blocks leads to preferable arrangement of block pavers at corner to stringer course.

Figure NGA12.6 Acceptable Loss of Module Pattern – Modules up to 300mm [Picture 3]

Use of cut 'half' blocks (100mm x 100mm) minimises apparent loss of local pattern (herringbone in this example)

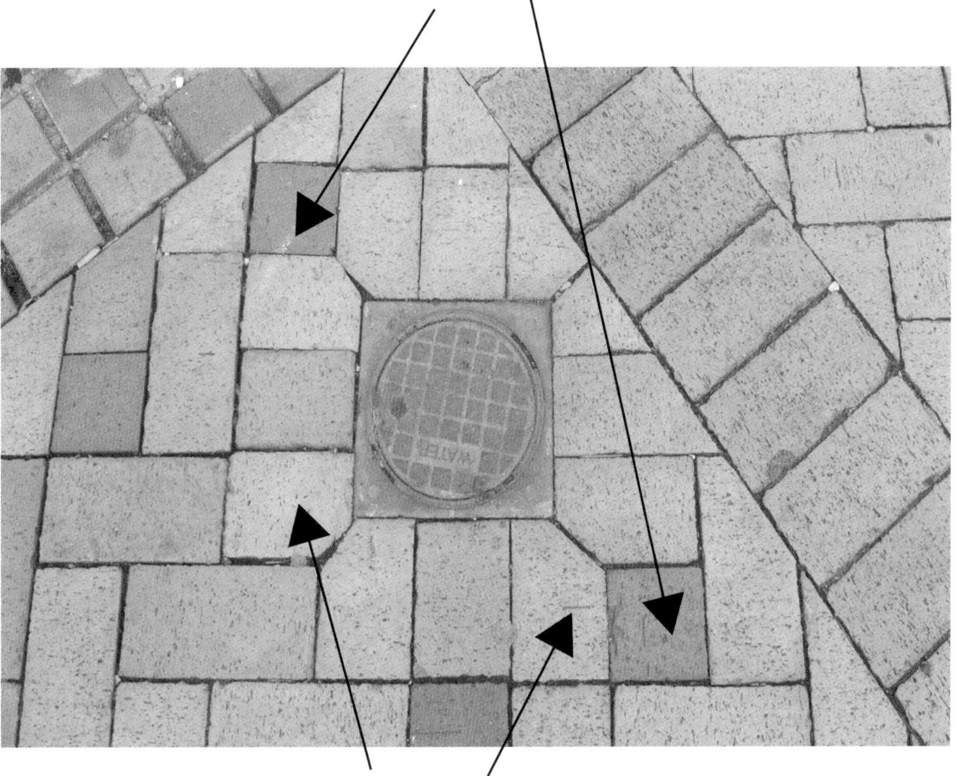

Use of larger cut and/or shaped blocks leads to preferable arrangement of block pavers as surround to small Stop-Cock type apparatus.

Index

I

J

L

M

N

O

P

R

S

T

U

V

W